Love Relations

Love
Relations

Normality and
Pathology

Otto F. Kernberg, M.D.

Yale University Press

New Haven and London

Published with assistance from the
foundation established in memory of
Philip Hamilton McMillan of the Class
of 1894, Yale College.

Designed by James J. Johnson. Set in
Trump type by Rainsford Type, Danbury,
Connecticut. Printed in the United
States of America by Vail-Ballou Press,
Binghamton, New York.

*Library of Congress Cataloging-in-
Publication Data*
Kernberg, Otto F., 1928–
   Love relations : normality and
pathology / Otto F. Kernberg.
      p.   cm.
   Includes bibliographical references and
index.
   ISBN 0-300-06031-9 (cloth: alk. paper)
        0-300-07435-2 (pbk.: alk. paper)
   1. Love. 2. Object relations.
   3. Psychoanalysis. I. Title.
BF175.5L68K470   1995
155.3'4—dc20   94-38369
                                   CIP

A catalogue record for this book is
available from the British Library.
   The paper in this book meets the
guidelines for permanence and durability
of the Committee on Production
Guidelines for Book Longevity of the
Council on Library Resources.

10 9 8 7 6 5 4 3 2

Contents

Preface

Years ago, when my writings about patients presenting borderline personality organization were stressing the importance of aggression in their psychodynamics, a colleague and good friend said to me, half jokingly: "Why don't you write about love? Everybody has the impression that you are concerned only with aggression!" I promised him I would do so when some of the puzzling questions in this area had become clearer to me. This book is the result, although I must admit that I have by no means found the answers to all those questions. Nevertheless, I believe I have come far enough in my thinking to share those answers I have found. I hope others will take the opportunity to illuminate what is still obscure.

Over the centuries the subject of love has received a great deal of attention from poets and philosophers. In more recent times it has been scrutinized by sociologists and psychologists. But surprisingly little about love can be found in the psychoanalytic literature.

Again and again, in my attempts to study the nature of love, the relation of the erotic to sexuality became inescapable. I discovered that, in contrast to the abundance of studies on the sexual response from a biological perspective, little had been written about it as a subjective experience. As I explored this subjective aspect with patients, I soon found myself dealing with unconscious fantasies and their roots in infantile sexuality—in short, back to Freud. Clinically I also found that it was through mutual projective identification that couples reenacted past "scenarios" (unconscious experiences and fantasies) in their relationships and that fantasied and real mutual "persecution" derived from the projection of the infantile superego—as well as the establishment of a joint ego ideal—powerfully influenced a couple's life.

I noticed that it was almost impossible to predict the destiny of a love relation or marriage on the basis of a patient's particular psychopathology. Sometimes different types and degrees of psychopathology in the partners seem to result in a comfortable match; at other times the differences seem to be the source of incompatibility. The questions "What keeps couples together? What destroys their relationship?" haunted me and were the impetus for my studying the underlying dynamics of couples in intimate relationships.

My sources of data are the treatment of patients by psychoanalysis and psychoanalytic psychotherapy, the evaluation and treatment of couples suffering from marital conflict, and particularly the long-term follow-up study of couples through the window of the psychoanalysis and psychoanalytic psychotherapy of individual patients.

It did not take me long to discover that it was just as impossible to study the vicissitudes of love without the vicissitudes of aggression in the relationship of the couple as in the individual. Aggressive aspects of the couple's erotic relationship emerged as important in all intimate sexual relations, an area in which the pioneering work of Robert J. Stoller has provided significant clarification. But I found the aggressive components of the universal ambivalence of intimate object relations equally important, as well as the aggressive components of superego pressures unleashed in the couple's intimate life. A psychoanalytic object relations theory facilitated the study of the dynamics linking intrapsychic conflicts and interpersonal relations, the mutual influences of the couple and its surrounding social group, and the interplay of love and aggression in all these fields.

So, despite the best of intentions, the incontrovertible evidence forces me to focus sharply on aggression in this treatise on love. But, by the same token, the acknowledgment of the complex ways in which love and aggression merge and interact in the couple's life also highlights the mechanisms by which love can integrate and neutralize aggression and, under many circumstances, triumph over it.

Acknowledgments

It was Dr. John D. Sutherland, former Medical Director of the Tavistock Clinic in London and for many years senior consultant to the Menninger Foundation, who first directed my attention to the work of Henry Dicks. Dicks's application of Fairbairn's object relations theory to the study of marital conflicts provided me with a frame of reference that became essential when I first tried to disentangle the complex interactions of borderline patients with their lovers and marital partners. The work of Drs. Denise Braunschweig and Michel Fain on the group dynamics within which erotic tensions are played out throughout the early years of life and adulthood initiated my contact with the French psychoanalytic contributions to the study of normal and pathological love relations. During two sabbatical periods in Paris, where I first developed ideas included in this book, I was privileged to be able to consult with many psychoanalysts who had concerned themselves with the study of normal and pathological love relations, particularly Drs. Didier Anzieu, Denise Braunschweig, Janine Chasseguet-Smirgel, Christian David, Michel Fain, Pierre Fedida, André Green, Béla Grunberger, Joyce McDougall, and Francois Roustang. Drs. Serge Lebovici and Daniel Widlocher were extremely helpful in clarifying my thinking about affect theory. Later Drs. Rainer Krause, of Saarbrücken, and Ulrich Moser, of Zurich, helped to clarify further the pathology of affect communication in intimate relations.

I have been privileged to count among my close friends some of the most important contributors to the psychoanalytic study of love relations in the United States: Drs. Martin Bergmann, Ethel Person, and the late Robert Stoller. Ethel Person helped acquaint me with the important work that she and Dr. Lionel Ovesey had done on core gender identity and sexual pathology; Martin Bergmann helped me to acquire a historical perspective on the nature of love relations and their expression in art; and Robert Stoller encouraged me to pursue the analysis of the intimate relations between eroticism and aggression that he had so brilliantly pioneered. The contributions in this area of Drs. Leon Altman, Jacob Arlow, Martha Kirkpatrick, and John Munder-Ross further stimulated my thinking.

As before, a group of close friends and colleagues within the psychoanalytic community have been of great help with their critical, yet always encouraging and stimulating, reactions to my work: Drs. Harold Blum, Arnold Cooper, William Frosch, William Grossman, Donald Kaplan, Paulina Kernberg, Robert Michels, Gilbert Rose, Joseph and Anne-Marie Sandler, and Ernst and Gertrude Ticho.

As before, I am deeply grateful to Louise Taitt and Becky Whipple for their cheerful and patient work throughout the many steps leading from early drafts to the final manuscript. Ms. Whipple's unwavering concern with every small detail of this manuscript has been essential in its production. Rosalind Kennedy, my administrative assistant, continued to provide the overall care, organization, and coordination of the work in my office that permitted the manuscript to emerge in the middle of many competing tasks and deadlines.

This is now the third book I have written with the close collaboration of Natalie Altman, my editor over many years, and Gladys Topkis, senior editor at Yale University Press. Their strong yet always encouraging, tactfully critical review of my writing has once again been an enlightening experience.

My deeply felt gratitude goes to all the friends, colleagues, and coworkers I have mentioned, and to my patients and students, who have provided me with more insight in a relatively few years than I dared hoped to acquire throughout my life span. They have also taught me to accept the limits of my understanding of this vast and complex area of human experience.

I am grateful also to the original publishers for permission to reprint material in the following chapters. All of this material has been largely reworked and modified.

Chapter 2: Adapted from "New Perspectives in Psychoanalytic Affect Theory," in *Emotion: Theory, Research, and Experience*, ed. R. Plutchik and H. Kellerman (New York: Academic Press, 1989), 115–130, and from "Sadomasochism, Sexual Excitement, and Perversion," *Journal of the American Psychoanalytic Association* 39(1991): 333–362. Published with the permission of Academic Press and the *Journal of the American Psychoanalytic Association.*

Chapter 3: Adapted from "Mature Love: Prerequisites and Characteristics," *Journal of the American Psychoanalytic Association* 22 (1974): 743–768, and from "Boundaries and Structure in Love Relations," *Journal of the American Psychoanalytic Association* 25 (1977): 81–114. Published with the permission of the *Journal of the American Psychoanalytic Association*.

Chapter 4: Adapted from "Sadomasochism, Sexual Excitement, and Perversion," *Journal of the American Psychoanalytic Association* 39 (1991): 333–362, and from "Boundaries and Structure in Love Relations," *Journal of the American Psychoanalytic Association* 25 (1977): 81–114. Published with the permission of the *Journal of the American Psychoanalytic Association*.

Chapter 5: Adapted from "Barriers to Falling and Remaining in Love," *Journal of the American Psychoanalytic Association* 22 (1974): 486–511. Published with the permission of the *Journal of the American Psychoanalytic Association*.

Chapter 6: Adapted from "Aggression and Love in the Relationship of the Couple," *Journal of the American Psychoanalytic Association* 39 (1991): 45–70. Published with the permission of the *Journal of the American Psychoanalytic Association*.

Chapter 7: Adapted from "The Couple's Constructive and Destructive Superego Functions," *Journal of the American Psychoanalytic Association* 41 (1993): 653–677. Published with the permission of the *Journal of the American Psychoanalytic Association*.

Chapter 8: Adapted from "Love in the Analytic Setting," accepted for publication by the *Journal of the American Psychoanalytic Association*. Published with the permission of the *Journal of the American Psychoanalytic Association*.

Chapter 11: Adapted from "The Temptations of Conventionality," *International Review of Psychoanalysis* 16 (1989): 191–205, and from "The Erotic Element in Mass Psychology and in Art," *Bulletin of the Menninger Clinic* 58, no. 1 (Winter, 1994). Published with the permission of the *International Review of Psychoanalysis* and the *Bulletin of the Menninger Clinic*.

Chapter 12: Adapted from "Adolescent Sexuality in the Light of Group Processes," *Psychoanalytic Quarterly* 49, no. 1 (1980): 27–47, and from "Love, the Couple and the Group: A Psychoanalytic Frame," *The Psychoanalytic Quarterly* 49, no. 1 (1980): 78–108. Published with the permission of the *Psychoanalytic Quarterly*.

Love Relations

The Sexual Experience

That sex and love are closely associated is hardly debatable. It should therefore come as no surprise that a book about love should start with a discussion of the biological and psychological roots of the sexual experience, which are intimately related. Because the biological aspects constitute the matrix within which the psychological aspects may develop, let us begin by exploring the biological factors.

The Biological Roots of Sexual Experience and Behavior

In tracing the development of human sexual characteristics, we see that as we advance along the biological scale of the animal kingdom (particularly when comparing low-order mammals with primates and humans) the psychosocial interactions between infant and caregiver play an increasingly significant role in determining sexual behavior, and there is a relative decrease in control by genetic and hormonal factors. My principal sources for the overview to follow are Money and Ehrhardt's (1972) pioneering work in this area and the subsequent advances summarized by Kolodny et al. (1979), Bancroft (1989), and McConaghy (1993).

In the early stages of its development, the mammalian embryo has the potential to be male or female. Undifferentiated gonads differentiate into either testes or ovaries, depending on the genetic code represented by the different characteristics of the 46, XY chromosome pattern for males and the 46, XX pattern for females. Primitive gonads in the human may be detected from about the sixth week of gestation, when, under the influence of the genetic code, testicular hormones are secreted in males: the Müllerian duct inhibiting hormone (MIH), which has a defeminizing effect on the gonadal structure, and testosterone, which promotes the growth of internal and external masculine organs, particularly the bilat-

1

eral Wolffian ducts. If a female genetic code is present, ovarian differentiation begins at the twelfth gestational week.

Differentiation always occurs in the female direction, regardless of genetic programming, unless an adequate level of testosterone is present. In other words, even if the genetic code is masculine, an inadequate amount of testosterone will result in the development of female sexual characteristics. The principle of feminization takes priority over masculinization. During normal female differentiation, the primitive Müllerian duct system develops into the uterus, the fallopian tubes, and the inner third of the vagina. In males, the Müllerian duct system regresses, and the Wolffian duct system develops, becoming the vasa deferentia, seminal vesicles, and ejaculatory ducts.

Whereas the internal precursors of both male and female sexual organs are thus present for potential development, the precursors for the external genitals are unitypic, that is, the same precursors may develop into either masculine or feminine external sexual organs. Without the presence of adequate levels of androgens (testosterone and dehydrotestosterone) during the critical period of differentiation, beginning with the eight-week fetus, a clitoris, vulva, and vagina will develop. But with the presence of adequate levels of androgen stimulation, the penis, including its glans, and the scrotal sack will form, and the testes will develop as organs within the abdomen. They normally migrate into their scrotal position during the eighth or ninth month of gestation.

Under the influence of circulating fetal hormones, a dimorphic development of certain areas of the brain takes place following the differentiation of internal and external genitals. The brain is ambitypic, and in it the development of female characteristics also prevails unless there is an adequate level of circulating androgens. Specific hypothalamic and pituitary functions that will be differentiated into the cyclic in women and noncyclic in men are determined by this differentiation. Male/female differentiation of the brain occurs only in the third trimester, after differentiation of external sex organs has taken place, and possibly continues during the first postnatal trimester. In nonprimate mammals, the prenatal hormonal differentiation of the brain preorders subsequent mating behavior. In primates, however, early social communication and learning are overridingly important in determining sexual behavior; the control of actual mating behavior is therefore determined largely by the earliest social interactions.

The secondary sexual characteristics, which emerge during puberty—distribution of body fat and hair, change of voice, development of breasts, and significant growth of the genitals—are triggered by central nervous system factors and controlled by a significant increase of circulating androgens or estrogens, as are the specific female functions of menstruation, gestation, and lactation.

Hormonal imbalances may alter the secondary sexual characteristics, bringing about, with lack of androgens, gynecomastia in males and, with excessive androgens, hirsutism, voice deepening, and clitoral hypertrophy in females. But the influences of alterations in hormonal levels on sexual desire and behavior are much less clear.

Exactly how the central nervous system affects the onset of puberty is also still unclear; a reduction in the sensitivity of the hypothalamus to negative feedback has been considered to be one mechanism involved (Bancroft 1989). In males, inadequate availability of circulating androgens reduces the intensity of sexual desire; but when circulating androgens are at normal or above-normal levels, sexual desire and behavior are remarkably independent of these fluctuations. Prepubertal castration in human males who do not receive testosterone replacement leads to sexual apathy. Exogenous testosterone during adolescence in males with primary failure of androgenization restores normal sexual desire and behavior. The response to replacement therapy with testosterone in later years, however, when apathy has become established, is less satisfactory: critical time sequences seem to play a part here. Similarly, although studies of women indicate a heightened sexual desire just before and after the menstrual cycle, the dependency of sexual desire on fluctuations of hormonal levels is insignificant when compared with psychosocial stimuli. In fact, McConaghy (1993) thinks that female sexual desire may be more influenced by psychosocial factors than male sexual desire.

In primates and lower forms of mammals, however, sexual interest as well as sexual behavior are strongly controlled by hormones. Mating behavior in rodents is determined by hormonal status alone, and early postnatal injection of hormones may crucially influence it. Postpubertal castration leads to a decrease of erection and sexual interest progressing gradually over weeks or even years; testosterone injections immediately reverse this indifference. Androgen injections in postmenopausal women increase their sexual desire, without in any way changing their sexual orientation.

In short, androgens appear to influence the intensity of sexual desire in human males and females, but within the context of a clear predominance of psychosocial determinants for sexual arousal. Although in low-order mammals such as rodents sexual behavior is controlled largely by hormones, in primates such control is somewhat modified by psychosocial stimuli. Male rhesus monkeys are stimulated by the odor of a vaginal

hormone secreted during ovulation. Female rhesus monkeys are most interested in mating at the time of ovulation, but they are interested at other
times as well, with individual preferences noticeable; here again, androgen
levels influence the intensity of females' sexual presenting behavior. The
injection of testosterone in the preoptic area of male rats elicits maternal
and mating behavior in them, but their copulation with females persists.
Testosterone seems to release maternal behavior, a potential that males
also contain in their brain and that speaks to the central nervous system's
control of discrete aspects of sexual behavior. This biological finding suggests that sexual behaviors ordinarily characteristic of one gender or more
charactcristic of onc gender can potentially exist in the other gender as
well.

The intensity of sexual arousal, the focused attention on sexual stimuli, the physiological responses of sexual excitement—increased blood
flow, tumescence, and lubrication of sexual organs—are all under hormonal influence.

Psychosocial Factors

The preceding discussion covers what is more or less accepted as biological; we now move into controversial, less understood areas in which
biological and psychological determinants overlap or interact. One such
area is that involving core gender identity and gender-role identity. In
humans the core gender identity (Stoller 1975b)—that is, the individual's
sense of being either male or female—is determined not by biological
characteristics but by the gender assigned it by its caretakers during the
first two to four years of life. Money (1980, 1986, 1988; Money and Ehrhardt 1972) and Stoller (1985) have offered convincing evidence in this
regard. Similarly, gender-role identity—that is, the individual's identification with certain behaviors as typical for males or females in a given
society—is also heavily influenced by psychosocial factors. Further,
psychoanalytic exploration reveals that the selection of the sexual object—the target of sexual desire—is also strongly influenced by early psychosocial experience.

In what follows, I examine salient evidence regarding the roots of these
constituents of human sexual experience. They are:

Core gender identity: whether an individual considers himself/herself
to be male or female.
Gender role identity: the particular psychological attitudes and interpersonal behaviors—general patterns of social interactions as well as

specifically sexual ones—that are characteristic for either men or women and therefore differentiate them.

Dominant object choice: the selection of a sexual object, whether heterosexual or homosexual, and whether focused on a broad range of sexual interactions with the sexual object, or restricted to a particular part of the human anatomy or a nonhuman or inanimate object.

Intensity of sexual desire: reflected in the dominance of sexual fantasy, alertness to sexual stimuli, desire for sexual behavior, and physiological excitement of genital organs.

Core Gender Identity

Money and Ehrhardt (1972) offer evidence that parents, under ordinary circumstances, even if they believe they are treating baby boys and baby girls exactly the same way, show gender-determined differences in their behavior toward their infants. Although there are male/female differences based on prenatal hormonal history, these differences do not automatically determine postnatal male/female behavioral differentiation: feminizing hormonal pathology in males and masculinizing hormonal pathology in females, except under conditions of extreme degrees of hormonal abnormality, may influence gender-role identity more than core gender identity.

Excessive androgens in a girl's prenatal period may be responsible, for example, for tomboyism and increased expenditure of energy in recreation and aggression. Inadequate prenatal androgen stimulation in a boy may cause a certain passivity and nonaggressiveness but does not influence core gender identity. Further, hermaphrodite children who are reared unambiguously as girls or boys will develop a solid identity as male or female in consonance with rearing practices, regardless of their genetic endowment, hormonal production, and even—to some extent—the external appearance of genital development (Money and Ehrhardt 1972; Meyer 1980).

Stoller (1975b) and Person and Ovesey (1983, 1984) have explored the relationship between early pathology in the child-parent interaction and the consolidation of core gender identity. Transsexualism—that is, the establishment of a core gender identity contrary to the biological one in individuals with a clearly defined biological gender—has not been found to be related to genetic, hormonal, or genital physical abnormalities. Although the research on subtle biological variables, particularly in female transsexuals, raises the question of some possible hormonal influences, the overriding evidence is of severe pathology in early psychosocial interactions.

In this regard, psychoanalytic exploration of children with abnormal sexual identity, as well as of the history of transsexual adults, provides information about significant patterns first described by Stoller (1975b). These include, for male transsexuals (biological males who experience themselves as having a core identity as a woman), a mother with strong bisexual personality components who is distant from her passive or unavailable husband and who engulfs her son as a symbolic provision of completeness for herself. Blissful symbiosis, which implicitly eliminates the boy's maleness leads him both to excessive identification with the mother and rejection of the male role that has been unacceptable to her and inadequately modeled by the father. In female transscxuals, the mother's rejecting behavior and the unavailability of the father propel the daughter, who feels not reinforced as a little girl, into becoming a substitute male and ameliorating her mother's sense of loneliness and depression. Her masculine behavior is encouraged by the mother, whose despondency then lifts, and leads to improved family solidarity.

Early parental behavior (particularly maternal) that influences core gender identity, and sexual functioning in general, is not exclusive to humans. Harlow and Harlow (1965), in their classic work with primates, demonstrated that an adequate attachment by means of secure, physically close contact between infant and mother is essential for the development of a normal sexual response in adult monkeys: the absence of normal mothering and, secondarily, of interaction with peer groups in critical developmental phases disrupts the later capacity for adult sexual response. These monkeys are also maladaptive in other social interactions.

Although Freud (1905, 1933) proposed a psychological bisexuality for both genders, he postulated that the earliest genital identity for both boys and girls was masculine. He proposed that girls—first fixated on the clitoris as a source of pleasure parallel to the penis—switched their primary genital identity (and implicit homosexual orientation) from mother to father in a positive oedipal orientation as an expression of disappointment at not having a penis, castration anxiety, and the symbolic wish to replace a penis by means of father's child. Stoller (1975b, 1985), however, suggested that, given the intense attachment and symbiotic relationship with the mother, the earliest identification of both male and female infants is feminine, with a gradual shift, as part of separation-individuation, in the infant male from a female to a male identity. But Person and Ovesey (1983, 1984), on the basis of their studies of patients with homosexual orientation, transvestism, and transsexualism, postulated an original gender identity that is male or female from the very start. I believe that their view dovetails with the studies of core gender identity in hermaphrodites by Money and Ehrhardt (1972) and Meyer (1980), as well as with observations of interactions between mothers and male and female infants from the beginning of life and with the psychoanalytic observations of normal children in addition to those with sexual disturbances, particularly studies that consider the conscious and unconscious sexual orientations of the parents (Galenson 1980; Stoller 1985).

Braunschweig and Fain (1971, 1975), in agreement with Freud's hypothesis of an original psychological bisexuality in both genders, argue persuasively in favor of a psychological bisexuality derived from the infant's unconscious identification with both parents, a bisexual identification that is controlled by the nature of the mother-infant interaction in which core gender identity is established. According to Money and Ehrhardt (1972), it does not matter "if father cooks the dinner and mother drives the tractor"; that is, socially defined gender roles of the parents are irrelevant as long as their gender identity is strongly differentiated.

The assignment and adoption of a core gender identity determine, for practical purposes, the reinforcement of gender roles considered male or female. Insofar as an unconscious identification with both parents—an unconscious bisexuality that is a universal finding in psychoanalytic exploration—also implies unconscious identification with roles socially assigned to one or the other gender, there exist strong tendencies toward bisexual attitudes and behavior patterns, as well as toward bisexual orientation as a universal human potential. It may well be that the strong social and cultural emphasis on core gender identity ("You must be either a little boy or a little girl") is reinforced or codetermined by the intrapsychic need to integrate and consolidate a personal identity in general, so that the core gender identity cements core ego identity formation; in fact, as Lichtenstein (1961) suggested, sexual identity may constitute the core of ego identity. Clinically, we find that a lack of integration of identity (the syndrome of identity diffusion) regularly coexists with problems of gender identity, and, as Ovesey and Person (1973, 1976) have stressed, transsexuals usually show severe distortions in other areas of identity as well.

Gender-Role Identity

In a classic study, Maccoby and Jacklin (1974) conclude that there are unfounded beliefs about these differences, some that are fairly well established and some that are open to question or are ambiguous. The unfounded beliefs include the assumptions that girls are more "social" and "suggestible" than boys, have lower self-esteem, lack achievement motivation, and are better at rote learning and simple repetitive tasks. Boys are assumed to be better at tasks that require higher cognitive processing and the inhibition of previous learned responses and to be more "analytic." Girls are assumed to be more affected by heredity, boys by environment; girls are more auditory, boys more visual.

Established gender differences include the following: girls have greater verbal ability than do boys, boys excel in visual-spatial and mathematical tasks, and boys are more aggressive. Open to question are differences in tactile sensitivity; fear, timidity, and anxiety; activity level; competitiveness; dominance; compliance; nurturance; and "maternal" behavior.

Which of these psychological differences are genetically determined, which are socially determined by socializing agents, and which are spontaneously learned through imitation? Maccoby and Jacklin argue (and there is much evidence to support them) that biological factors have been clearly implicated in gender differences regarding aggression and visual-spatial ability. There is evidence of greater male aggression in both humans and subhuman primates; this seems cross-culturally universal, and evidence suggests that levels of aggression are linked to sex hormones. It is probable that male predisposition toward aggression extends to such behaviors as dominance, competitiveness, and activity level, but the evidence is not decisive. Maccoby and Jacklin conclude that a genetically controlled characteristic may take the form of a greater readiness to display a particular kind of behavior. This includes but is not limited to learned behaviors.

Friedman and Downey (1993) reviewed the evidence on the influence of prenatal hormonal virilizing pathology in girls with regard to postnatal sexual behavior. They examined the findings from a study of girls with congenital adrenal hyperplasia and of girls whose mothers had ingested sex-steroidlike hormones during pregnancy. These children were raised as girls; although their core gender identity was female, the question was the extent to which the dominance of prenatal male hormones would influence their core gender identity and their gender-role identity during childhood and adolescence.

Although a modest association of excessive prenatal androgens and an increased prevalence of homosexuality was found, more significant was the finding that, regardless of rearing circumstances, girls with congenital adrenal hyperplasia showed more tomboyish behavior, had less interest in doll play, infants, and self-adornment, and tended to prefer such toys as cars and guns more than the controls did. They had a greater preference for boys as playmates and displayed higher energy expenditure and more rough-and-tumble activity at play. The findings suggest that childhood gender-role behavior is influenced by prenatal hormonal factors. Friedman (personal communication) agrees with Maccoby and Jacklin (1974) that the majority of traits differentiating boys and girls are in all likelihood culturally determined.

Richard Green (1976) studied the upbringing of effeminate boys. He found that the dominant factors determining the development of effeminate behavior are parental indifference to or encouragement of feminine behavior, cross-dressing of the child by a female in parental function, maternal overprotection, father's absence or rejection, the child's physical beauty, and the lack of male playmates. The crucial common feature seemed to be a failure to discourage feminine behavior. Follow-up showed a high percentage of bisexuality and homosexuality among the effeminate boys—up to 75 percent of two-thirds of the original sample (Green 1987).

Behavior characteristic of the other gender—tomboyishness in girls, effeminacy in boys—is often but not necessarily linked with a homosexual object choice. In fact, one might consider gender-role identity to be related as closely to core gender identity as to object choice: a sexual orientation toward one's own gender may influence the adoption of roles socially identified with the other gender. Conversely, a predominant acculturation toward gender roles that coincide with those of the other gender might predispose a child toward homosexuality. This brings us to our next constituent, object choice.

The Dominant Object Choice

Money (1980) and Perper (1985) use the term *templates* of human behavior in referring to the object of the individual's sexual arousal. Perper believes that such templates are not encoded but derive from developmental processes, including genetic regulation of neural development and later neurophysiological construction of the image of the desired other. Money designates as *lovemaps* the development of the sexual objects one selects; he sees these as derived from schemata implanted in the brain and complemented by environmental input before age eight. One can hardly fail to notice that the language of these major researchers in early human sexual development remains very general when they are discussing the nature of sexual object choice. A review of the literature reveals that little if any actual research has been done on the sexual experiences of children, in contrast to the extensive research completed on gender-role and core gender identity.

Behind this dearth of research and well-documented knowledge lies, I believe, the resistance to recognizing the existence of childhood sexuality, the taboo that Freud so daringly defied. This is linked with the prohibitions against infantile sexual behavior in Western culture. Cultural anthropology (Endleman 1989) provides evidence that in the absence of such prohibitions children engage spontaneously in sexual behavior. Galenson and Roiphe (1974), observing children in a naturalistic nursery setting, found that boys begin genital play at about the sixth or seventh month, girls at the tenth or eleventh month, and that masturbation is established at fifteen to sixteen months for both genders. Working-class children are twice as likely to masturbate as are middle-class children, suggesting that class structure and culture influence sexual behavior.

Fisher (1989) has reported how children's ability to think logically about their genitals lags dramatically behind their general level of logic; how girls tend to ignore the clitoris and mystify the nature of the vagina; and how parents unconsciously repeat with their children their own childhood experiences of sexual suppression. Evidence also exists of ignorance regarding sexual matters persisting throughout adolescence.

Money and Ehrhardt (1972) and Bancroft (1989) speak of a widespread fear of investigating childhood sexuality. But in view of the rising public concern about child sexual abuse, Bancroft suggests, it is conceivable "that a need for better understanding of childhood sexuality will be more widely recognized and research into this aspect of childhood may become easier to carry out in the future" (p. 152). Even psychoanalysis did not until recently discard the concept of the "latency years," a phase during which very little sexual interest and activity are supposedly in evidence. There is a growing awareness among child analysts that these years are in fact characterized by greater internalized control and suppression of sexual behavior (Paulina Kernberg, personal communication).

The evidence, it seems to me, points overwhelmingly to the conclusion that psychological or, rather, psychosocial factors determine core gender identity and significantly if not exclusively influence gender-role identity; there is less clear-cut evidence that these factors influence sexual object choice. The sexual life of primates tells us of the importance of early learning, mother-infant contact, and peer relations in the development of sexual behavior and the relatively diminishing role of hormones in determining sexual object choice in comparison with nonprimate mammals. In the human infant, as we have seen, this process evolves further.

Meyer (1980) has suggested that, just as the infant and small child unconsciously identify with the parent of the same gender in establishing core-gender and gender-role identities, so they identify with that parent's sexual interest in the other parent. Money and Ehrhardt (1972) also emphasize that the rules of male/female behavior are learned and stress the child's identification with reciprocal and complementary aspects of the relationship between men and women. The striking clinical evidence of mutual seductive behavior between child and parents is often bypassed in academic studies of gender identity and gender role, perhaps because of the persisting cultural taboo against childhood sexuality.

Two specific contributions of psychoanalytic observations and theory are relevant to these issues. The first is a psychoanalytic object relations theory that permits the incorporation of identification processes and complementarity of roles into a single model of development. The second, Freud's theory of the Oedipus complex, I discuss later in another context. Here I refer to my earlier work, in which I proposed that identity formation derives from the earliest relationship between infant and mother, particularly when the infant's experiences involve intense affect, either pleasurable or painful.

Memory traces established under these affective conditions leave core schemata of the infant's self representation interacting with the object representation of the mother under the impact of either pleasurable or unpleasurable affect. As a consequence, two parallel and originally separate series of self and object representations and their corresponding positive and negative affect dispositions are built up. These respectively "all-good" and "all-bad" representations of self and object eventually are integrated into a representation of the total self and a representation of total significant others, a process that constitutes normal identity integration. In earlier writings (1976, 1980a, 1992), I have also stressed my conviction that identity is built from identifications made with a *relationship* to an object rather than with the object itself. This implies an identification with both the self and the other in their interaction and an internalization of the reciprocal roles of that interaction. The establishment of core gender identity—that is, of an integrated concept of self that defines the individual's identification with one or the other gender—cannot be seen as separate from the establishment of a corresponding integrated concept of the other that includes a relationship to this other as desired sexual object. This link between core gender identity and the choice of the sexually desired object explains, at the same time, the intrinsic bisexuality of human development: we identify both with our own self and with our object of desire.

Insofar as the male child, for example, experiences himself as a male child loved by his mother, he identifies with the male-child role and with the female-mother role. He thus acquires the ability, in later interactions, to actualize his self representation while projecting the representation of mother onto another woman, or—under certain circumstances—to enact the role of mother while projecting his self representation onto another man. The dominance of the self representation as male child as part of ego identity will assure the dominance of a heterosexual orientation (including the unconscious search for mother in all other women). The dominance of the identification with mother's representation may determine one type of homosexuality in men (Freud 1914).

In the female child, insofar as her first relationship with the mother cements her core gender identity by identifying with both her own and her mother's role in their interaction, her later wish to replace father as mother's love object as well as her positive choice of father in the oedipal relation consolidate her unconscious identification with him, too. She thus also establishes an unconscious bisexual identification. Identification with a relationship rather than with a person and the building up of reciprocal role dispositions in the unconscious mind suggest that bisexuality is psychologically determined, reflected in the capacity for acquiring both a core gender identity and a sexual interest in a person of the other (or the same) gender at the same time. This also facilitates the integration of gender roles of the other gender with one's own and the identification with socially transmitted gender roles corresponding to one's own and the other gender.

This view of early sexuality suggests that Freud's (1933) concept of an original bisexuality was correct, as was his questioning of its apparent linkage with the known biological structural differences of the genders. In other words, we still lack evidence of a direct connection between the dimorphic anatomical disposition to bisexuality and the psychic bisexuality derived from early experience.

Intensity of Sexual Desire

As we have seen, the biological machinery for sexual arousal, sexual excitement, and sexual intercourse including orgasm is relatively well understood. It is the stimuli that evoke a sexual response, the subjective quality of arousal, that are still an open question. Also, we still lack consensus regarding how to measure the quantitative factors of intensity of arousal. Another problem is the comparative study of male and female arousal; again, although their physiological concomitants are well known, their psychological similarities and differences remain controversial.

In summary, an adequate level of circulating androgens appears to be a prerequisite for the human capacity for sexual response, thus influencing sexual desire in both males and females; but at normal and above-normal hormonal levels, sexual desire and behavior are remarkably independent of hormonal fluctuations. For humans, the dominant factor determining the intensity of sexual desire is cognitive—the conscious awareness of sexual interest reflected in sexual fantasies, memories, and alertness to sexual stimuli. The experience itself is not purely "cognitive"; it contains a strong affective element. In fact, the sexual experience is above all an affective-cognitive one.

Physiologically, affective memory is related to the limbic system, which is the neural substrate of sexuality, as it is of other appetitive functions (Maclean 1976). Animal studies have demonstrated that selected limbic areas determine erection and ejaculation and the existence of both excitatory and inhibitory mechanisms affecting the peripheral response of erection. Mounting behavior in male rhesus monkeys has been induced by electrical stimulation of the lateral hypothalamus and the dorsomedial nucleus of the hypothalamus, leading to coital sequences and ejaculation when the monkeys are freely moving.

According to Bancroft (1989), human sexual arousal is a global response that includes specific sexual fantasies, memories, and desires, and an increased awareness of and search for reinforcing external stimuli that are relatively specific to the individual's sexual orientation and sexual object. Sexual arousal, according to Bancroft, includes the activation of the limbic system under the influence of this cognitive-affective state, which stimulates the central spinal and peripheral neural control centers that determine engorgement, lubrication, and heightened local sensitivity of the genital organs, providing a central feedback of awareness of this genital activation. I am suggesting that sexual excitement is a specific affect that fulfills all the characteristics of affective structures and constitutes the central "building block" of the sexual or libidinal drive as an overall motivational system.

Terminology in this area may need some clarification. Biologically, the sexual response can be divided into sexual arousal, sexual excitement, and orgasm. But because sexual arousal may occur without the activation of specific genital responses, and genital responses are possible with limited or minimal sexual arousal, it seems preferable to use *sexual arousal* to refer to general awareness of, thinking about, interest in, and response to sexual stimuli. *Genital excitement* would refer to a full-fledged genital response: vascular engorgement and tumefaction leading to erection in the male and the corresponding erectile processes and vaginal lubrication, with engorgement of the breasts and nipple erection in the female.

Sexual excitement seems an appropriate term for the total response, including the specific cognitive aspects and subjective experience of sexual arousal, genital excitement, and orgasm, and the corresponding neurovegetative and facially expressive aspects (part of what Freud called the discharge process) of this affect. I consider sexual excitement, in turn, to be the basic affect of a more complex psychological phenomenon, namely, *erotic desire*, in which sexual excitement is linked to an emotional relationship with a specific object. Let us now examine the nature of sexual excitement and its elaboration into erotic desire.

2.

Sexual Excitement and Erotic Desire

Affects are, in phylogenetic terms, a relatively recent characteristic of mammals, and their basic biological function is infant-caregiver communication, as well as general communication among individuals that serve basic instincts (Krause 1990). If feeding, fight-flight, and mating are basic instinctive organizations, the corresponding affect states may be considered their components, which acquire hierarchically supraordinate roles as we ascend the evolutionary ladder, particularly in primates and, of course, in humans.

Sexual excitement occupies a very particular place among affects. That it is rooted in biological functions and in structures serving the biological instinct of reproduction in the animal kingdom and that it occupies a central position in the human psychological experience as well seem self-evident. But sexual excitement does not develop as early and is not as uniform in its manifestations as such primitive affects as rage, elation, sadness, surprise, and disgust. In its cognitive and subjective constituents, it resembles the complex affects, such as pride, shame, guilt, and contempt.

Psychoanalysis and psychoanalytically inspired infant observation provide abundant evidence that sexual excitement originates in the context of the pleasurable experiences of early infant-caregiver and familial relationships, and culminates in the full-fledged centrality of genital sensations in puberty and adolescence. The diffuse excitability of the skin involved in early attachment behavior, the sexually exciting qualities of what Freud described as the erotogenic zones, and the cognitive imprints and unconscious fantasy developments linked to intense pleasurable affect activation from infancy forward culminate in the specific cognitive-affective experience of sexual excitement.

15

The particular conscious and unconscious focus of an individual's sexual object choice transforms sexual excitement into *erotic desire*. Erotic desire includes the wish for a sexual relationship with a particular object. Sexual excitement, however, is not objectless. Like other affects, it exists in relation to an object, but the object is a primitive "part-object," unconsciously reflecting the fusional experiences of symbiosis and the merger wishes of early separation-individuation.

In its origins, in the first year or two of life, sexual excitement is diffuse and linked to the stimulation of erogenous zones. In contrast, the affect of erotic desire is more elaborated, and the specific nature of the object relation is cognitively more differentiated.

Erotic desire is characterized by sexual excitement linked to the oedipal object; the desire is for symbiotic fusion with the oedipal object in the context of sexual merger. Under normal circumstances, sexual excitement in the mature individual is activated in the context of erotic desire, so that my distinction between these two affects may appear forced or artificial. Under pathological circumstances, such as severe narcissistic pathology, dismantling the internal world of object relations may lead to the incapacity for erotic desire, with a diffuse, nonselective, and perpetually dissatisfied random manifestation of sexual excitement, or even to a lack of the capacity to experience sexual excitement.

Mature sexual love, which we shall explore in subsequent chapters, expands erotic desire into a relationship with a specific person in which the activation of unconscious relationships from the past and conscious expectations of a future life as a couple combine with the activation of a joint ego ideal. Mature sexual love implies a commitment in the realms of sex, emotions, and values.

The proposed definitions immediately raise certain questions: if sexual excitement and erotic desire develop in the context of the early relationship between infant and caregiver and the evolving oedipal situation, are they secondary to the development of these object relations? Are biological dispositions "recruited," so to speak, in the service of the developing world of internalized and actual object relations? Or is the gradual maturation of the biological apparatus, which permits the development of sexual excitement, the organizer of early and later object relations? Here we enter the controversial territory of psychoanalytic theory regarding the relationships among biological instincts, psychological drives, and internalized object relations. It will be necessary to explore these issues before returning to the particular cognitive structures involved in erotic desire—the early fantasy structures that transform sexual excitement into erotic desire.

Instincts, Drives, Affects, and Object Relations

As Holder (1970) pointed out, Freud clearly differentiated drives from instincts. He saw drives as psychological motivators of human behavior, constant rather than intermittent. He saw instincts, on the other hand, as biological, inherited, and intermittent in the sense that they are activated by physiological and/or environmental factors. Libido is a drive, hunger an instinct.

Laplanche and Pontalis (1973) appropriately stress Freud's referring to instincts as behavior patterns that vary little from one member of the species to another. It is impressive to see how closely Freud's concept of instinct resembles modern instinct theory in biology as represented, for example, by Tinbergen (1951), Lorenz (1963), and Wilson (1975). These investigators consider instincts hierarchical organizations of biologically determined perceptual, behavioral, and communicative patterns, triggered by environmental factors that activate inborn releasing mechanisms. This biological-environmental system is considered to be epigenetic. As Lorenz and Tinbergen illustrated in their animal research, the organization of the maturational and developmental linkage of discrete inborn behavior patterns within a particular individual is very much determined by the nature of environmental stimulation. Instincts, in this view, are hierarchically organized, biological motivating systems. Usually classified along the lines of feeding or fight-flight or mating behavior, and perhaps along other lines as well, they represent the integration of inborn dispositions and environmentally determined learning.

Although Freud recognized the ultimate biological sources of the drives, he repeatedly stressed the lack of available information regarding the processes that transform these biological predispositions into psychic motivation. His concept of libido or the sexual drive was of a hierarchically supraordinate organization of developmentally earlier "partial" sexual drives. The dual-drive theory of sexuality and aggression (1920) represents his final conception of drives as the ultimate source of unconscious psychic conflict and psychic structure formation. Freud described the biological sources of sexual drives according to the excitability of the erotogenic zones, but he did not describe such concrete biological sources for aggression. In contrast to the fixed sources of libido, he characterized the aims and objects of both sexual and aggressive drives as changing throughout psychic development: the developmental continuity of sexual and aggressive motivations could be recognized in a broad variety of complex psychic developments.

Freud had proposed (1915b,c,d) that drives are manifested by means of psychic representations or ideas—that is, the cognitive expression of the drive—and an affect. Freud changed his definition of affects at least twice (Rapaport 1953). He originally (1894) thought that affects were pretty much equivalent to drives. He later (1915b,d) considered them discharge products of drives (particularly their pleasurable or painful, psychomotor, and neurovegetative features). These discharge processes may reach consciousness but do not undergo repression; only the mental representation of the drive is repressed, together with the memory of or a disposition toward activating the corresponding affect. Eventually (1926) Freud described affects as inborn dispositions (thresholds and channels) of the ego and emphasized their signal functions.

If affects and emotions (that is, cognitively elaborated affects) are complex structures, including subjective experiences of pain or pleasure with particular cognitive and expressive-communicative ingredients and neurovegetative discharge patterns, and if they are present—as infant researchers have found (Emde et al. 1978; Izard 1978; Emde 1987; Stern 1985)—from the earliest weeks and months of life, are they the primary motivational forces of psychic development? If they include both cognitive and affective components, what is left in the broader concept of drive that is not contained in the concept of affect? Freud implied that the drives are present from birth on, but he also implied that they matured and developed. It may be argued that the maturation and development of affects are expressions of the underlying drives, but if all the functions and manifestations of drives can be included in the functions and manifestations of developing affects, a concept of independent drives underlying the organization of affects would be difficult to sustain. In fact, the transformation of affects throughout development, their integration with internalized object relations, their overall developing dichotomy into pleasurable ones building up the libidinal series and painful ones building up the aggressive series, all point to the richness and complexity of their cognitive as well as affective elements.

I view affects as instinctive structures (see Kernberg 1992), psychophysiological in nature, biologically given, and developmentally activated, which include psychic components. I believe that this psychic aspect becomes organized to constitute the aggressive and libidinal drives Freud described. The partial sexual drives, in my view, are more limited, restricted integrations of corresponding affect states, whereas libido as a drive is the result of the hierarchically supraordinate integration of these states—that is, the integration of all erotically centered affect states. Therefore, in contrast to the still quite prevalent psychoanalytic view of affects as merely discharge products, I consider them the bridging structures between biological instincts and psychic drives. I believe that affective development is based on affectively imbued object relations in the form of affective memory. Emde, Izard, and Stern all point to the central function of object relations in the activation of affects. This association supports my proposal that early affect states fixed in memory include such object relations.

I think that the activation of different affect states toward the same object occurs under the influence of a variety of developmental tasks and biologically activated, instinctive behavior patterns. The resulting variety of affect states directed to the same object may provide an economical explanation of how affects are linked and transformed into a supraordinate motivational series that becomes the sexual or aggressive drive. For example, the pleasurable oral stimulations during nursing and the pleasurable anal stimulations during toilet training may result in a condensation of pleasurable interactions of infant and mother that link such oral and anal libidinal developments. And the infant's enraged reaction to frustrations during the oral period and the power struggles characteristic of the anal period may link consonant aggressive affect states, resulting in the aggressive drive. Further, the infant's intense positive affective investment of mother during the practicing stage of separation-individuation (Mahler et al. 1975) may become linked with a sexually imbued longing for her derived from the activation of genital sensations in the oedipal stage of development.

But if we view affects as the primary, psychobiological "building blocks" of drives and as the earliest motivational systems, we still have to explain how they become organized into hierarchically supraordinate systems. Why not say that the primary affects themselves are the ultimate motivational systems? Because I believe that affects undergo a multitude of secondary combinations and transformations throughout development, a theory of motivation based on affects rather than on two basic drives would be complicated and clinically unsatisfactory. I also believe that the unconscious integration of affectively determined early experience requires assuming a higher level of motivational organization than that represented by affect states per se. We need to assume a motivational system that does justice to the complex integration of all affective developments in relation to the parental objects.

Similarly, an effort to replace both drive and affect theory with an attachment theory or an object relations theory that rejects the concept of drives leads to reducing the complexity of intrapsychic life by stressing only the positive or libidinal elements of attachment and neglecting the unconscious organization of aggression. Although in theory this should not be necessarily so, in practice object relations theoreticians who have rejected drive theory have, in my view, also seriously neglected the motivational aspects of aggression.

For these reasons, I think we should not replace a drive theory by an affect theory or by an object relations theory of motivation. It seems eminently reasonable and preferable to consider affects the building blocks of drives. Affects are thus the link between biologically determined instinctive components, on the one hand, and intrapsychic organization of the drives, on the other. The correspondence of the series of rewarding and aversive affect states with the dual lines of libido and aggression makes sense both clinically and theoretically.

This concept of affects as the building blocks of drives resolves, I believe, some persisting problems in the psychoanalytic theory of drives. To think of affects this way broadens the concept of erogenous zones as the "source" of libido into a general consideration of all psychologically activated functions and body zones that become involved in affectively invested interactions of the infant and child with mother. These functions include the shift from concerns with bodily functions to concerns with social functions and role enactments. My proposed concept also provides the missing links, within psychoanalytic theory, of the "sources" of aggressively invested infant-mother interactions, the "zonal" function of aggressive rejection of oral ingestion, anal control, direct physical power struggles linked with temper tantrums, and so forth. Affectively invested object relations are what energize physiological "zones."

The sequential psychophysiological activation of early distress, rage, fear—and later of depression and guilt—determines the corresponding series of aggressive self and object investments. These investments are reactivated in the unconscious conflicts with respect to aggression that are expressed in the transference. The direct internalization of libidinal and aggressive affective dispositions as part of self and object representations (in technical terms, "internalized object relations") integrated within ego and superego structures represents, in my formulation, the libidinal and aggressive investments of these structures.

The id, according to this concept of the relation between drives and affects, consists of repressed intensely aggressive or sexualized internalized object relations. The condensation and displacement characteristic of the mental processes of the id reflect the linkage of affectively related self and object representations of the corresponding aggressive, libidinal, and, later on, combined series.

This concept of drives also permits us to do justice to the biologically determined input of new affective experiences throughout life. These experiences include the activation of sexual excitement during adolescence, when erotically exciting affect states become integrated with genital excitement and with erotically charged emotions and fantasies derived from the oedipal stage of development. In other words, the intensification of drives (both libidinal and aggressive) at various stages of the life cycle is determined by the incorporation of new psychophysiologically activated affect states into the preexistent hierarchically organized affect systems.

More generally, in my view, once the organization of drives as the supraordinate hierarchical motivational systems has been consolidated, any particular activation of drives in the context of intrapsychic conflict is represented by the activation of corresponding affect states. The affect state includes an internalized object relation, basically a particular self representation relating to a particular object representation under the impact of a particular affect. The reciprocal role relation between self and object that is framed by the corresponding affect is usually expressed as a fantasy or wish. Unconscious fantasy consists of such units of self representation, object representation, and an affect linking them. Affects, in short, are the signals or representatives of drives—as Freud (1926) had suggested—as well as their building blocks.

Freud (1905) described libido as a drive, one originating in the stimulation of the erogenous zones and characterized by a particular aim, pressure, and object. As I have stated, I believe that libido originates in primitive affect states, including a state of elation found in the early infant-mother relation and characteristic of symbiotic experience and fantasy. Affectionate and generally pleasurable experiences with mother, occurring under quotidian conditions and quiescent states are also integrated into libidinal strivings.

Sexual excitement is a later and more differentiated affect; it enters as a crucial component of the libidinal drive, but its origin as an affect resides in the integration of erotically tinged experiences resulting from stimulation of the various erogenous zones. Indeed, insofar as sexual excitement as an affect involves the total field of psychic experience, it is not limited to the stimulation of any particular erogenous zone but is manifested as pleasurable sensations in the entire body.

Just as libido, or the sexual drive, results from the integration of positive or rewarding affect states, so the aggressive drive results from the integration of a multitude of negative or aversive affective experiences—rage, disgust, and hatred. Rage may in fact be considered the central affect of aggression. The early characteristics and development of rage have been documented extensively by infant researchers; around it clusters the complex affective formation of aggression as a drive. Infant research documents the primordial function of rage as an attempt to eliminate a source of pain or irritation. In the unconscious fantasies that develop around rage reactions, rage comes to signify both the activation of the "all-bad" object relationship and the wish to eliminate it and restore an "all-good" one, represented by object relations under the impact of positive, libidinal affect states. But the psychopathology of aggression is not limited to the intensity and frequency of rage attacks: the affect that comes to dominate aggression as a drive in pathology is the complex or elaborated affect of hatred, a stable, structured, object-directed rage.

Aggression also enters into the sexual experience itself. We shall see that penetrating and being penetrated incorporate aggression in the service of love, utilizing the erotogenic potential of the experience of pain as a necessary contributor to gratifying fusion with the other in sexual excitement and orgasm. This normal capability for transforming pain into erotic excitement miscarries when severe aggression dominates the mother-infant relationship and is probably a crucial bridge to the erotic excitement produced by inducing suffering in others.

I believe that this formulation of the relationships between drive and affects does justice to Freud's dual-drive theory and at the same time links psychoanalytic theory harmoniously with contemporary instinct theory in biology and with developmental observations on infancy and early childhood.

If sexual excitement is the basic affect around which clusters the constellation of affects that jointly constitute libido as a drive, erotic desire— that is, sexual excitement directed to a particular object—links sexual excitement to the world of internalized object relations in the context of the oedipal structuring of psychic reality. Erotic desire, in fact, contributes to integrating part object into total object relations—that is, split-off or dissociated representations of self and object into total or global ones. This development deepens the nature of the sexual experience, a process that will eventually culminate in mature sexual love.

Clinical and Genetic Aspects of Erotic Desire

What are the clinical characteristics of erotic desire as they become manifest in the course of psychoanalytic exploration? First is a search for pleasure, always oriented to another person, an object to be penetrated or invaded or to be penetrated or invaded by. It is a longing for closeness, fusion, and intermingling that implies both forcefully crossing a barrier and becoming one with the chosen object. Conscious or unconscious sexual fantasies refer to invasion, penetration, or appropriation and include the relations between body protrusions and openings—penis, nipple, tongue, finger, feces on the penetrating or invasive site, and vagina, mouth, anus on the receptive or encompassing site. The erotic gratification promised by the rhythmic stimulation of these body parts decreases or vanishes when the sexual act does not serve the broader unconscious function of fusion with an object. "Container" and "contained" are not to be confused with masculine and feminine, active and passive; erotic desire includes fantasies of actively incorporating and passively being penetrated, together with actively penetrating and passively being incorporated. I have suggested that psychological bisexuality in the sense of identification with both self and object in the specific sexual interaction is universal for men and women. One might say that bisexuality is first of all a function of identification with both participants in a sexual relationship, or with all three (the "excluded third party") in the triangulation of sexual experience (Liberman 1956).

A second characteristic of erotic desire is identification with the partner's sexual excitement and orgasm, in order to enjoy two complementary experiences of fusion. The primary element here is the pleasure derived from the desire of the other, the love expressed in the other's response to the sexual desire of the self, and the associated experience of fusion in ecstasy. There is also the sense of becoming both genders at the same time, of temporarily overcoming the ordinarily unbreachable barrier separating the genders, and the sense of completion and enjoyment of the penetrating and encompassing, penetrated and enclosed aspect of sexual invasion. In this connection, a symbolic displacement of all "penetrating" parts of the anatomy and of all "encompassing" or "penetrable" openings signals the condensation of eroticism from all zones, an expected regression in sexual excitement to "zonal confusion" (Meltzer 1973), and the consequent confluence, in sexual activity or contact, of fantasies and experiences reflecting the entire body surface of both participants. In this identification with the other, there is gratification of the wish for fusion, of homosexual longings, and of oedipal rivalry—by implication, all other relationships disappear in the unique and fused sexual pair. By the same token, unconsciously identifying with both genders eliminates the need to envy the other gender, and, in remaining oneself while becoming the other as well, one has a sense having achieved intersubjective transcendence.

A third characteristic of erotic desire is a sense of transgression, of overcoming the prohibition implied in all sexual encounters, a prohibition derived from the oedipal structuring of sexual life. This sense takes many forms, and the simplest and universal is transgression against the ordinary social constraints that protect the intimacy of body surfaces as well as the intimacy of sexual excitement from public display. Stendhal (1822) first pointed out that the very act of undressing repeals social notions of shame and permits lovers to face each other without shame; getting dressed after the sexual encounter is a return to conventional shamefulness. Conventional morality (Kernberg 1987) tends to suppress or regulate those aspects of sexual encounters most directly related to infantile polymorphous sexual aims, and it is these aims, prototypically framed in the sexual perversions, that most directly express sexual excitement and erotic intimacy and the transgression of social conventions.

Basically, transgression includes violating oedipal prohibitions, thus constituting a defiance of and a triumph over the oedipal rival. But transgression also includes transgression against the sexual object itself, experienced as seductive teasing and withholding. Erotic desire includes a sense that the object is both offering and withholding itself, and sexual penetration or engulfing of the object is a violation of the other boundaries. In this sense, transgression involves aggression against the object as well, aggression that is exciting in its pleasurable gratification, reverberating with the capacity to experience pleasure in pain, and projecting that capacity onto the object. The aggression is also pleasurable because it is being contained by a loving relationship. And so we have the incorporation of aggression into love and the assurance of safety in the face of unavoidable ambivalence.

The ecstatic and aggressive features of the effort to transcend the boundaries of the self represent a complex aspect of erotic desire. Bataille (1957) proposed, in a different context, that the most intense experiences of transcendence occur under the "sign" of love and under the "sign" of aggression. He suggests that one of the most dramatic characteristics of human functioning is that the breakdown of boundaries between self and other occurs at moments of deepest regression into ecstatic love and under conditions of extreme pain. The intimacy that develops between torturer and tortured and the lasting effects on the psychic experience of both participants may well originate in the most primitive, ordinarily dissociated or repressed awareness of fused, "all-bad" relations between self and object, which constitute the counterpart of the split-off "all-good" object in the symbiotic stage of development.

Erotic desire transforms genital excitement and orgasm into an experience of fusion with the other that provides an ultimate sense of fulfillment, of transcending the limits of the self. This fusion also facilitates, in the experience of orgasm, a sense of oneness with the biological aspects of personal experience. By the same token, however, to be the object of pain induced by another and to identify with the aggressive object as well as to experience oneself as its victim create a sense of union in pain that reinforces the fusion in love. To induce pain in the other and to identify with the other's erotic pleasure in pain is erotic sadism, the counterpart of erotic masochism. Erotic desire, in this regard, also includes an element of surrender, of accepting a state of enslavement to the other, as well as being master of the other's fate. The extent to which this aggressive fusion will be contained by love is mediated by the superego, the guardian of the love that contains aggression. Both in pleasure and in pain, there is a search for an intense affective experience that temporarily erases the boundaries of the self, an experience that may give a fundamental meaning to life, a transcendence that links sexual engagement and religious ecstasy, an experience of freedom beyond the constraints of daily existence.

Idealization of the body of the other or of the objects that symbolically represent it is an essential aspect of erotic desire. Lussier (1982) and Chasseguet-Smirgel (1985) have pointed to the central function of idealization in, respectively, fetishism and perversion in general. This idealization is a defense and represents the denial of anal regression in perversion and the denial of castration anxiety. I agree with them regarding the important function of idealization as a mechanism in pathology; I also believe (1989a) that idealization of the sexual partner's anatomy, of the surface of his or her body, is a crucial aspect of the normal integration of tender and erotic strivings in both heterosexual and homosexual love relations. This erotic idealization parallels the normal idealization processes in romantic love described by Chasseguet-Smirgel (1985), namely, the projection of the ego ideal onto the loved object with a simultaneous increase in self-esteem. In mature sexual love, replication of the ego ideal in the form of the idealized love object creates a sense of harmony with the world, actualization of one's value system and aesthetic ideals: morality and beauty are actualized in the love relation.

Meltzer and Williams (1988) have proposed the existence of an early "aesthetic conflict" linked to the infant's attitude to mother's body. The infant's love for mother, they say, is expressed by idealizing the surface of her body and, by introjection of the mother's love expressed in her idealizing the infant's body, by identifying with her in this self-idealization. Such idealization would give rise to the earliest sense of aesthetic value, of beauty. Meltzer and Williams see the split-off aggression toward mother, in contrast, as directed mainly toward the inside of her body; by projection, the infant experiences the inside of mother's body as dangerous. Accordingly, the desire for and fantasy of violent invasion of mother's body are an expression of aggression, of envy of her outside beauty as well as of her capacity to give life and love. The idealization of mother's body surface is a defense against the dangerous aggression lurking under that surface. Chasseguet-Smirgel's (1986) contribution on the archaic aspects of the Oedipus complex (the fantasied destruction of the interior of mother's body, father's penis, and father's babies, and the transformation of mother's inside into a limitless cavity) is an important clarification of the nature of primitive aggression and fears directed to the interior of mother's body.

For these authors, the origin of men's idealization of women's bodies is consistently traceable to the idealization of and excitement evoked by the surface of mother's body; similarly, the origins of the unconscious fears linked to the vagina and the interior of women's bodies can be traced to the early relationship with mother.

Also, in men, idealization of the body parts of homosexual partners can regularly be traced back to idealization of mother's body. The idealization of male body parts is originally much less prominent in women, but this capacity develops in the context of a gratifying sexual relation with a man, who unconsciously represents the oedipal father in reaffirming the beauty and value of a woman's body, thus liberating her genital sexuality from its early infantile inhibition. In both genders, the integration of the tender and erotic elements of object relations provides more depth and complexity to the idealization of body surfaces as well.

The body of the beloved becomes a geography of personal meanings, so that the fantasied early polymorphous perverse relations to the parental objects are condensed with the admiring and invasive relation to the lover's body parts. Erotic desire is rooted in the pleasure of unconsciously enacting polymorphous perverse fantasies and activities, including symbolic activation of the earliest object relations of the infant with mother and of the small child with both parents. All this is expressed in the perverse components of intercourse and sexual play—in fellatio, cunnilingus, and anal penetration, and in exhibitionistic, voyeuristic, and sadistic sexual play. Here the links between the early relationship with mother of both genders and the enjoyment of the interpenetration of body surfaces, protuberances, and cavities is central. Mother's physical ministrations activate the infant's erotic awareness of his or her own body surfaces and, by projection, the erotic awareness of the body surfaces of mother. Love received in the form of erotic stimulation of body surfaces becomes the stimulus for erotic desire as a vehicle for the expression of love and gratitude.

A woman who loves a man will become erotically aroused by intimate aspects of the geography of his body, and characteristically, if that love ends, her interest in and idealization of his body will be extinguished. Correspondingly, narcissistic men who give the appearance of rapidly losing their interest in previously idealized aspects of a woman's body will be able to maintain that interest if and when, as a consequence of psychoanalytic treatment, the unconscious deterioration of internalized object relations (typically related to profound envy of women) can be resolved. I am suggesting that in both genders, and despite the differences related to the different history of their sexual development, idealization of body surfaces, a central aspect of erotic desire, is a function of the availability of primitive internalized object relations. And the personal history of a love relation becomes symbolically inscribed in aspects of the loved object's anatomy.

The lack of activation or the extinction of body-surface eroticism when intense aggression and a parallel lack of pleasurable body-surface stimulation combine in such a way as to interfere with the development of early idealization processes as part of erotic stimulation determines a primary sexual inhibition. Such an inhibition is illustrated in the case of the woman patient whose intense transference love was connected with the wish that I kill her. The secondary repression of sexual excitement linked to later superego functioning and later oedipal prohibitions is much less severe and has a much better prognosis in treatment.

The wish to tease and be teased is another central aspect of erotic desire. This wish cannot be completely separated from the excitement at going beyond the barrier of something forbidden, which is experienced as sinful or amoral. The sexual object is always, au fond, a forbidden oedipal object and the sexual act a symbolic repetition and overcoming of the primal scene. But here I am stressing the object's withholding itself—teasing as a combination of promise and withholding, of seductiveness and frustration. A naked body may be sexually stimulating, but a partially hidden body becomes much more so. There are good reasons why complete nudity at the end of a striptease show is followed by the performer's rapid exit.

Sexual teasing is typically though not exclusively linked to exhibitionistic teasing and illustrates the intimate connection between exhibitionism and sadism: the wish to excite and frustrate the significant other. By the same token, voyeurism is the simplest response to exhibitionistic teasing and constitutes a sadistic penetration of an object that withholds itself. Like the other perversions, exhibitionistic perversion is a typical sexual deviation of men; exhibitionistic behavior, on the other hand, is much more frequently interwoven with the character style of women.

Psychoanalytic interpretations of female exhibitionism as a reaction formation to penis envy should be amended to incorporate our recent recognition of the step the little girl undertakes in shifting her object choice from mother to father: exhibitionism can be a plea for sexual affirmation at a distance. Father's love and acceptance of his little girl and her vaginal genitality reconfirm her feminine identity and self-acceptance (Ross 1990).

The experience of women's sexuality as both exhibitionistic and withholding—that is, as teasing—is a powerful stimulus to erotic desire in men. And the experience of being teased also provokes aggression, a motive for the aggressive implication of invading a woman's body, a source of the voyeuristic aspects of the sexual relation that contain the wish to dominate, expose, encounter, and overcome barriers of true and false shamefulness in the woman who is loved. Overcoming shamefulness is not the same as humiliation; the desire to humiliate usually includes a third party, a witness to the humiliation, and implies a greater degree of aggression, which threatens the capacity for an exclusive sexual object relation.

The voyeuristic impulse to observe a couple in sexual intercourse—the symbolic expression of a wish to violently interrupt the primal scene—is a condensation of the wish to penetrate the privacy and secrecy of the oedipal couple and to take revenge against the teasing mother. Voyeurism is an important component of sexual excitement in the sense that every sexual intimacy implies an element of privacy and secrecy and, as such, an identification with and a potential triumph over the oedipal couple. The many couples who cannot enjoy sex in their own home, in proximity to their children, but only in a secluded area elsewhere illustrate the inhibition of this aspect of sexual intimacy.

This leads us to one more aspect of erotic desire, namely, the oscillation between the wish for secrecy, intimacy, and exclusiveness, on one hand, and the wish to shift away from sexual intimacy, for a radical discontinuity (André Green, personal communication), on the other. Contrary to the popular belief that it is the woman who wants to preserve intimacy and exclusiveness and the man who wants to break away after sexual gratification, clinical evidence shows many men whose dependent longings are frustrated by their perception of their wife's affectionate dedication to their infants and small children and as many women who complain about their husband's failure to maintain sexual interest in them.

Although it is true that there are different types of sexual discontinuity in men and women, the very fact of discontinuity in sexual involvement and repeated disengagements even within a continuous, loving relationship are important counterparts to secrecy, intimacy, and fusional aspects of erotic desire and behavior. The loss of this discontinuity, a sexual relation that merges with ordinary life and replaces it, may well create an accumulation of aggressive elements of fusional experiences that ends up threatening the entire relationship. The Japanese film *In the Realm of the Senses*, by Nagisa Oshima (1976), illustrates the gradual deterioration into unbridled aggression of the relationship of two lovers whose sexual encounter becomes all-consuming, eliminating their contact with the external world.

Erotic desire and mature sexual love absorb and express all aspects of the ordinary ambivalence of intimate object relations. The intensity of affectionate, tender, polymorphous perverse—particularly sadomasochistic—aspects of the sexual relation reflects the expression of this ambivalence and constitutes a basic cement for love relations. But in a more specific way, that ambivalence is illustrated by what I describe as the direct and reverse triangulation of sexual relations (see chap. 6)—in essence, the unconscious and conscious fantasies that accompany erotic desire and sexual intercourse. The wish to be the unique, preferred, triumphant, exclusive love object of one's sexual partner, with actualized triumphs over the oedipal rival in each sexual encounter, is the counterpart of that other desire to be involved with two partners of the opposite sex, in revenge against the frustrating, teasing, withholding oedipal parent. In these oedipal dynamics, the primitive precursors of deep ambivalence toward mother and elimination of father bring about the threat of a fusion in aggression with destruction of the loved object, the threatening negative to the idyllic world of ecstatic fusion with the idealized primitive mother (A. Green 1993).

Throughout this discussion I have referred to some of the genetic roots of these components of erotic desire. Braunschweig and Fain (1971, 1975) offer an appealing idea regarding the characteristics of erotic desire in terms of the development of the infant's and small child's relation to mother. I offer a brief summary of their ideas. The early relationship of the infant of both genders with mother determines the child's later capacity for sexual excitement and erotic desire. Mother's ministrations and her expression of pleasure in the physical stimulation of the male infant's body surface while emotionally communicating her love for him foster the infant's erotic desire; the infant identifies with mother under such stimulation and also when he feels abandoned after mother leaves him to return as a sexual woman to father. Infants realize that mother's attitude is not quite the same in father's presence as in his absence (Paulina Kernberg, personal communication).

Braunschweig and Fain attribute a crucial role to the mother's psychological turning away from the infant. It is at this moment that the infant identifies himself with the frustrating yet stimulating mother, with her erotic stimulation, and with the sexual couple—that is, father as mother's object. This identification of the infant with both parents provides the basic frame for a psychic bisexuality and consolidates the triangular situation in the child's unconscious fantasy.

The male infant's acknowledgment of this frustration and of the implicit censorship of his erotic desire for mother shifts his erotic stimulation into masturbatory fantasy and activity, including the desire to replace father and, in primitive symbolic fantasy, to become the father's penis and the object of mother's desire.

In the little girl, mother's subtle and unconscious rejection of the sexual excitement that she would freely experience in relation to a little boy gradually inhibits the girl's direct awareness of her original vaginal genitality; she therefore gradually becomes less aware of her own genital impulses while being less directly frustrated by the discontinuity in the relationship with mother. The identification with mother's eroticism takes more subtle forms, derived from mother's tolerance and fostering the little girl's identification with her in other areas. The little girl has a tacit understanding of the "underground" nature of her own genitality, and her deepening identification with mother also strengthens her longing for father and her identification with both members of the oedipal couple.

The little girl's change of object from mother to father determines her capability for developing an object relation in depth with the loved and admired yet distant father and the secret hope of eventually being accepted by him and becoming free once more in the expression of her genital sexuality. This development fosters the little girl's capacity to commit herself emotionally to an object relationship. Thus the woman's capacity for such a commitment in her sexual life is greater, from early on, than a man's.

The explanation resides in the early exercise of trust, in the little girl's turning from mother to father, in his love and affirmation of her femininity "from a distance," in her capacity to transfer her dependency needs to an object physically less available than mother, and also, by the same change of object, in her escape from preoedipal conflicts and ambivalence toward mother. Men, in whom continuity of the relationship from mother to later female objects signifies potential perpetuation of both preoedipal and oedipal conflicts with mother, would have greater difficulty in dealing with ambivalence toward women and would evince a slower development than women in the capacity to integrate their genital with their tender needs. Women, in contrast, tend to develop their later capacity for a full genital relation in the context of their earlier capacity for a love relationship in depth with a man. In short, men and women develop in opposite order their capacity for full sexual enjoyment and for an object relation in depth.

Braunschweig and Fain's theory, it seems to me, provides a new psychoanalytic approach to the observations of early genital masturbation in both genders (Galenson and Roiphe 1977) and to the consistent clinical observations in the psychoanalysis of women regarding the erotic aspects of mothers' reactions to their infants. The implications of their theory for our understanding of erotic desire seem evident: the relationship between erotic desire and the wish for fusion as an expression of the symbiotic longings for mother (Bergmann 1971); the search for the teasing object, and the revengeful quality of the aggressive elements of sexual excitement; the polymorphous perverse quality of erotic desire as an expression of its origin in the earliest developmental stages, the different development of male and female attitudes regarding genital and tender aspects of eroticism; the connection between the sexualization of pain and the search for fusion in pain and the aggressive aspects of erotic desire; psychic bisexuality; the unconscious conflicts over an "excluded third party"; and the discontinuity regarding sexual relations.

3.

Mature Sexual Love

Now we come to the most complex stage of the developmental transformations that, starting from sexual excitement as a basic affect, lead to erotic desire for another person and culminate eventually in mature sexual love. Poets and philosophers have undoubtedly described the prerequisites for and components of mature love better than a psychoanalytic dissection could achieve. And yet, the wish to better understand limitations in achieving the capacity for mature love relations warrants, I believe, an attempt to carry out such a dissection.

In essence, I propose that mature sexual love is a complex emotional disposition that integrates (1) sexual excitement transformed into erotic desire for another person; (2) tenderness that derives from the integration of libidinally and aggressively invested self and object representations, with a predominance of love over aggression and tolerance of the normal ambivalence that characterizes all human relations; (3) an identification with the other that includes both a reciprocal genital identification and deep empathy with the other's gender identity; (4) a mature form of idealization along with deep commitment to the other and to the relationship; and (5) the passionate character of the love relation in all three aspects: the sexual relationship, the object relationship, and the superego investment of the couple.

Some Further Considerations about Erotic Desire

In the preceding chapter, I referred to sexual excitement as an affect linked from the start with the stimulation of the skin and bodily openings, and gradually becoming concentrated in particular body zones and orifices; the context is the object relations in the preoedipal and oedipal stages of development. The lifelong yearning for physical closeness and stimulation, for the intermingling of body surfaces, is linked to the longing for symbiotic fusion with the parental object and, by the same token, to the earliest forms of identification.

The infant's enjoyment of intimate bodily contact with mother in the context of their gratifying, loving relationship, his/her love for mother, accompanies the development of a primitive fantasy of gratification of polymorphous sexual longings. The baby builds up an internalized world of fantasy, of exciting and gratifying symbiotic experiences, which eventually will constitute the core of libidinal strivings in the dynamic unconscious.

At the same time, the aggressive, sadomasochistic component of sexual excitement, which represents the incorporation of aggressive affect not only as part of the polymorphous infantile sexual response per se but as a complementary component of the search for fusion, penetration, and being penetrated, is also part of the erotic response in the broadest sense. I have already referred to Meltzer and Williams' (1988) proposal that idealization of the surface of mother's body acquires a defensive function against the fantasied projection of aggression into the interior of mother's body, and directly expresses the integration of love for the ideal image of mother with earliest sensual gratification. The primitive idealization of the surface of mother's body leads, by way of early introjection and primitive identification with her, to idealization of the infant's own body. The primitive idealization characteristic of splitting processes that dissociate such idealization from "all-bad" or persecutory experiences preserves the sexual disposition toward the idealized object and protects sexual excitement from being overwhelmed by aggressive impulses.

Whereas the vicissitudes of sexual excitement in the context of the preoedipal mother-infant relationship represent the origin of erotic desire, this desire culminates in the oedipal stage of development. Freud proposed (1905) that infantile psychology leads to the dominance of genital impulses directed to the parent of the opposite gender and the simultaneous activation of intense ambivalence toward and rivalry with the parent of the same gender. Unconscious patricidal or matricidal wishes for the parent of the same gender are the counterpart of the incestuous wishes for the other parent and the fear of castration, accompanied by unconscious fantasies of threat and punishment. This constellation, the positive Oedipus complex, is parallel to the negative Oedipus complex, that is, sexual love for the parent of the same gender and the sense of rivalry and aggression directed at the other parent. Freud considered the negative Oedipus complex a defense against the castration anxiety activated by the positive Oedipus complex—in other words, a defensive homosexual submission, an important but not exclusive motive for the negative Oedipus complex, the roots of which reside in preoedipal bisexuality.

This theory, by providing an explanation for a patient's intense attachment to the analyst as an ideal, unavailable, forbidden object, illuminated the nature of transference love. But Freud (1910a,b,c, 1915a), astonished by the intensity and violence of transference and its unmistakable relation to falling in love, also concluded that the unconscious search for the oedipal object is part of all normal love relations and provides the undercurrent of longings for and idealization of the love object. As Bergmann (1982) has pointed out, however, Freud never formulated a comprehensive theory that would clearly differentiate transference love from erotic love and normal love. What interests us here is the centrality of oedipal longings in the unconscious content of erotic desire.

Erotic Desire and Tenderness

Tenderness reflects the integration of libidinal and aggressive self and object representations and the tolerance of ambivalence. Balint (1948) was the first to emphasize the importance of tenderness, which he suggested derives from the pregenital phase: "The demand for prolonged, perpetual regard and gratitude forces us to regress to, or even never to egress from, the archaic infantile form of tender love" (p. 114). In terms of the internalization of relationships with significant others that will constitute the complex world of internalized object relations (and eventually determine the structure of the ego, superego, and id), there are two major currents influencing the capacity for the development of mature sexual love. One is the regressive pull toward establishing fusion with the loved object, in a search for the at least transitory recovery of a desired symbiotic oneness in an ideal relationship with mother. The other is the progressive tendency toward consolidation of the differences, first between self and object representations, and later toward integration of "all-good" with "all-bad" representations of self into a consolidated self concept and the corresponding integration of "all-bad" with "all-good" representations of significant others into integrated conceptions that include a clear differentiation of their sexual roles.

The search for symbiotic fusion is already implied, as I said earlier, in the psychodynamics of erotic desire; the capacity for establishing an intimate relationship with a differentiated, integrated, or "total" object is the complementary aspect of the capacity for developing a mature love relationship. This integration of "part" into "total" internalized object relations   crystallizes   toward   the   end   of   the   stage   of   separation-individuation and signals the beginning of object constancy, the initiation of the oedipal phase. This marks the completion of the preoedipal developmental phases and brings about what Winnicott (1955, 1963) described as the prerequisite for developing the capacity for concern. It is a development that implies the fusion of aggression with love in early object relations, replicating, we might say, the integration of libidinal and aggressive strivings that occurred when sexual excitement and erotic desire prevailed. The feeling of tenderness is an expression of the capacity for concern about the love object. Tenderness expresses love for the other and is a sublimatory (reparative) outcome of reaction formations against aggression.

The nature of preoedipal influences on the capacity for sexual love has been the subject of significant psychoanalytic exploration. Bergmann (1971), following the developmental schemata of Mahler (1968, Mahler et al. 1975), proposed that the capacity to love presupposes a normally developing symbiotic experience and separation-individuation phase. He notes a natural continuity from the early narcissistic function of establishing an ideal relationship with a loved object to the later narcissistic gratification in the primitive oedipal relationship. Bergmann (1987) points to the search, in the love relation, for the lost oedipal object, the wish to repair the oedipal trauma in the relationship to the new object, and the search for a fusion, underneath this oedipal longing, that replicates the search for symbiotic fusion. Bak (1973), stressing the relation between being in love and mourning, saw being in love as an emotional state based on the separation of mother from child and directed toward undoing this as well as later separations and losses of important objects.

Wisdom (1970), reviewing some of the basic findings and dilemmas in the psychoanalytic approach to the understanding of love and sex, suggested that Melanie Klein's theory of the depressive position accounted for fundamental components, though not for all of them, in adult love. He suggested that the idealization of love arises through neutralization of the bad aspect of the object by reparation, rather than through keeping the idealized object wholly good by splitting it off from what is bad. In this connection, Wisdom described the difference between idealization of the "paranoid-schizoid position" and of the "depressive position" (a difference, it seems to me, related to the difference between the borderline patient's idealization of love objects and that of the neurotic patient). He enumerated the aspects of falling in love related to the capacity for developing mourning and concern. Josselyn (1971) suggested that parents who deprive their children of opportunities to mourn the loss of loved objects contribute to the atrophy of the capacity to love.

May (1969) stressed the importance of "care" as a prerequisite to love in a mature way. Care, he said, "is a state composed of the recognition of another, a fellow human being like oneself; of identification of one's self with the pain or joy of the other; of guilt, pity, and the awareness that we all stand on the base of a common humanity from which we all stem" (p. 289). He considers "concern" and "compassion" to be possible other terms. Indeed, his description of care is closely related to Winnicott's (1963) description of concern.

Identification with the Other

Balint (1948) suggested that, in addition to genital satisfaction, a true love relation includes idealization, tenderness, and a special form of identification. He suggests calling the last "genital identification," within which the "interests, wishes, feelings, sensitivity, shortcomings of the partner attain—or are supposed to attain—about the same importance as our own" (p. 115). In short, he suggests that what we call genital love is a fusion of genital satisfaction and pregenital tenderness and that genital identification is the expression of this fusion.

Balint's idea was a shift from the then dominant focus on "genital primacy" per se as the basis of ideal love relations, pointing to the important preoedipal elements influencing genital identification, and to the importance of integrating pregenital tenderness with genital satisfaction.

Evolving psychoanalytic thinking then questioned "genital primacy," defined as the capacity for sexual intercourse and orgasm, not as the equivalent of sexual maturity or even necessarily representing relatively advanced psychosexual development. Lichtenstein (1970) examined this issue and concluded that "clinical observations do not confirm a clear correlation between emotional maturity (i.e., the capacity to establish stable object relations) and the ability to obtain full satisfaction through genital orgasm (genital primacy)." He suggested that "sexuality is the earliest and most basic way available for the growing human personality to experience an affirmation of the reality of his existence." And he added that "the concept of genital primacy in the classical sense can no longer be maintained" (p. 317).

In addition to emphasizing the relation between the capacities for tenderness and for concern, May (1969) puts the capacity for "genital identification" (in Balint's terms)—that is, for full identification without losing one's identity in the love relation—in a central position. In addition, May stresses the presence of sadness in the love relation (which is a potential link between his thoughts and the theory of consolidation of total object relations and the corresponding activation of concern, guilt, and reparation). He also discusses the importance of the genital experience itself, which provides a shift in consciousness, a new union wherein develops a oneness with nature.

Genital identification implies coming to terms with the heterosexual and homosexual identifications derived from preoedipal and oedipal conflicts. Careful analysis of the emotional reactions during sexual intercourse, particularly in patients who have reached a stage of working through the various levels of pregenital and genital conflicts as expressed in their sexual engagements, reveals the manifold, simultaneous and/or shifting heterosexual and homosexual, pregenital and genital, identifications activated in that context.

One aspect of those emotional reactions is the excitement and gratification derived from the orgasm of the sexual partner. This corresponds to the gratification of other needs, such as the capacity to provide oral gratification or reconfirmation of the identification with the oedipal figure of the same gender, which reflect heterosexual components. At the same time, the excitement accompanying the partner's orgasm reflects an unconscious identification with that partner and, in heterosexual intercourse, a sublimated expression of homosexual identifications from both pregenital and genital sources. Sexual foreplay may include identification with the fantasied or real wishes of the object of the other gender, so that passive and active, masochistic and sadistic, voyeuristic and exhibitionistic needs are expressed in the simultaneous reconfirmation of sexual identity and tentative identification with the complementary one of the sexual partner.

Such simultaneous and intense identification with one's own sexual role and the object's complementary role during orgasm also represents a capacity for entering and becoming one with another person in a psychological as well as a physical sense and the reconfirmation of emotional closeness, linked to the activation of the ultimately biological roots of human attachment. In contrast to the primitive fusion of self and object representations during the symbiotic phase of development (Mahler 1968), the fusion of orgasm is based upon and reconfirms one's own individuality and particularly a mature sexual identification.

Thus, sexual identification with one's own and one's partner's complementary sexual roles implies a sublimated integration of heterosexual and homosexual identity components. This integrative function of intercourse and orgasm is also carried out in the polarity of love and hate because the capacity for fully experiencing concern for the loved person (which underlies an authentic, deep human relationship) presupposes the integration of love and hatred—that is, the tolerance of ambivalence. It seems to me that such ambivalence, which is characteristic of stable significant human relations, is activated in sexual intercourse when sexual and aggressive excitement are blended.

A mature sexual relationship, I believe, includes some sexual encounters in which the partner is utilized as a "pure sexual object"; sexual excitement may be maximal during expression of the need to "use" and "be used" by the other person sexually. Mutual empathy and implicit collusion with such sexual expression are counterparts to empathy and collusion in connection with violent anger, attack, and rejection in the relationship. The confidence that all these conditions can be contained within an overall loving relation, which also has periods of quiet, mutual contemplation and sharing of the participants' internal life, provides significance and depth to human relations.

Idealization and Mature Sexual Love

Balint (1948), expressing his agreement with Freud (1912), discards idealization "as not absolutely necessary for a good love relation." He particularly agrees with Freud's statement that in many cases idealization does not help and even hinders the development of a satisfactory form of love.

David (1971) and Chasseguet-Smirgel (1973), however, stress the importance of idealization in the love relation. They believe that the state of being in love enriches the self and increases the libidinal investment of the self because it fulfills an ideal state of self and because the relation of the exalted self to the object at that point reproduces the optimum relation between the self and the ego ideal.

Van der Waals (1965) emphasizes the simultaneous increase of object and narcissistic libidinal investment in normal love. Chasseguet-Smirgel suggests that in mature love, in contrast with transitory adolescent falling in love, there is a limited projection of a toned-down ego ideal onto the idealized love object and a simultaneous enhancement of narcissistic (self) investment from the sexual gratification provided by the loved object. These observations are, I believe, compatible with my thinking that normal idealization constitutes an advanced developmental level of the mechanism by which infantile and childhood morality is transformed into an adult ethical system. Idealization, thus conceived, is a function of the mature love relation, establishing continuity between "romantic" adolescent and mature love. Under normal conditions, it is not the ego ideal that is projected but ideals that stem from structural developments within the superego (including the ego ideal).

David (1971) stresses how very early the oedipal longings in children of both genders arrive, the intuition of an exciting, gratifying, and forbidden relationship that links the parents and excludes the child, and the child's longing for and excitement about forbidden knowledge—particularly sexual knowledge—as a crucial prerequisite for and part of the quality of sexual love. In both genders, longing, envy, jealousy, and curiosity finally propel an active search for the idealized oedipal object.

As I pointed out in chapter 2, the intimate fusion of longed-for erotic gratification and symbiotic fusion also includes the sexual function of early idealization. I have referred to Meltzer and Williams' (1988) proposal that idealization of the surface of mother's body acquires a defensive function against the fantasied projection of aggression into the interior of mother's body. It also directly expresses the integration of love for the ideal image of mother and earliest sensual gratification. Thus, the earliest idealization, the primitive idealization characterized by the predominance of splitting processes that dissociate such idealization from "all-bad" or persecutory experiences, preserves the sexual disposition toward the idealized object and protects sexual excitement from being overwhelmed by aggressive impulses.

Later on, idealization occurring in the context of integrated or total object relations and the corresponding capacity for experiencing guilt, concern, and reparative trends when total object relations are achieved will facilitate the integration of sexual excitement and erotic desire with an idealized view of the love object and the integration of erotic desire with tenderness. Tenderness, as we have seen, reflects the capacity for the integration of love and aggression in the domain of internalized object relations and includes an element of concern for the loved object that should be protected from dangerous aggression. Gradually, the early idealization of the body of the loved other and the later idealization of the total person of the other evolve into the idealization of the value systems of the love object—an idealization of ethical, cultural, and aesthetic values—a development that will guarantee the capacity for romantic falling in love.

These gradual transformations of idealization processes in the context of psychological development also reflect the vicissitudes of passage through the oedipal stage of development—the original prohibitions against erotic desire for the oedipal object, a major reason for the sharp defensive cleavage between erotic desire and idealized object relations. Evolving idealization processes eventually culminate in the capacity for reconfirming the linkage between erotic desire and romantic idealization of the same person and at the same time represent the integration of the superego at a higher level, including sophisticated capacity for integrating tender and sexual feelings, which reflects the overcoming of the oedipal conflict. In this establishment of identification with the values of the love object, a transcendence is achieved from the interrelationship of the couple to a relationship with their cultural and social background. The experiences of the past, the present, and the imagined future are linked through the experience of the present relationship with the love object.

Commitment and Passion

Passion in the realm of sexual love is, I propose, an emotional state that expresses the crossing of boundaries, in the sense of bridging intrapsychic structures that are separated by dynamically or conflictually determined boundaries. In what follows, I use the term *boundary* to mean boundaries of self, except where explicit references are made to the broader use of the term as the active, dynamic interface of hierarchically related (particularly social) systems.

The most important boundaries crossed in sexual passion are those of the self.

The central dynamic feature of sexual passion and its culmination is the experience of orgasm in intercourse; in the experience of orgasm, mounting sexual excitement culminates in an automatic, biologically determined response with a primitive, ecstatic affect, which requires for its full experience a temporary abandonment of the boundaries of the self, or, rather, an expansion—or an invasion—of the boundaries of the self into awareness of the subjectively diffuse biological roots of existence. I have already explored the relationships among biological instincts, affects, and drives; here I would stress the key functions of affects as subjective experiences at the boundary (in a general-systems context) between the biological and the intrapsychic realms, and their crucial function in organizing internal object relations and psychic structures in general.

But if sexual excitement constitutes a basic affect that lies at the core of passionate love, this does not mean that the capacity for passionate love is "wired in" as part of the orgastic experience. The longing for fusion with mother and the subjective experience of merger with her that characterize the symbiotic stage of development infiltrate the search for body contact, for intermingling of body surfaces. But the ecstatic experience of orgasm only gradually acquires a central organizing function; the genital phase of infantile sexuality recaptures and focuses, we might say, the diffuse excitement connected with merger experiences and fantasies in the pregenital phase of symbiotic attachment.

Clinical experience demonstrates that the affective quality of orgasm varies widely and, particularly in patients with severe narcissistic pathology and significant deterioration of internalized object relations, is often dramatically reduced so that orgasm provides a sense of frustration as well as relief. In passionate love, the orgastic experience is maximal, and it is here that we may examine the significance of the experience for the individual and for the couple.

In passionate love, orgasm integrates the simultaneous crossing of the boundary of the self into awareness of biological functioning beyond the control of the self, and the crossing of boundaries in a sophisticated identification with the loved object while maintaining the sense of separate identity. The shared experience of orgasm includes, in addition to temporary identification with the sexual partner, transcendence from the experience of the self to that of the fantasied union of the oedipal parents, as well as transcendence from the repetition of the oedipal relation to abandonment of it in a new object relation that reconfirms one's separate identity and autonomy.

In sexual passion, time-determined boundaries of the self are crossed, and the past world of object relations is transcended into a new, personally recreated one. Orgasm as part of sexual passion may also represent symbolically the experience of dying, of maintaining self-awareness while being swept into passive acceptance of neurovegetative sequences including excitement, ecstasy, and discharge. And the transcendence from self to a passionate union with the other person and the values for which both stand also is a challenge to death, to the transitory nature of individual existence.

But acceptance of the experience of merger with the other also replicates, unconsciously, the forceful penetration of the dangerous interior of the other's body (of mother's body)—that is, the mysterious realm of primitive projected aggression. Merger is therefore a dangerous venture that implies a dominance of trust over mistrust and fear, delivering the self to the other in the search for an ecstatic merger always threatened by the unknown (merger in aggression).

Similarly, in the domain of the activation of internalized object relations from preoedipal and oedipal stages of development, dissolving the protective barriers against primitive, diffuse affects while still remaining separate—that is, aware of oneself—and leaving behind the oedipal objects again implies the acceptance of the danger, not only of losing one's identity, but of the liberation of aggression against these internal and external objects and their retaliation.

Sexual passion therefore implies a courageous delivery of the self to a desired union with the ideal other in the face of unavoidable dangers. Hence it includes accepting the risks of abandoning oneself fully in relation to the other, in contrast to the fear of the dangers from many sources that threaten when amalgamating with another human being. It includes a basic hope in terms of giving and receiving love and thus being reconfirmed in one's own goodness, in contrast to guilt about and fear of the danger of one's aggression toward the loved object. And in sexual passion, crossing the time boundaries of the self also occurs in the commitment to the future, to the loved object as an ideal that provides personal meaning to life. In perceiving the beloved other as the incorporation not only of the desired oedipal and preoedipal object and the ideal relationship with another, but also of the ideas, values, and aspirations that make life worth living, the individual who experiences sexual passion expresses the hope for the creation and consolidation of meaning in the social and cultural world.

Sexual passion is a central issue in the study of the psychology and psychopathology of love relations, an issue that seems to bear in many ways on the question of the stability or instability of love relations. The question is often raised whether sexual passion is a characteristic of romantic falling in love or of the early stages of love relations that is gradually replaced by a less intense, "affectionate" relationship, or whether it is a basic ingredient of what keeps couples together, an expression (as well as guarantee) of the active, creative functions of sexual love. Could it be that sexual passion, a potential condition for the couple's stability, is also a potential source of threat to it, so that a creative love relation is by implication also more threatened than one characterized by a relatively quiet, nonpassionate harmony and feeling of security?

The contrast between the affection in a stable love relation or marriage and the passion in a love affair has been debated by poets and philosophers throughout the centuries. On the basis of my evaluation of patients in long-standing relationships, following the vicissitudes of the relationship of couples over many years, I believe this dichotomy to be an oversimplified convention. Passionate love characterizes some couples during many years of life together.

I believe that sexual passion cannot be equated with the ecstatic mood characteristic of adolescence. The subtle yet deep, self-contained, and self-critical awareness of love for another person, combined with a clear awareness of the final mystery separating one from any other person, the acceptance of unfulfillable longings as part of the price to pay for a total commitment to a loved other, also reflect sexual passion.

Nor is sexual passion limited to, although it is typically expressed in, sexual intercourse with orgasm. To the contrary: sexual love expands, from the intuitive awareness of intercourse and orgasm as its final liberating, consuming, and reconfirming aim, into the broad field of sexual longing for the other, of heightened erotic desire and the appreciation of the physical, emotional, and general human values represented by the other. There are normal oscillations in intensity and abrupt discontinuities in the relationship of a couple, which I shall explore later. But in a satisfactory sexual relationship, sexual passion is an available structure characterizing their relationship simultaneously in the sexual, object relational, and ethical and cultural realms.

I have said that an essential aspect of the subjective experience of passion at all levels is crossing the boundaries of the self, merging with the other. This experience of merger and fusion has to be contrasted with regressive merger phenomena, which blur self-nonself differentiation: what is characteristic of sexual passion is the simultaneous experience of merger and maintenance of a separate identity.

Crossing the boundaries of self, thus defined, is the basis of the subjective experience of transcendence. Psychotic identifications (Jacobson 1964) with their dissolution of self and object boundaries, interfere with the capacity for passion. However, because transcendence implies the danger of losing oneself, of being faced with threatening aggression, passion is related to the fear of aggression in psychotic merger. And it is when there is an intensity of aggression, with a split between idealized and persecutory object relations, in the primitive idealizations of borderline patients, that passionate love may suddenly turn into passionate hatred. The lack of integration of "all-good" and "all-bad" internalized object relations fosters dramatic and sudden changes in the relationship of a couple. The prototypal experience of the spurned lover who kills his or her rival and the betraying love object and then kills himself or herself signals this relationship among passionate love, splitting mechanisms, and primitive idealization and hatred.

There is an intrinsic contradiction in the combination of these two crucial features of sexual love: the firm boundaries of the self and the constant awareness of the indissoluble separateness of individuals, on the one hand, and the sense of transcendence, of becoming one with the loved person, on the other. The separateness results in loneliness and longing and fear for the frailty of all relations; transcendence in the couple's union brings about the sense of oneness with the world, of permanence and new creation. Loneliness, one might say, is a prerequisite for transcendence.

To remain within the boundaries of the self while transcending them in identification with the loved object is an exciting, moving, and yet painful condition of love. The Mexican poet Octavio Paz (1974) has expressed this aspect of love with an almost overwhelming conciseness, stating that love is the point of intersection between desire and reality. Love, he says, reveals reality to desire and creates the transition from the erotic object to the beloved person. This revelation is almost always painful because the beloved presents himself or herself simultaneously as a body which can be penetrated and a consciousness which is impenetrable. Love is the revelation of the other person's freedom. The contradictory nature of love is that desire aspires to be fulfilled by the destruction of the desired object, and love discovers that this object is indestructible and cannot be substituted.

Here is a clinical illustration of a maturing capacity for the experience of sexual passion, the development of a romantic longing in a previously inhibited, obsessive man in psychoanalytic treatment. I omit the dynamic and structural aspects of this change in order to focus on the subjective experience of integrating eroticism, object relations, and value systems.

A college professor, in his late thirties, shortly before setting out on a professional trip to Europe, had become engaged to a woman he felt very much in love with. On his return, he described an experience he had when visiting the Louvre and seeing there for the first time Mesopotamian miniature sculptures from the third millennium BCE. At one point, he had the uncanny experience that one of these sculptures, the body of a woman whose nipples and navel were marked by tiny precious stones, resembled the body of the woman he loved. He had been thinking about her, longing for her, as he walked through the almost deserted halls, and while he was looking at the sculpture, a wave of erotic stimulation seized him, together with an intense feeling of closeness to her. He also was very much moved by what he considered the extreme simplicity and beauty of the sculpture, and he felt that he could empathize with the unknown artist, who had died more than four thousand years ago. He had a sense of humility and yet of reassuring communication with the past and felt as if he had been allowed to share the understanding of the eternal mystery of love expressed in that work of art. The sense of erotic desire had become fused with the sense of oneness, of longing for and yet closeness to the woman he loved, and through that oneness and love he had been permitted entrance into the transcendent world of beauty. At the same time, he had a strong sense of his own individuality, together with gratitude for the opportunity to share the experience of this work of art and with humility.

Sexual passion reactivates and contains the entire sequence of emotional states that assure the individual of his own, his parents', the entire world of objects' "goodness" and the hope of the fulfillment of love despite frustration, hostility, and ambivalence. Sexual passion assumes the capacity for continued empathy with—but not merger into—a primitive state of symbiotic fusion (Freud's [1930] "oceanic feeling"), the excited reunion of closeness with mother at a stage of self-object differentiation, and the gratification of oedipal longings in the context of overcoming feelings of inferiority, fear, and guilt regarding sexual functioning. Sexual passion is the facilitating core of a sense of oneness with a loved person as part of adolescent romanticism and, later, mature commitments to the beloved partner in the face of the realistic limitations of human life, the unavoidability of illness, decay, deterioration, and death. It is an important source of empathy with the loved person. Hence, the crossing of boundaries and the reconfirmation of a basic sense of goodness in spite of many risks link biology, the emotional world, and the world of values in one immediate system.

Crossing the boundaries of the self in sexual passion, and the integration of love and aggression, homosexuality and heterosexuality, in the internal relationship to the loved person are illustrated eloquently in Hans Castorp's declaration of love to Claudia Chauchat in Thomas Mann's *Magic Mountain* (1924). Breaking away from his humanist, rational, and mature "mentor," Settembrini, Castorp declares his love in French, which becomes an almost private and intimate language in the German text of the book. Excited and liberated by Madame Chauchat's warm though slightly ironic response, he tells her that he has always loved her and hints at his past homosexual relation with a friend of his youth who resembled her and whom he had once asked for a pencil just as he had asked Madame Chauchat for one earlier in the evening. He tells her that love is nothing if it is not madness, something senseless, forbidden, and an adventure in evil. He tells her that the body, love, and death—all three—are but one thing. He talks about the miracle of organic life and physical beauty, which is composed of living and corruptible matter.

But crossing the boundaries of the self implies that certain conditions must exist: as mentioned before, there has to be an awareness of and a capacity for empathy with the existence of a psychological field outside the boundary of the self. Hence, the erotically tinged states of manic excitement and grandiosity characteristic of psychotic patients cannot be called sexual passion, and the unconscious destruction of object representations and external objects that is so predominant in narcissistic personalities destroys their capacity to transcend into the intimate union with another human being, therefore eroding and eventually destroying their capacity for sexual passion.

Sexual excitement and orgasm also lose their function of boundary crossing into biology referred to before when mechanical, repetitive sexual excitement and orgasm are built into the self experience dissociated from the deepening of internalized object relations. This is where sexual excitement becomes differentiated from erotic desire and sexual passion; basically, masturbation may (and usually does) express an object relation—typically, the various aspects of oedipal relations from early childhood on. But masturbation as a compulsive, repetitive activity, functioning defensively against forbidden sexual impulses and other unconscious conflicts in the context of a regressive dissociation from conflictual object relations, loses its transcendent function. I am suggesting that it is not the endless, compulsively repetitive gratification of instinctual urges that brings about a deterioration of the excitement, pleasure, and satisfaction derived from them but the loss of the crucial function of crossing self-object boundaries that is guaranteed by the normal investment in the world of object relations. In other words, it is the world of internalized and external object relations that keeps sexuality alive and provides the potential for lasting gratification.

The integration of loving and hating self representations and object representations and affects in the transformation of part into total object relations (or object constancy) is a basic requirement for the capacity to establish a stable object relation. It is necessary for crossing the boundary of a stable ego identity into identification with the loved object.

But the establishment of object relations in depth also liberates primitive aggression in the relationship, in the context of the reciprocal activation in both partners of repressed or dissociated pathogenic object relations from infancy and childhood. The more pathological and aggressively determined the repressed or dissociated internalized object relations, the more primitive the corresponding defensive mechanisms; these, particularly projective identification, may induce experiences or reactions in the partner that reproduce the threatening object representations; idealized and devaluated, mourned-for and persecutory object representations are superimposed on the perception of and interaction with the loved object and may threaten—as well as strengthen—the relationship. As both partners become increasingly aware of the effects of distortions in their perceptions and behavior toward each other, they may grow painfully aware of mutual aggression without necessarily being able to resolve their interactive patterns; thus the unconscious cement of the couple's relationship also may endanger it. It is at this point that superego integration and maturation, expressed in the transformation of primitive prohibitions and guilt feelings over aggression into concern for the object—and the self—protect the object relation and the capacity for crossing boundaries toward the loved object. The mature superego fosters love and commitment to the loved object.

One general implication of the proposed definition of sexual passion is that it constitutes a permanent feature of love relations rather than an initial or temporary expression of the "romantic" idealization of adolescence and early adulthood; it has the function of providing intensity, consolidation, and renovation to love relations throughout life; and it provides permanence to sexual excitement by linking it with the couple's total human experience. This leads us to the erotic aspects of stable sexual relations. I think that clinical evidence clearly indicates how intimately sexual excitement and enjoyment are linked with the quality of the couple's total relationship. Although statistical studies of large populations show a decrease of frequency of sexual intercourse and orgasm over the decades, clinical study of couples indicates the significant effect of the nature of their relationship on the frequency and quality of sexual intercourse; the sexual experience remains a constant, central aspect of love relations and marital life. Under optimal circumstances, the intensity of sexual enjoyment has an ongoing renovative quality that depends not on sexual gymnastics but on the couple's intuitive capacity to weave changing personal needs and experiences into the complex net of heterosexual and homosexual, loving and aggressive aspects of the total relationship expressed in unconscious and conscious fantasies and their enactment in the couple's sexual relations.

4.

Love, Oedipus, and the Couple

The Impact of Gender

In my earlier discussion of core gender identity, I reviewed the controversy as to whether an original psychological bisexuality for both genders can be sustained or whether the earliest identity of both genders is either masculine, as postulated by Freud (1905), or feminine, as proposed by Stoller (1975a, 1985). I expressed my agreement with Person and Ovesey (1983, 1984), whose view that infants establish a core gender identity that is male or female from the very start dovetails with the findings of studies of hermaphrodites and with observations of early childhood. Braunschweig and Fain (1971, 1975), presenting psychoanalytic evidence for an original psychological bisexuality derived from the unconscious identification of the infant and small child with both parents, convincingly propose that this unconscious bisexual potential is gradually controlled by the dominant nature of the mother-infant interaction, in which one core gender identity is established. This idea is in agreement with Money and Ehrhardt's (1972) view that the parental definition of the infant's gender identity is the key organizer of that identity, a view strengthened by Stoller's observations on transsexuality.

In further developing Braunschweig and Fain's theories, I earlier pointed to mother's ministrations and her expression of enjoyment in the physical stimulation of the infant as essential in fostering the infant's body-surface erotism and, later, erotic desire. For both the girl and the boy, the early erotic experience with mother kindles the potential for sexual excitement, but while mother's implicitly "teasing" erotic relation to her little boy remains a constant aspect of male sexuality and contributes to the boy's ordinarily continuous capacity for genital excitement, her subtle and unconscious rejection of this sexual excitement regarding her daughter gradually inhibits the little girl's awareness of her original vaginal genitality. This different treatment of boy and girl in the erotic realm powerfully cements their respective core gender identities while contributing to their difference in the assertion of genital excitement throughout childhood—continuous for the little boy, inhibited in the little girl.

For this reason, men—fixated unconsciously to their primary object—have greater difficulties in dealing with their ambivalence toward women and are to develop the capacity to integrate genital and tender needs while women—inhibited early in their genital awareness—are slower to integrate a full genital relationship in the context of a loving relationship.

Braunschweig and Fain's (1971) observations are extremely useful in explaining the significant differences that can be found between men and women in mature sexual love. In summarizing some of their salient points, I shall attempt to remain as close as possible to their own language.

For the boy, the pregenital relationship with mother already involves a special sexual orientation of her toward him, which stimulates his sexual awareness and the narcissistic investment of his penis. The danger is that excessive pregenital gratification of the boy's narcissistic needs by mother may bring about a fantasy that his small penis is fully satisfactory to her and thus may contribute to his denial of its difference from the powerful penis of the father. Under these circumstances, such narcissistic fixation may later on, in men, determine a kind of infantile, playful sexual seductiveness toward women without full identification with the penetrating power of the paternal penis. This fixation will interfere with full genital identity, with the internalization of the father into the ego ideal, and will foster the repression of excessive castration anxiety.

For these men, unresolved competition with father and the defensive denial of castration anxiety are expressed in narcissistic enjoyment of infantile dependent relations with women, representing mother images. This constellation, for Braunschweig and Fain as well as for Chasseguet-Smirgel (1973, 1974), is an important origin of narcissistic fixation (I would say, fixation at a level of normal infantile narcissism) and lack of normal resolution of the oedipal complex in boys, and is fostered by those aspects of mother's behavior by which she rebels against the "predominance" of the paternal penis and the "paternal law" in general. The implication is that an unconscious collusion exists between eternally little boys—Don Juans—and seductive maternal women, who utilize the rebelliousness of the Don Juan against father's "law and order" to express their own competitiveness with and rebelliousness against the father.

Braunschweig and Fain state that normally, mother's periodically turning away from the male child to return to father frustrates the little boy's
narcissism and stimulates him to competitive identification with father,
thus initiating or reinforcing the positive oedipal constellation in boys.
One consequence is the boy's heightened feelings of frustration at being
sexually rejected by mother, so that his orally derived—and projected—
aggression toward her is reinforced by early oedipally derived aggression.
This development will have a crucial influence on the love life of men
who unconsciously do not change their first sexual object—mother.

Chasseguet-Smirgel (1970) and Braunschweig and Fain (1971) also emphasize the little girl's vaginal excitability and her feminine sexuality in
general. In this regard, their observations are similar to those of Jones
(1935), Klein (1945), and Horney (1967) and to research in the United
States indicating early vaginal masturbatory activities of little girls and
the intimate connection between clitoral and vaginal erotic responsiveness (Barnett 1966; Galenson and Roiphe 1977). These studies suggest that
a very early vaginal awareness exists in the little girl and that this vaginal
awareness is inhibited and later repressed.

The French writers stress evidence indicating that the attitudes of parents, particularly mothers, toward baby boys and girls differ, and that the
role induction of early mother-child interaction has a powerful influence
on gender identity (see also Stoller 1973). According to the French group,
mother, in contrast to her early stimulation of the little boy's genitality,
does not particularly invest the little girl's genitals because mother maintains her own sexual life, her "vaginal sexuality," as part of her separate
domain as a woman relating to father; even when mother narcissistically
invests her little daughter, this narcissism has pregenital rather than genital features (except in women with strong homosexual tendencies). The
mother's not investing her daughter's female genitals is also a response
to the culturally determined pressures and shared inhibitions regarding
the female genitals that stem from male castration anxiety.

Blum (1976) emphasizes the importance of the oedipal rivalry and conflicts around self-esteem as a woman that the little girl arouses in her
mother: if mother has devalued herself as a woman, she will devalue her
daughter, and mother's self-esteem will strongly influence her daughter's
self-esteem. Mother's unresolved conflicts about her own genitality and
her admiration of her little boy's penis will lead her daughter to merge
penis envy with sibling rivalry. Normally, the little girl turns toward father, not only from disappointment in mother, but also in identification
with her.

A general implication of the French line of thought is that castration anxiety is not a primary determinant in the little girl's turning from mother to father but a secondary complication reinforcing the primary inhibition or repression of vaginal genitality under the influence of mother's implicitly denying attitude. The intensity of castration anxiety in women depends largely on a three-step displacement of pregenital aggression: first projected onto mother, then reinforced by oedipal competitiveness with her, and finally displaced onto father. Penis envy in little girls reflects mostly reinforcement of oedipal conflicts under the effect of the displacement of pregenital aggression and envy onto the penis.

Chasseguet-Smirgel (1974), relating to Horney's (1967) ideas, has suggested that the little boy's fantasy of a phallic mother may serve not only as a reassurance against, or denial of, perceiving the female genitals as a product of castration, but also against the awareness of the adult vagina that would prove his little genitals highly inadequate.

From all these developments various developmental stages evolve that the little girl and the little boy have to pass through on their road to identifying with adult genitality. For the boy, the identification with father implies that he has overcome his pregenital envy of women, the projection of this envy in the form of primitive fears of women (Kernberg 1974), and his fears of inadequacy regarding the female genitals. For the French writers, the Don Juan is midway between inhibiting the sexual drive toward women who represent the oedipal mother, on the one hand, and identifying with father and the paternal penis in an adult sexual relation with a woman, on the other: Don Juan, Braunschweig and Fain suggest, affirms genitality without paternity.

I do not think the Don Juan syndrome in men has a single etiology. Like promiscuity in women—the cause of which may range from severely narcissistic character pathology to relatively mild masochistically or hysterically determined pathology—male promiscuity exists along a continuum. The promiscuous narcissistic personality is a much more severe type of Don Juan than the infantile, dependent, rebellious, but effeminate type described by the French.

I think that the next step toward the normal boy's sexual identification with father is the conflictual identification with the primitive, controlling, and sadistic male who represents the fantasied jealous and restrictive father in the early oedipal period. The final overcoming of the oedipal complex in men is characterized by identification with a "generous" father who no longer operates by means of repressive laws against the son. The capacity to enjoy the growth of a son without having to submit him to punishing initiation rites, reflecting unconscious envy of him, signifies that the father has definitely overcome his own oedipal inhibitions. The practical implication of these formulations is that one important source of instability in the love relations of adult men is incomplete identification with the paternal function, with various fixations along the way.

For the little girl, the lack of direct stimulation of her genital eroticism in her early relation with mother and, above all, the mother's conflicts over the value of her own genitals and feminine functions would result in inhibited psychosexual development, which is then secondarily reinforced by the development of penis envy and the repression of sexual competitiveness with the oedipal mother. However, the mother's depreciation of men and her little boy's genitals may radically alter the sexual perceptions and conflicts of her children of both genders.

For the French writers, the little girl's genitality is private, in contrast to the socially reinforced "public display" of male genitality in little boys' pride in the penis; the girl is alone in the realm of her sexual development. Her silent and secret unconscious hope resides in turning from mother to father and in her intuitive longing for the paternal penis, which, in penetrating the vagina, would eventually re-create the affirmation of vaginal genitality and female sexuality in general. Braunschweig and Fain suggest that because the road of female sexual development is lonelier and more secretive, it is more courageous than the little boy's, whose male genitality is for various reasons stimulated by both parents. Perhaps because the little girl has had to change her first erotic object in turning from mother to father and has thus had to cross from pregenital to genital developments earlier, more definitely, and in a lonely way, the adult woman has potentially greater courage and capacity for heterosexual commitment than the adult man.

In a different context, Altman (1977) has pointed out that, in contrast to the permanence of the first object in men, the change of object in women may be one important source of the generally greater difficulty men have in committing themselves to a stable love relation. Men are inclined to search eternally for the ideal mother and more prone to reactivate pregenital and genital fears and conflicts in their relations with women, which predisposes them to avoid commitments in depth. Women, having already renounced their first object, are more able to commit themselves to a man who is willing to establish a full genital and "paternal" relationship with them. An additional, crucial factor in women's capacity for commitment may be their concern for the stability of care and protection of the young, involving biological and psychosocial determinants, mostly the identification with maternal functions and related sublimatory superego values (Blum 1976).

These differences in the development of the capacity for erotic desire and sexual love notwithstanding, men and women do have experiences in common stemming from the oedipal situation as a fundamental organizer both for individuals and for all areas of a couple's interaction.

I agree with David (1971) that the quality of longing for the unavailable and forbidden oedipal object, which energizes sexual development, is a crucial component of sexual passion and love relations. In this regard, the oedipal constellation may be considered a permanent feature of human relations, and it may be important to stress that neurotic solutions to oedipal conflicts have to be differentiated from their normal manifestations.

Crossing the boundaries of sexual and generational prohibitions might be formulated as the active reconstruction, on the part of the individual in love, of his or her history of oedipal relations, including the defensive and creative fantasies that transform the reencounter into the new encounter with the love object. Crossing the social and sexual boundaries transforms unconscious fantasies into subjective experience in reality; in the reciprocal activation of their world of internal object relations, the couple reactivates the oedipal myth as a social structure (Arlow 1974).

In both genders, oedipal longings, the need to overcome the fantasies of oedipal prohibitions and satisfy curiosity about the mysterious relations between the parents, stimulate sexual passion. Because of the considerations already mentioned, women probably cross the final boundary of identification with the oedipal mother earlier in their affirmation of female sexuality in the change of erotic object from mother to father. Men have to cross the final boundary of identification with the oedipal father in their capacity to establish a sexual relation with a loved woman and to carry out the functions of paternity and "generosity" in this context. Clinical experience reveals how guilt-ridden men feel when they decide to terminate a relationship with a woman, whereas women usually feel free in letting a man know when they do not love him. This difference probably reflects men's deep-seated guilt over aggression toward mother, which is so frequently reenacted in their relationships with women (Edith Jacobson, personal communication). But in women, unconscious guilt because of the pregenital and genital mother's fantasied prohibitions against vaginal genitality requires a fully erotic, genital affirmation in the sexual relation with a man. The condensation of sadistic superego forerunners related to the introjection of primitive, preoedipal maternal images with the later, prohibitive aspects of the oedipal mother may be one factor contributing to the great frequency of genital inhibitions in women. It may also be an important element in what is generally referred to as "female masochism."

There has been a growing questioning of the earlier psychoanalytic assumptions regarding the inborn disposition to masochism in women and an increasing awareness of the various psychological and social factors contributing to their masochistic tendencies and sexual inhibitions. Person (1974) and Blum (1976) have reviewed the pertinent literature and stress the developmental and psychosocial determinants of feminine masochism. Blum concludes that there is no evidence that the human female has a greater endowment than the male to derive pleasure from pain and that the girl's earliest identifications and object relations are of crucial importance in determining her later sexual identity, feminine role, and maternal attitudes: masochism is more likely to be a maladaptive solution for feminine functions.

Stoller (1974) has suggested that because of the original merging with mother, the sense of femininity is more firmly established in women than the sense of maleness in men. Men, because of their original merger with mother—a female—may be more vulnerable regarding their bisexuality and more prone to the development of perversion.

I have found that, after full analysis of a woman's pregenital and genital sources of penis envy and loathing of her own genitals, one regularly encounters an earlier capacity for full enjoyment of vaginal eroticism, an affirmation of the full value of her own body, simultaneously with the capacity to love the man's genitality without envy. I do not think that normal female sexuality implies the need or capacity to renounce the penis as the most appreciated genital, and I think there is good evidence that men's fear of female genitals is not only secondary to oedipal castration anxiety in the most severe cases but has profound pregenital roots. In short, overcoming fear and envy of the other gender represents, for both men and women, the exhilarating experience of overcoming the prohibitions against sexuality.

From a broader perspective, the couple's discovery of the enjoyment of full genitality may cause them to change radically from submitting to the predominant cultural conventions and the ritualized prohibitions and superstitions that erect barriers against mature genitality. This degree of sexual freedom, combined with the final overcoming of oedipal inhibitions, may reflect the ultimate potential for sexual enjoyment in love relations and reinforce passion by creating a new mystery of sexual secrets shared by the couple and freeing it from its surrounding social group. From a developmental point of view, the elements of secrecy and opposition characteristic of sexual passion derive from the oedipal constellation as a basic organizer of human sexuality.

From a sociocultural viewpoint, I think that the relation of sexual love to social convention is always ambiguous, and love's "harmony" with social norms easily deteriorates into conventionality and ritualization. But by the same token, the couple's sexual freedom in love cannot be exported easily into social norms, and efforts to "free sexual love" on the basis of massive education and "cultural change" usually conclude in a conventionalized mechanization of sex. I think that opposition between the couple and the group is inevitable; Braunschweig and Fain (1971) have thoughtfully discussed this issue.

The tragic incapacity to identify with the paternal function, so that all love relations are doomed to failure in spite of "genital primacy," and the rationalization of this failure in terms of a predominant myth of a male-dominated culture are dramatically illustrated in Henry de Montherlant's book *Les Jeunes Filles* (1936). Speaking through his young hero (or anti-hero) Pierre Costals, Montherlant bitterly resents the pressures derived from the desire that brings men and women together in an eternal misunderstanding. For women, he says (pp. 1010–1012), love begins with sexual gratification, whereas for men, love ends with sex; women are made for one man, but man is made for life and for all women. Vanity is the dominant passion of man, while the intensity of feelings related to the love for a man represents a major source of happiness for women. The happiness of women comes from man, but that of man comes from himself. The sexual act is surrounded by dangers, prohibitions, frustrations, and disgusting physiology.

It would be easy to dismiss Montherlant's description of the aesthetically oriented, anguished, proud, old-fashioned, cruel, and self-destructive Costals as the product of a paternalistic ideology; but this would miss the deeper sources of the intensity of longing and the fear and hatred of women that underlie this rationalization.

The predominant pathology interfering with a stable, fully gratifying relationship with a member of the opposite gender is represented by pathological narcissism, on the one hand, and by the incapacity to resolve oedipal conflicts with a full genital identification with the parental figure of the same gender, on the other. Narcissistic pathology is relatively similar in men and women. Pathology derived mainly from oedipal conflicts differs in men and women. In women, unresolved oedipal conflicts are manifested most frequently in various masochistic patterns, such as persistent attachment to unsatisfactory men and an incapacity to enjoy or maintain a relationship with a man who potentially would be fully satisfactory to them. Men also attach themselves to unsatisfactory women, but culturally they used to be freer to dissolve such unsatisfactory relationships. And women's value systems, their concern and sense of responsibility for their children, may reinforce whatever masochistic tendency they have. However, the natural ego ideal and maternal concerns are not masochistic goals (Blum 1976) in the "ordinary devoted mother."

In men, the predominant pathology of love relations derived from oedipal conflicts takes the form of fear of and insecurity vis-à-vis women and reaction formations against such insecurity in the form of reactive or projected hostility toward them; these combine in various ways with pregenital hostility and guilt toward the maternal figure. Pregenital conflicts, particularly conflicts around pregenital aggression, are intimately condensed with genital conflicts. In women, this condensation appears typically in the exacerbation of conflicts around penis envy; the orally determined envy of the pregenital mother is displaced onto the idealized genital father and his penis, and onto the oedipal rivalry with mother. In men, pregenital aggression, envy, and fear of women reinforce oedipal fears and feelings of inferiority toward them: the pregenital envy of mother reinforces the oedipally determined insecurity of men regarding idealized women.

The universal nature of the oedipal constellation makes for the reemergence of oedipal conflicts in various stages of the relationship, so that psychosocial circumstances may sometimes induce and at other times protect the couple from the reactivation of neurotic expression of oedipal conflicts. For example, a woman's dedicated commitment to her husband's interests may reflect an adaptive expression of her ego ideal, but it may also compensate adaptively for masochistic tendencies related to unconscious guilt over taking the place of the oedipal mother. When the husband no longer depends on her and their economic and social relations no longer require or warrant her "sacrifice," unconscious guilt reflecting unresolved oedipal conflicts may no longer be compensated; a variety of conflicts may be triggered—perhaps her unconscious need to destroy the relationship out of guilt, or unresolved penis envy and related resentment of male success. Or a man's failure at work may decompensate his previous sources of narcissistic affirmation, which have protected him from oedipal insecurity toward women and pathological rivalries with men, and may bring about a regression toward sexual inhibition and conflictual dependency on his wife, further reactivating his oedipal conflicts and their neurotic solutions.

The social, cultural, and professional development and success of women in Western society, then, may threaten the traditional, culturally sanctioned and reinforced protection of men against their oedipal insecurity and fears and envy of women; and the changing reality confronts both participants with the potential reactivation of conscious and unconscious envy, jealousy, and resentment, which dangerously increase the aggressive components of the love relation.

These sociocultural dimensions of the couple's unconscious conflicts are subtly, yet dramatically illustrated in a series of films by Eric Rohmer dealing with love and marriage, particularly *My Night at Maude's* (Rohmer 1969; Mellen 1973). Jean-Louis, the conventional, intelligent, sensitive, but timid, rigid young Catholic, does not dare to become involved with Maude, the vivacious, professionally active, emotionally deep and complex divorcée. He prefers to remain "faithful" to the idealized, rather flat, secretive, and submissive Catholic girl he has decided he will marry. He appears to be a man of commitment and consistency, but underneath he is afraid to commit himself to a full although uncertain relationship with a woman who is his equal. And Maude, with all her charm and talent and capacity for personal fulfillment, is unable to recognize that Jean-Louis will not give her anything because he is afraid and unable to do so; after rejecting Jean-Louis' friend Vidal, who does love her, she enters into yet another unsatisfactory marriage to still another man. The tragedy is one of lost opportunities—counterparts to the potential happiness and fulfillment of a stable love relation or marriage within which both partners are able to transcend the unconsciously determined dangers to their relationship.

Falling in Love and Becoming a Couple

The capacity to fall in love is a basic pillar of the relationship of the couple. It implies the capacity to link idealization with erotic desire and the potential for establishing an object relationship in depth. A man and a woman who discover their attraction and longing for each other, who are able to establish a full sexual relationship that carries with it emotional intimacy and a sense of fulfillment of their ideals in closeness with the loved other, are expressing their capacity not only to unconsciously link eroticism and tenderness, sexuality and the ego ideal, but also to recruit aggression in the service of love. A couple in a fulfilling love relationship defies the ever-present envy and resentment of the excluded others and the distrustfully regulating agencies of the conventional culture in which they live. The romantic myth of the lovers who find each other in a hostile crowd expresses an unconscious reality for both partners. Some cultures may highlight romanticism (the emotional, heroic, idealized aspects of love) and others may rigorously deny it, but the emotional reality is revealed in art and literature throughout history (Bergmann 1987).

Another important dynamic is the couple's defiant rupture of the submission to the unconsciously homosexual groups of latency and early adolescence (Braunschweig and Fain 1971): the man defies the anally tinged devaluation of sexuality and the defensive depreciation of women of latency and early adolescent male groups, the groups' defense against profound dependent longings and oedipal prohibitions; the woman overcomes the fear of male aggression, of latency and adolescent female groups, their collusion in denying the longing for sexual intimacy, and the defensive idealization of partially desexualized men as a shared group ideal.

A man and a woman may have known each other from childhood, may have constituted a couple in the minds of everybody who knows them, they may marry, and still not really be a couple. Or they may become one secretly sooner or later: many if not most marriages are several marriages, and some consolidate only long after they have faded from the attention of their social group.

If the couple can incorporate their polymorphous perverse fantasies and wishes into their sexual relationship, discover and uncover the sadomasochistic core of sexual excitement in their intimacy, their defiance of conventional cultural mores may become a conscious element of their pleasure. In the process, a full incorporation of their body eroticism may enrich each partner's openness to the aesthetic dimension of culture and art and to the experience of nature. The joint stripping away of the sexual taboos of childhood may cement the couple's emotional, cultural, and social life as well.

In patients with significant character pathology, the capacity for falling in love indicates certain psychological achievements: in narcissistic personalities, falling in love marks the beginning of the capacity for concern and guilt and some hope for overcoming the deep, unconscious devaluation of the love object. With borderline patients, primitive idealization may be the first step toward a love relation different from the love-hate relation with the primary objects. This occurs if and when the splitting mechanisms responsible for this primitive idealization have been resolved and this love relation, or a new one replacing it, is able to tolerate and resolve the pregenital conflicts against which primitive idealization was a defense. Neurotic patients and patients with relatively mild character pathology develop a capacity for a lasting love relation if and when successful psychoanalytic or psychotherapeutic treatment resolves the unconscious, predominantly oedipal, conflicts.

Being in love also represents a mourning process related to growing up and becoming independent, the experience of leaving behind the real objects of childhood. In this process of separation, there is also reconfirmation of the good relations with internalized objects of the past as the individual becomes confident of the capacity to give and receive love and sexual gratification simultaneously—with a growth-promoting mutual reinforcement of both—in contrast to the conflict between love and sex in childhood.

Achievement of this developmental stage permits the development of the capacity to transform falling in love into a stable love relationship, implying a capacity for tenderness, concern, and idealization more sophisticated than that of earlier developmental levels, and a capacity for identification and empathy with the love object. Now tenderness may expand into full sexual enjoyment, concern deepens with full sexual identification and empathy, and idealization becomes a mature commitment to an ideal represented by what the loved person is or stands for, or what the couple, united, might become.

Mature Sexual Love and the Sexual Couple

Henry Dicks (1967) has provided, on the basis of research on the conflicts of marital couples, what I consider the most comprehensive psychoanalytic frame for the study of the characteristics of normal as well as psychopathological love relations. He approached the study of the capacity for a mature love relation in terms of dimensions of interaction established in a marital relationship. By examining marital couples individually and jointly from a psychoanalytic perspective, he mapped out a frame of reference that permitted an analysis of the reasons for chronic marital conflict as well as the outcome of such conflicts, whether the destruction of the couple, the maintenance of an unsatisfactory and conflictual equilibrium, or resolution of the conflict.

Dicks found that there were three major areas in which couples related to each other: their conscious mutual expectations of what a marital relationship should provide; the extent to which their mutual expectations permitted harmonizing their own cultural expectations and also integrating them in their cultural environment; and the unconscious activation of past pathogenic internalized object relations in each partner and their mutual induction of roles complementary to these past object relations. Dicks found that couples established a compromise formation between their unconscious object relations, which were often in sharp conflict with their conscious wishes and mutual expectations.

This mutual role induction was achieved by projective identification and proved to be a strong factor in determining the couple's capacity to obtain gratification. Dicks emphasized how sexual conflicts between the

partners were the usual territory in which marital conflicts and unconsciously activated object relations were expressed, and he pointed to the
sharp contrast between these activated object relations and the couple's
initial mutual idealization.

The vicissitudes Dicks described of the activation of mutual projective
identification as part of the couple's object relations and the influence of
their ego ideals on the relationship have significantly influenced my own
thinking on the relationship of couples. He stated that "paradoxically to
common sense, the unconscious commitment—the mutual collusive in-
terlocking of the partners—appears more powerful and inescapable in the
kind of disturbed marriage we are now considering than in the free and
flexible interdependence of 'whole persons' " (p. 73).

In my view, the areas of the couple's interaction Dicks outlined may
be reformulated and expanded to at least the following three areas: (1)
their actual sexual relations, (2) their consciously and unconsciously predominant object relations, and (3) their establishment of a joint ego ideal.
The capacity for mature sexual love that I have described is played out in
these three areas.

What I would like to stress is the importance of the integration of
libido and aggression, love and hatred, with the predominance of love over
hatred, in all three of these major areas of a couple's interaction. In this
regard, I am indebted to Stoller (1979, 1985), who made sweeping contributions to the psychoanalytic understanding of sexual excitement, the
perversions, and the nature of love. He pointed to the essential presence
of aggression as a component of sexual excitement, independently reaching conclusions similar to those I have reached in studying the sexual
experiences of borderline patients. He also emphasized the importance of
mystery in sexual excitement and described anatomical and physiological
factors that, in interaction with oedipal desires and dangers, contribute to
the exciting and frustrating qualities that are so much a part of mystery.
Mystery both induces and reflects sexual fantasy. Stoller stressed the function of sexual excitement in re-creating dangerous and potentially frustrating situations and overcoming them by the gratification of the specific
sexual fantasy and act. Thus, in terms of the capacity both for sexual
excitement and erotic desire and for integration of preoedipal and oedipal
object relations as part of love relations, the integration of libido and aggression, love and hatred, gradually emerged as a major aspect of the capacity for, as well as the pathology of, love relations.

The sadomasochistic aspects of polymorphous perverse sexuality provide an important impetus to the striving for sexual fusion; and an excessive predominance of lack of tender bodily care or traumatic

experiences, physical or sexual abuse, may erase the capacity for sexual response and interfere with the consolidation and development of the affect of sexual excitement. Conversely, an excessive repression of aggression, unconscious prohibitions against the early, aggressive components of polymorphous perverse infantile sexuality, may inhibit it significantly and impoverish the sexual response.

Clinically, in fact, it is my observation that some degree of suppression or repression of polymorphous perverse infantile sexuality is the most frequent type of sexual inhibition, importantly contributing to impoverishing the love life of couples whose emotional relations are otherwise very satisfactory. In practice, we find that couples may have genital intercourse regularly, with sexual excitement and orgasm, but with a developing monotony, a vague sense of dissatisfaction and boredom. In the area of sexual excitement, then, both a lack of integration of aggression and an excess of aggression may inhibit the love relation.

The same process appears in the dominant object relations of the couple. The lack of integration of "all-good" and "all-bad" internalized object relations leads to primitive idealization in the love relations of borderline personality organization; the unrealistic quality of the idealization easily leads to conflict and destruction of the relationship. An idealization that does not tolerate ambivalence, that is easily destroyed by any aggression in the relationship, is by definition a frail and unsatisfactory one, and the partners lack the capacity for mutual identification in depth. But the integration of object relations that heralds the dominance of advanced oedipal conflicts with the corresponding tolerance of ambivalence also signifies the emergence of aggression in the relationship that has to be tolerated and is potentially dangerous to the relationship.

The tolerance of ambivalence facilitates the activation of unconscious scenarios and mutual projective identification of past pathogenic internalized object relations, so that the tolerance of aggression as part of the ambivalent relationship of the couple enriches it enormously and ensures the depth that has been pointed to as part of Balint's "genital identification" or Winnicott's "concern." But excessive aggression threatens the couple with intolerable conflict and potential rupture of the relationship.

Let us turn from object relations to the couple's mutual projection of the ego ideal. The joint establishment of an idealization of each other as well as of the couple's relationship not only may serve defensive purposes against a more realistic appreciation of their needs and their relationship but also carries with it the ascendance of superego functions in general and of the infantile superego, with its remnant of prohibition against oedipal desires and infantile sexuality. The normal development of superego functions protects the couple and adds a powerful element—the sense of mutual responsibility and concern—to that derived from their emotional depth. But it also creates the possibility, when aggression predominates in the superego, for mutual persecution and suppression of freedom.

Obviously, the quality and development of a love relation depend on the nature of the match and, by implication, on the selection process that joins them. The same features that imply maturation of the capacity for love relations influence the selection process. The capacity for freedom of sexual enjoyment constitutes, if available to at least one of the two partners, an early test situation of the extent to which they are able to achieve jointly freedom, richness, and variety in their sexual encounters. Standing up to the partner's sexual inhibition, limitation, or rejection is an expression of a stable genital identification, in contrast to angry rejection, devaluation, or masochistic submission to the partner's sexual inhibition. Naturally, the response of the sexually inhibited partner to such a challenge will become an important element of the developing dynamics of the sexual couple. Behind early sexual incompatibilities of a couple lie usually significant unresolved oedipal issues, and the extent to which the relationship may contribute to resolving them will depend mostly on the attitude of the healthier partner. But avoiding the choice of a partner who obviously would impose severe limitations on the expectation of sexual gratification is one aspect of a normal selection process.

The development of the capacity for total or integrated object relations implies the achievement of ego identity and, by the same token, of object relations in depth, which facilitates selecting intuitively a person who corresponds to one's desires and aspirations. There will always be unconscious determinants of the selection process, but under ordinary circumstances the discrepancy between unconscious wishes and fears and conscious expectations will not be so extreme as to make the dissolution of early idealization processes in the couple's relationship a major danger.

In addition, mature selection of the person one loves and with whom one wants to spend one's life involves mature ideals, value judgments, and goals, which, in addition to satisfaction of the needs for love and intimacy, give a broader meaning to life. It may be questioned whether the term *idealization* still applies here, but insofar as a person is selected who corresponds to an ideal to be striven for, there is an element of transcendence in the choice, a commitment to a person that comes naturally because it is a commitment to a certain type of life as represented by what the relationship with that person might be or will be.

But here we come back to the basic dynamic, according to which the integration of aggression in the areas of the sexual relation, the object relation, and the ego ideal of the couple guarantees the depth and intensity of the relationship and yet may threaten it. The fact that the equilibrium between love and aggression is a dynamic one makes that integration and depth potentially unstable. A couple cannot take their future for granted even under the best of circumstances; much less so when significant unresolved conflict in one or both partners threatens the equilibrium between love and aggression. Sometimes, even under conditions that seem auspicious and safe, new developments change that equilibrium.

The very fact that the requirement for a deep and lasting relation between two people is the achievement of a capacity for depth in relation to one's self as well as to others—for empathy and understanding, which open the deep pathways of the unspoken multiple relations between human beings—creates a curious counterpart. As one becomes more capable of loving in depth and better able to realistically appreciate someone else over the years as part of his or her personal and social life, he or she may find others who realistically could serve as an equally satisfactory or even better partner. Emotional maturity is thus no guarantee of nonconflictual stability for the couple. A deep commitment to one person and the values and experiences of a life lived together will enrich and protect the stability of the relationship, but if self-knowledge and self-awareness are deep, each partner may experience, from time to time, a longing for other relations (the potential of which may be a realistic assessment) and repeated renunciations. But renunciation and longing also may add depth to the life of the individual and the couple, and the redirection of longings and fantasies and sexual tensions within the couple's relationship may constitute an additional, obscure, and complex dimension of their love life. In the final analysis, all human relationships must end, and the threat of loss and abandonment and, in the last resort, of death is greatest where love has most depth; awareness of this also deepens love.

5.

Psychopathology

In what follows, I provide clinical illustrations of how significant psychopathology interferes with the development of mature love relations. I contrast the consequences of severe and less severe borderline conditions, narcissistic, and neurotic psychopathology by means of typical clinical cases.

In some of the most severe cases of borderline personality organization, particularly patients with significant self-destructive and self-mutilating tendencies, or with narcissistic pathology, antisocial tendencies, and ego-syntonic aggression, a remarkable absence of the capacity for sensual pleasure and skin eroticism may prevail. Both male and female patients may experience an absence of any sexual outlet, no pleasure in masturbation, no sexual desire linked to any object, and an incapacity to achieve excitement, let alone orgasm, in sexual intercourse. These are patients who manifest no sense of having established the repressive mechanisms seen in healthier patients (usually neurotic) who might present a repression-based, secondary inhibition of sexual excitement.

The patients I am describing are unable to achieve sexual excitement, although they are clearly equipped with a perfectly normal biological apparatus. Their history of early development conveys the impression that pleasurable activation of skin eroticism was not achieved or was interfered with from earliest infancy. Severely traumatic experiences, physical or sexual abuse, and the remarkable absence of any loving, concerned parental object dominate their history. Often self-mutilation—they pull their skin, hair, or mucosal surfaces—gives them sensual gratification of a kind, but pain by far overrides any evidence of erotic pleasure. Psychoanalytic exploration reveals a world of primitive fantasies dominated by sadomasochistic interactions, and a search for power is the only assurance of security as an alternative to total submission to a sadistic object. These patients have great difficulties achieving the capacity for sensual enjoyment. Paradoxically, psychoanalytic psychotherapy may enormously improve their personality difficulties but may contribute to further consolidating their sexual inhibition by introducing repressive mechanisms. Sex therapists rightly regard these patients as presenting extremely guarded prognoses for treatment.

The integration of primitive, split-off, idealized, and persecutory internalized object relations as part and consequence of psychotherapeutic treatment may make it possible for these patients to develop the capacity for idealization, to long for an idealized relation that may facilitate improvement in their capacity for emotional investment and commitment. They may finally be able to establish a committed love relation, but they typically show no capacity for passionate love.

A woman in her late twenties was hospitalized because of severe self-mutilating tendencies, with life-threatening implications. In the past, she had deeply cut her arms, presented multiple disfiguring scars, had burned herself with cigarettes, and seemed to be alive only miraculously after several suicide attempts. She had interrupted her university studies in the first semester to enter a drifting lifestyle in which she lived with men who provided her with illegal drugs, and she did not experience any sexual desire or sexual pleasure in her intimate relations with them. On the contrary, extremely suspicious of being exploited by men and, at the same time, tending herself to exploit men financially and emotionally, she obtained sensual gratification only from being held physically while sleeping with them at night or from feeling that they were providing her with drugs without asking questions or making any demands on her other than for her sexual favors. She presented, however, the capacity of loyalty to a man she lived with as long as her demands were met and she felt in control of the relationship; she reacted with sudden devaluation and abandonment of him only when she feared that she was being exploited or treated unfairly. Her history included physical abuse by her mother and sexual abuse by a stepfather. Early success in elementary school related to her high intelligence was followed by a gradual deterioration of her functioning because of lack of investment in her work during the later years of high school. She had been part of a marginal, somewhat antisocial group, but had not engaged in antisocial activities other than shoplifting during her early adolescence, which she stopped when she decided it was too dangerous.

Less severely ill borderline patients may present the capacity for sexual excitement and erotic desire, but suffer from the consequences of their pathology of internalized object relations. The splitting mechanisms of borderline personality organization divide the world of internal and external object relations into idealized and persecutory figures. They are capable, therefore, of idealizing relationships with "part objects." These relationships, however, are fragile and forever at risk of being contaminated by "all-bad" aspects that may shift an ideal into a persecutory relationship.

The love relations of these patients may present erotic desire along with primitive idealization of the love object. What we find here is the development of intense love attachments, with primitive idealization and a somewhat more enduring nature than the transitory involvements of narcissistic patients. The counterpart of these idealizations is a tendency to abrupt, radical disappointment reactions, the transformation of the idealized object into a persecutory one, and disastrous relations with previously idealized objects. These cases typically show the most dramatic aggressive features in divorce proceedings. Perhaps the most frequent type of this pathological relationship is displayed by women with infantile personalities and borderline personality organization who cling desperately to men idealized so unrealistically that it is usually very difficult to get any accurate picture of these men from the patients' description. On the surface, such involvements resemble those of much better integrated masochistic women who submit to idealized, sadistic men, but unrealistic, childlike idealization is much more marked in these cases. The following case, taken from my previous work (1976), illustrates these dynamics.

The patient was an obese eighteen-year-old girl. She habitually took a variety of drugs, and her performance at school was gradually deteriorating in spite of her high I.Q. Her rebelliousness caused her to be expelled from several schools and was expressed predominantly in violent scenes at home. In the hospital she conveyed the impression of an impulsive, hyperactive, disheveled, dirty adolescent. Her ruthless exploitation of most people contrasted sharply with her complete dedication and submission to a young man she had met in another hospital and to whom she daily wrote long, passionate love letters. He responded only occasionally and in a rather desultory manner; he was apparently having some difficulties, never specified, with the law, and in spite of careful efforts on the part of the patient's hospital physician to gain some realistic picture of this man, he remained a nebulous shadow, although, according to the patient, he was a perfect, ideal, loving, "beautiful" man.

In psychotherapy, the patient glowingly described intense sexual experiences with her boyfriend, her sense of complete fulfillment in their relationship, and her conviction that if she could just escape with him and live a life isolated from the rest of the world she would be happy and normal. She had seen several psychotherapists previously, and she came to our hospital "prepared" to fight off efforts on the part of staff to separate her from her boyfriend.

She was able to forgive, or rather to rationalize, the boyfriend's unresponsiveness, at the same time remaining highly sensitive, often even paranoid about other people's slights or neglects. Only after he had rejected her totally and obviously and after she found another young man in our hospital with whom she repeated this same relation could she disengage from the first one. This she did so completely that after a few months it was hard for her even to evoke the first one's face.

Paradoxically, this type of "falling in love" has a better prognosis than the ephemeral infatuations of narcissistic personalities, notwithstanding that narcissistic personalities appear to be so much more "reality oriented" than typical borderline patients without narcissistic personality structure.

There are several noticeable aspects of intense love relations of patients with borderline personality organization. First, they illustrate the full capacity for genital excitement and orgasm linked with a passionate commitment, showing that the development of "genital primacy" does not necessarily imply emotional maturity.

In these patients a certain integration seems to have taken the place of polymorphous perverse infantile sexuality and genital sexuality in that they seem able to integrate aggression with love—that is, to recruit the aggressive, sadomasochistic components of infantile sexuality in the service of libidinal erotic gratification. This integration of sexual excitement and erotic desire occurs before the subject has the capacity for integrating aggressively invested and libidinally invested internalized object relations. Splitting of object relations (into idealized and persecutory ones) persists, and intense erotic idealization of idealized objects serves the function of denying the aggressive segment of internalized object relations and protecting the idealized relationship from contamination with aggression.

Borderline patients evince a capacity for a primitive kind of falling in love, characterized by an unrealistic idealization of the love object, whom they do not perceive in any depth. This kind of idealization differs from mature idealization and illustrates the developmental processes the mechanism of idealization undergoes before culminating in the normal idealization of falling in love.

Intense sexual experiences that idealize intimate relations may be used to deny intolerable ambivalence and protect the splitting of object relations. This process illustrates what might be called a premature oedipalization of preoedipal conflicts in many patients with borderline personality organization: highly neurotic but intense love affairs obscure the underlying incapacity to tolerate ambivalence. Clinically, in both genders, the activation of genital modes of interaction may serve as an attempt to escape from the frightening, frustrating relations centering on oral needs and dependency. It is as if an unconscious hope for oral gratification by means of sexual activity and for an ideal relationship different from the frustrating pregenital one with mother fosters an escape into early sexualization of all relations.

Many patients with a narcissistic personality structure have a well-developed capacity for sexual excitement and orgasm in sexual intercourse and a broad spectrum of polymorphous perverse infantile trends without the capacity for a deep investment in a love object. Many of these patients have never fallen or been in love. Patients who are promiscuous and have intense feelings of frustration and impatience when desired sexual objects do not become immediately available to them may seem to be in love but are not. This becomes evident in their indifference once they have achieved their conquest.

For therapeutic and prognostic reasons, it is important to differentiate the sexual promiscuity of patients with a narcissistic personality structure from that of patients with a hysterical personality and strong masochistic trends. In the latter, sexual promiscuity usually reflects unconscious guilt over establishing a stable, mature, gratifying relationship because this would unconsciously represent the forbidden oedipal fulfillment. These hysterical and masochistic patients show a capacity for full and stable object relations in areas other than sexual involvement. For example, women with a hysterical personality and strong unconscious competitive strivings with men may develop stable, deep relations with them as long as no sexual component is present; only when sexual intimacy develops does unconscious resentment over fantasied submission to men or unconscious guilt over forbidden sexuality interfere with the relation.

In contrast, the sexual promiscuity of narcissistic personalities is linked with sexual excitement for a body that "withholds itself" or for a person considered attractive or valuable by other people. Such a body or person stirs up unconscious envy and greed in narcissistic patients, the need to take possession of, and an unconscious tendency to devalue and spoil, that which is envied. Insofar as sexual excitement temporarily heightens the illusion of the desirability of the object, a temporary enthusiasm for the desired sexual object may resemble the state of falling in love. Soon, however, sexual fulfillment gratifies the need for conquest, triggers the unconscious process of devaluing the desired object, and results in a speedy disappearance of both sexual excitement and personal interest.

The situation is complex, however, because unconscious greed and envy tend to be projected onto the desired sexual object, and as a consequence, fear of the possessive greed and potential exploitation by the sexual object becomes a threat, reinforcing the need to escape into "freedom." For the narcissistic patient, all relations are between exploiters and exploited, and "freedom" is simply an escape from a fantasied devouring possessiveness. In the course of psychoanalytic treatment, however, the driven promiscuity of narcissistic patients also reveals a desperate search for human love, as if it were magically bound up with parts of the body— breasts or penises or buttocks or vaginas. The narcissistic patient's endless, repetitive longing for such body parts may emerge, upon analysis, as a regressive fixation on split-off early symbiotic experiences involving erogenous zones and body-surface idealization to compensate for an incapacity to establish a total object relation or object constancy (Arlow et al. 1968).

Narcissistic patients' flight from sexual objects who have been "conquered" may also represent an effort to protect those objects from unconsciously sensed destructiveness. Riviere (1937), discussing the psychology of "Don Juans and Rolling Stones," stressed the oral sources of the envy of the other gender and the defenses of rejection and contempt as leading dynamic factors. Fairbairn (1954) emphasized the function of perversion as a replacement for a relationship with deeply split, idealized, and persecutory objects that could not be tolerated by the patient's "central" ego.

Narcissistic pathology, in short, illustrates how the original capacity for sexual excitement and idealization of body surfaces may proceed to full-fledged polymorphous perverse infantile sexuality and, eventually, to genital interests and the capacity for genital orgasm. This progression occurs in the context of the failure to develop in depth the capacity for intimate object relations, so that idealization remains restricted to the sexual realm and is largely undeveloped in the realm of actual object relations. The temporary idealization of significant others by narcissistic patients is inadequate for generating more than a "purely sexual" interest, an idealization of body surfaces that does not extend to the idealization of the total person. Some narcissistic personalities are able to experience idealization of the other person that extends from the body to the person, even if this interest is transitory and limited by unconscious mechanisms of defensive devaluation. The following cases, also originally described in my earlier work (1976), illustrate the psychopathological continuum within the range of narcissistic personality disturbances.

A man in his mid-twenties consulted me because of fear of impotence. Although he had had intercourse occasionally with prostitutes, when he attempted it for the first time with a woman he described as having been a platonic friend, he failed to achieve a full erection. This was a severe blow to his self-esteem and brought about an intense anxiety reaction. He had never fallen in love and had not been sexually or emotionally involved with either women or men. His masturbation fantasies reflected multiple perverse trends, with homosexual, heterosexual, sadomasochistic, exhibitionistic, and voyeuristic aspects.

Of high intelligence and culture, he worked effectively as an accountant, and several somewhat distant, yet stable relations with both men and women centered on common political and intellectual interests. He did not seem ambitious. He was satisfied with his work routine and was generally liked because of his friendly, flexible, highly adaptive behavior. His friends were amused by his occasional biting irony and haughty attitude toward other people.

This patient was seen initially as an obsessive personality, but psychoanalytic exploration revealed a typical narcissistic personality structure. He had the deep, mostly unconscious, conviction that he was superior to the petty, competitive struggles in which his colleagues and friends were involved. He was superior also, he felt, to the interests that his friends developed in mediocre, psychologically despicable, although physically attractive women. The fact that he was unable to perform when he graciously consented to have intercourse with his platonic friend was a terrible blow to his self-concept. He thought he should be able to perform sexually with men or women and was above the narrow, conventional morality of his contemporaries.

I would stress here, first, that the capacity for a sexual involvement, for falling in love—even in the form of a transitory infatuation—was absent, suggesting a reserved prognosis for psychoanalytic treatment. (In fact, the analysis of this patient ended in failure after more than five years of treatment.) The central dynamic feature in this case was intense envy of women and defenses against this envy by devaluation and a narcissistically determined homosexual orientation—a frequent characteristic of narcissistic personalities.

The next case illustrates both the presence of some capacity for falling in love and the deterioration of this capacity in a series of short-lived infatuations and promiscuity. It also illustrates the proposal that the advance from the fixation on body surfaces to falling in love with a person is linked to the development of the capacity for experiencing guilt and concern, depression and reparative trends. In contrast to the preceding case, this man in his early thirties showed some potential for falling in love. In the course of his psychoanalysis, this potential developed dramatically as he worked through a basic transference paradigm.

The patient originally consulted me because of intense anxiety when speaking in public and an increasingly unsatisfactory sexual promiscuity. He said he had fallen in love on a few occasions in his adolescence but found he soon tired of women he had originally idealized and longed for. After some sexual intimacy with a woman, he would lose all interest and move on to search for another. Shortly before starting treatment, he had begun a relationship with a divorced woman who had three small children. He found her much more satisfactory than most of his previous women. His sexual promiscuity nevertheless continued, and for the first time he experienced conflict between his wish to establish a more stable relation with a woman and his numerous affairs.

His desperate search for sexual experiences with women was the principal subject of the analysis from the beginning. At first, he proudly proclaimed his successes with women and what he thought were his extraordinary capacities for sexual activity and enjoyment. It soon became apparent, however, that his interest in women was geared exclusively to their breasts, buttocks, vaginas, soft skin, and, above all, to gratifying his fantasy that women were concealing and withholding all their "treasures" (as he used to call them). In conquering them, he felt he would "unwrap" them and "swallow them up." On a deeper level (he became aware of this only after many months of analysis) he had the frightening conviction that there was no way of incorporating women's beauty and that sexual penetration, intercourse, and orgasm represented only an unreal, illusionary incorporation of what he admired and wanted to make his.

The narcissistic gratification of having "made" a woman was wearing off rapidly, and his awareness of his complete loss of interest after a short period of sexual involvement was increasingly spoiling the entire anticipation and development of these ephemeral relations. In recent years he had frequently fantasied having intercourse with not-yet-conquered women while having intercourse with one who was already his and, therefore, on the road to devaluation. Married women were particularly attractive to him, not, as I first assumed, because of oedipal-triangular conflicts, but because other men's finding something attractive in such women bolstered this patient's waning interest in them as possessing a "hidden treasure."

Finally the patient became aware of the intensity of his envy of women, derived from his envy of and rage against his mother. His mother had chronically frustrated him; he felt she had withheld from him, bodily and mentally, all that was lovable and admirable. He still remembered clinging desperately to her warm, soft body while she coldly rejected his expression of love as well as his angry demands upon her.

During adolescence he struggled constantly to control his awareness and expression of his unconscious envy and hatred of women. He used to watch movies of World War II and was incensed when actresses exhibited themselves before a large audience of cheering soldiers. He felt that this was cruel and that the soldiers should have stormed the stage and killed the actresses. He brooded endlessly over the fact that women were aware of their breasts and genitals, and that when they took off their under-clothes at night—those marvelous, soft garments which had had the priv-ilege of lying close to their body—they would throw them—treasures neglected and unavailable to him—on the floor.

Analysis gradually uncovered sadistic masturbation fantasies the pa-tient had had as a child. He would see himself tearing up women, tortur-ing a large number of them, and then "freeing" the one within the group who seemed innocent and gentle, good, loving, and forgiving—an ideal, ever-giving, ever-forgiving, beautiful, and inexhaustible mother surrogate. In splitting his internal relations with women into dependency upon an ideal, absolutely good mother and retaliatory destruction of all other, bad mothers, he ended up without the capacity to establish a relation in depth within which he would have been able to tolerate and integrate his con-tradictory feelings of love and hate. Instead, the idealization of breasts, female genitals, and other parts of the body permitted him to regressively gratify primitive, frustrated erotism while symbolically robbing women of what was specific and unique to them. By means of his promiscuity, he also denied his frightening dependency upon a specific woman and unconsciously spoiled that which he was avidly attempting to incorpo-rate.

That he could "give" an orgasm to women, that they needed his penis, symbolically reassured him that he did not need them—that he had a giving organ superior to any breast. But the fact that a woman should then try to continue to be dependent on him evoked fear that she would want to rob him of what he had to give. Yet, in the midst of his desperate search for gratification of erotic longings to replace his need for love, the patient sensed his growing dissatisfaction and at one point became aware that he was actually searching for a relation with a person "underneath" the skin of a woman.

It was only by systematic examination of his oral demandingness, of his long-lasting dissatisfaction in the transference, that the patient rec-ognized his tendency to unconsciously spoil and destroy what he most longed for—namely, understanding and interest on the part of his analyst, and love as well as sexual gratification from women. Full awareness of his destructive tendencies toward the analyst and toward women led to the gradual development of guilt, depression, and reparative trends. Finally, concern for the object brought about a radical shift in his relation to the analyst, to his mother, and to the divorced woman whom (acting out unconscious guilt) he had married during his analysis.

As he gradually became aware of how much love and dedication he received from his wife, he began to feel unworthy of her. He noticed that he was becoming more interested in her thoughts and feelings, that he could enjoy her moments of happiness with her, that he was becoming deeply curious about the interior life of another human being. He finally realized how terribly envious he had been of his wife's independent interests, her friends, her belongings, the thousand little secrets he felt she shared with other women and not with him. He realized that by consistently depreciating and devaluating her, he had made her empty and boring for him and had made himself fearful lest he have to drop her as he had dropped other women.

At the same time, he experienced a dramatic change in his internal attitude during sexual intercourse. He described it as almost a religious feeling, a sense of overwhelming gratitude, humility, and enjoyment in finding her body and her person at the same time. He was now able to express this gratitude in the form of physical intimacy while experiencing her body (now representing her total person rather than a part object) with new excitement. In short, the patient was now able to experience romantic love linked with sexual passion for the woman he had been married to for more than two years. His sexual life left him fully satisfied—a contrast to his old pattern of rapid disappointment and an immediate search for a new woman. His previous need to masturbate compulsively after sexual intercourse disappeared.

Intense envy and hatred of women can be seen in many male patients. Indeed, clinically, its intensity in men seems to match that of penis envy in women. What distinguishes male narcissistic personalities is not only the intensity of this envy and hatred but the pathological devaluation of women (derived from devaluation of mother as a primary object of dependency).

Devaluation of female sexuality and denial of dependency needs for women contribute to an incapacity to sustain a deep personal and sexual involvement with women. We find a complete absence of sexual interest in women (a definite heterosexual orientation notwithstanding) in the most severely ill patients; less severe cases show a frantic search for sexual excitement and sexual promiscuity linked with an incapacity for establishing a more permanent relationship; still milder cases show a limited capacity for transitory infatuation.

Transitory infatuations may represent the beginning of a capacity for falling in love, but with idealization limited to the cherished physical sexual attributes of the women to be conquered. What these patients are not able to achieve, however, is the idealization characteristic of falling in love, when female genitality as well as the individual woman is idealized and gratitude for her love and concern for her as a person develop into the capacity for a more stable relation. The sense of fulfillment that goes with falling in love is lost for the narcissistic personality; at most, he may have a fleeting sense of fulfillment at having achieved a conquest.

Envy of and dependency on mother as the primary source of love is, of course, as intense in women as in men, and an important source of penis envy in women is their search for a dependent relation with father and his penis, dependency that serves as an escape and liberation from a frustrating relation with mother. The oral components of penis envy are predominant in women with a narcissistic personality structure, and so is their revengeful devaluation of men and women. Whether the prognosis for psychoanalytic treatment of such women is more guarded than for men is an open question: this question is explored in Paulina Kernberg's (1971) report on the case of a woman with a narcissistic personality reflecting these mechanisms.

A narcissistic patient in her early twenties was icily attractive (the iciness is typical of narcissistic women in contrast to the warm coquettishness of hysterical personalities), enough so she was able to replace one man after another as her slave. She exploited men ruthlessly. When they finally decided to leave her she reacted with anger and vindictiveness but without longing, mourning, or guilt.

With neurotic patients we enter the realm of the inhibition of the normal capacity for love relations under the influence of unresolved oedipal conflicts. The idealization processes involved in love relations have shifted from primitive, unrealistic idealization to the integration of "all-good" and "all-bad" internalized object relations, and the patient has achieved object constancy and a realistic capacity to assess both self and the love object in depth.

The typical pathology of love relations related to dominant oedipal conflicts is a full capacity for romantic idealization, for falling in love and remaining in love (that is, for a commitment in depth within the context of tolerance of ambivalence), in combination with the inhibition of direct genital and polymorphous infantile sexual longings for the oedipal object.

Patients in whom this type of psychopathology predominates typically are able to fall in love and have deep and stable love relations, in the context of some inhibition of their genital sexuality: impotence, premature and retarded ejaculation (although in these cases pregenital psychopathology also tends to play an important role), and frigidity (particularly inhibition of a woman's capacity for sexual excitement and orgasm in intercourse) are preponderant symptoms.

An alternate defense against the unconscious prohibition against sexual involvement because of its oedipal implications is the dissociation between tender and erotic longings, so that one "sexual" love object is chosen in contrast to another, desexualized and idealized one. The incapacity to integrate erotic desire and tender love shows in the capacity for an intensely gratifying sexual relation with one object, dissociated from intense nongenital love for another object. Expiation of unconscious guilt over forbidden oedipal longings may be expressed by the selection of frustrating, unavailable, or punishing love objects or by being able to fully combine sexual and tender love only in frustrating love relations. One might say, in fact, that whereas narcissistic types of love relations represent the typical psychopathology of preoedipal conflicts in the area of love relations, masochistic love relations represent the typical pathology of the oedipal level of development. The following case, first described in my earlier work (1976), illustrates aspects of these issues.

A man in his mid-thirties consulted me because of obsessive doubts about whether his fiancée was attractive or unattractive. To the first session he brought a suitcase containing oversized photographs of his fiancée, carefully sorted into those in which she appeared attractive to him and those in which she appeared unattractive. He asked whether I saw any difference in the two series of photographs. I saw no difference at all with regard to the degree of "attractiveness" in the different photographs, and the patient later told me that this was the same reaction he had received from friends to whom he had confided his difficulty. He later revealed that his fiancée always appeared unattractive to him whenever he suspected she might be sexually excited about him.

The patient presented a typical obsessive character structure, with strong reaction formations against aggression, a consistent overpoliteness, and a pedantic way of expressing himself. He had an important position at a local university but was handicapped in his work because he was shy and fearful of his more senior colleagues and insecure regarding his students, whom he suspected of secretly making fun of him because of his "correct, conservative" ways.

His domineering, nagging mother controlled the household, according to the patient, with the help of her "female army" (his several older and younger sisters). His father was an overtly tense, somewhat explosive man, but submissive to his wife. Throughout his childhood, the patient had felt he lived in a house full of women, full of secrets and places he could not enter, drawers he could not open, subjects he could not listen to. He was reared in an extremely religious atmosphere, where everything related to sex was considered dirty. In his childhood, his mother spied on him while he was involved in sex play with his younger sister's friends; afterward she punished him severely.

The patient was very proud of his "moral purity" and quite shocked when I failed to appreciate "as a moral achievement" the fact that he had had no sexual intercourse throughout his life, nor any sexual excitement about the women with whom he had felt "in love." He later admitted that there were women who had excited him sexually during his adolescence, generally women of lower socioeconomic status. He idealized and completely desexualized women of his own social group. He had never had any symptoms, he claimed, until he started dating his fiancée, about two years before consulting me, and the obsessive doubt over whether she was attractive or repulsive developed as she was pressing for a physically more intimate relation, such as kissing or caressing him.

In the transference, his obsessive-compulsive perfectionism at first interfered seriously with free association and gradually became the major focus of the analytic work in the first two years of analysis. Behind his perfectionistic submission to psychoanalysis lay an unconscious mockery of the analyst as supposedly powerful but actually weak and impotent—an unconscious reaction similar to the one the patient had toward his senior colleagues and projected onto his students (whom he saw as mocking him). Intense defiance of and rebelliousness against father figures gradually emerged in the transference and took the specific form of deep suspicion that I wanted to corrupt the patient's sexual morality (a view the patient attributed to all psychoanalysts).

Later, the patient felt that the analyst was also an agent of his fiancée, wanting to push the patient into her arms: he consulted a number of ministers about the dangers psychoanalysis posed for sexual morality and for the purity of his relationship with his fiancée. After thus seeing the analyst as repeating father's superficially controlling but deeply submissive behavior to mother (the analyst being an agent of the fiancée), he gradually shifted into perceiving the analyst as his mother—that is, as spying on him and only pretending to be sexually tolerant in order to have him express his sexual feelings and then punish him. During the second and third years of analysis, this mother transference became predominant, and the same conflicts could be analyzed in his relation to his fiancée and in his general view of women as dangerous mothers who were out to tease young men, to provoke them into sexual behavior in order to later take revenge on them.

This transference paradigm shifted, in turn, to a still deeper level at which sexual excitement in connection with his sisters, and particularly his mother, came into the foreground, with deeply repressed fears of retaliation from father. The perception of a hostile mother was a displacement from his even more frightening perception of a hostile father.

At that juncture the characteristic neatness, politeness, and overconcern with cleanliness became the focus of the analytic work. These character traits now appeared to represent a reaction formation against sexual feelings of any kind; they also represented a quiet, stubborn protest against the "excited" and disorderly, overpowering mother. Finally, they represented his aspiration to be a neat little boy who would be loved by father at the price of renouncing his competitiveness with father and with men in general.

In the fourth year of his psychoanalysis, the patient began, for the first time, to feel erotic desire for his fiancée. Previously, when he had found her attractive, she represented the idealized, pure, unavailable woman—a counterpart of the sexually exciting but repulsive mother image. During the fifth and final year of analysis, the patient started to have intercourse with his fiancée and, after a period of premature ejaculation (linked with fear of his genitals' being damaged in the vagina, and a reactivation of paranoid fears of the analyst as the combined vengeful father-mother figure), his potency became normal. It was only then that the patient discovered he had always had a compulsive need to wash his hands frequently, because this symptom disappeared in the context of his sexual experiences with his fiancée. It is this latter episode that I wish to focus on further.

The patient used to meet with his fiancée on Sunday mornings, originally to join his parents and other members of his family at church. Later on, the two met in his office rather than in his apartment—which was close to where his parents lived—and spent Sunday mornings together instead of going to church. One Sunday morning the patient was able, for the first time in his life, as part of sexual play, to perform cunnilingus and feel excited. He marveled at her reaching an orgasm this way. He was profoundly impressed that she could be so free and open with him. He realized how terribly prohibitive and frowning he had envisioned all women (mother) to be about sex. He also realized, with a feeling of exhilaration, that the warmth, humidity, odor, and taste of his fiancée's body and genitals excited rather than repelled him, and his feeling of shame and disgust turned into sexual excitement and satisfaction. To his surprise, he did not have a premature ejaculation while having intercourse with her, and he understood that this was related to his having lost, at least temporarily, the feeling of anger and resentment against her as a woman.

He recognized during the ensuing weeks that his staying at his office and being involved sexually with his fiancée represented a rebellion against his father and his mother and against those aspects of his religious convictions that represented a rationalization of superego pressures. This patient, in his adolescence, had had the fantasy that Jesus was watching him, particularly when he was spying on his sisters' girlfriends, trying to glimpse their bodies while they were undressing. It was dramatic to observe how his attitude to religion changed and how he now began to perceive Jesus as not so much concerned with whether human beings "behaved well" sexually but rather as representing the search for love and human understanding.

The patient also became aware that those aspects in his fiancée which at times seemed disgusting to him represented, in his mind, aspects of his mother when, during his childhood, she had appeared sexually excited with his father. These aspects of his fiancée now became unimportant, and he recognized other ways in which she had real features in common with his mother, such as her cultural and national background. When his fiancée sang songs of her native region, he was deeply moved; the songs gave him the feeling of communicating with a part of his past—not with his mother as a person but with the background from which she stemmed. He felt that in reaching such total fulfillment in his relation with his fiancée he was also reaching a new connection with his past, a past he had previously rejected as part of his repressed rebelliousness against his parents.

Penis envy can always be traced to the original envy of mother (basically, of mother's "breasts" as the symbol of the capacity for giving life and nourishment and symbolizing the first good object), so that it has as an important root that unconscious envy of mother, displaced onto father's penis and then reinforced by the aggressive components of oedipal conflicts, including particularly the displacement of aggression from mother onto father. Behind penis envy we regularly find a woman's devaluation of her own genitals, reflecting a combination of the primary inhibition of vaginal genitality in the unconscious relationship between mother and daughter, the culturally promoted and reinforced infantile fantasy of male superiority, and the indirect effects of unconscious guilt over the positive relation to father's penis.

A woman with significant masochistic character pathology consulted me because of sexual inhibitions she could overcome only by having sex with men who debased her. In the first two years of her analysis, it was possible to focus on the self-defeating needs in her relations with men and with the analyst, linked with deep, unconscious guilt feelings over her sexual activities and wishes, which represented oedipal strivings.

In the third year of analysis, her wish to have the analyst—and men in general—need her underwent a gradual change into the emergence of early dependent longings for her stepmother, whom she had experienced as cold and rejecting. She had turned to her father in an effort to receive sexual love from him to replace the lack of oral gratification from mother. The idealization of her real mother, who had died at the height of the patient's oedipal period, now appeared to be a defense not only against oedipal guilt but against earlier orally determined rage against her.

The analyst was now seen as a mother image, cold and rejecting, and the patient developed a strong wish to be protected, cuddled, and loved by him as a good mother who would reassure her against the fears about her bad mother. She had sexual fantasies about performing fellatio, related to the feeling that the orgasm of men represented symbolically the giving of love and milk, protection and nourishment. The desperate clingingness in her relations with men and her frigidity now came into focus as an expression of these oral longings toward men, of her rageful wish to control and incorporate them, and her fear of letting herself experience full sexual gratification, because that would mean total dependency on and, therefore, total frustration by cruel "motherly" men.

It was at this stage of her analysis that the patient was able for the first time to establish a relation with a man who seemed a more appropriate love object than most of those she had previously chosen. (She married him some time after the completion of her analysis.) Because her capacity to achieve full sexual gratification with this man marked a dramatic change in her relation with him, with the analyst, with her family, and in her general outlook on life, I shall examine this episode more closely.

During analysis, the patient became capable of achieving orgasm on a regular basis in intercourse with this man. To her surprise, she found herself crying the first few times after achieving a full orgasm, crying with a sense of embarrassment and, at the same time, relief. She felt deeply grateful to him for giving her his love and his penis; she felt grateful that she could enjoy his penis fully, and at one point during intercourse she had the fantasy that she was embracing a huge penis, spinning around it with a sense of exhilaration while feeling that she was rotating around the center of the universe, the ultimate source of light. She felt that his penis was hers, that she could really trust that he and his penis belonged to her.

At the same time, she was no longer envious that he had a penis and she did not. If he separated from her, she could tolerate it because what he had been giving her had become part of her inner life. Her new experience was something that belonged to her now and could not be taken away. She felt grateful and guilty at the same time for the love this man had given her while she had been, as she now realized, so envious and suspicious of him, so bent upon not giving herself fully to him to avoid his supposed "triumph" over her as a woman. And she felt she had been able to open herself up to enjoying her body and her genitals in spite of the internal prohibitions stemming from the fantasied orders of her mother and stepmother. She had become free of the terror of becoming sexually excited with an adult man who treated her like an adult woman (thus breaking the oedipal taboo).

She also felt exhilarated at being able to expose her body to this man and did not secretly fear that her genitals were ugly, mutilated, and distasteful. She was able to say to him, "I cannot imagine what, if heaven exists, heaven could offer beyond this," referring to their sexual experience. She could enjoy his body, become sexually excited playing with his penis, which was no longer the hated instrument of male superiority and dominion. She now could walk about feeling she was equal to other women. She no longer needed to envy the intimacy of others, because she had her own intimate relation with a man she loved. But above all, the capacity to enjoy sex jointly and to be fully aware that she was receiving love from him while giving it—feeling grateful for it and no longer afraid of fully expressing her needs to depend upon him—were expressed in her crying after orgasm.

The central feature in this case was overcoming penis envy: both its oral roots (envy of the giving mother and the giving penis, and fear of a hateful dependency upon it) and its genital roots (the childhood conviction of the superiority of male sexuality and men) were worked through in the context of a total object relation in which guilt over the aggression toward the object, gratitude for love received, and the need to repair guilt by giving love were all expressed together.

6.

Aggression, Love, and the Couple

Having explored how sexual excitement incorporates aggression in the service of love, I now turn to the interplay of love and aggression in the couple's emotional relationship.

With sexual intimacy comes further emotional intimacy, and with emotional intimacy, the unavoidable ambivalence of oedipal and preoedipal relations. We might say, to put it in a condensed and simplified way, that the man's ambivalence toward the exciting and frustrating mother from early childhood on, his deep suspicion of the teasing and withholding nature of mother's sexuality, become issues interfering with his erotic attachment, idealization, and dependency on the woman he loves. His unconscious oedipal guilt and his sense of inferiority to the idealized oedipal mother may result in sexual inhibition with or intolerance of a woman who becomes sexually free and toward whom he may no longer feel reassuringly protective. Such a development may perpetuate the dichotomy between erotized and desexualized idealized relations to women, a dichotomy typical of boys in early adolescence. Under pathological circumstances, particularly in men with narcissistic pathology, the unconscious envy of mother and the need to take revenge against her may bring about a catastrophic unconscious devaluation of the woman as the longed-for sexual object, with consequent estrangement and abandonment.

In a woman who did not have an early satisfactory relationship with a mother who tolerated her daughter's sexuality, the unconscious experience of a hostile and rejecting mother who interfered with the little girl's early development of bodily sensuality, and, later on, with her love for her father, may result in exaggerated unconscious guilt about sexual intimacy in conjunction with commitment in depth to a man. In these circumstances, the little girl's normal shift in object from mother to father is unconsciously distorted, and her relationship with men becomes a sadomasochistic one. If a narcissistic personality structure evolves, the girl may express her intense unconscious envy of men by a defensive devaluation of the men who love her, by emotional distancing, and perhaps by a narcissistically determined promiscuity which parallels that in narcissistic men. The experience of an unavailable, sadistic, sexually rejecting, or seductive and teasing oedipal father will exacerbate these early conflicts and their effects on a woman's love life.

Granting the frequency of severe unconscious oedipal guilt and of narcissistic defenses derived from both oedipal and preoedipal sources, we might well ask what factors are responsible for creating and maintaining a successful relation between a man and a woman. Two standard and conventional answers are that social mores protect the structure of marriage, and insofar as cultural and social structures now seem to be disintegrating, the institution of marriage is in danger; and second, that "mature" love implies friendship and comradeship, which gradually replace the passionate intensity of initially romantic love and assure the continuity of the couple's life together.

From a psychoanalytic viewpoint, the longing to become a couple and thereby to fulfill the deep unconscious needs for a loving identification with one's parents and their roles in a sexual relationship is as important as the aggressive forces that tend to undermine intimate relationships. What destroys passionate attachment and may appear to be a sense of imprisonment and "sexual boredom" is actually the activation of aggression, which threatens the delicate equilibrium between sadomasochism and love in a couple's relationship, both sexual and emotional.

But more specific dynamics come into play as emotional intimacy develops. The unconscious wish to repair the dominant pathogenic relationships from the past and the temptation to repeat them in terms of unfulfilled aggressive and revengeful needs result in their reenactment with the loved partner. By means of projective identification, each partner tends to induce in the other the characteristics of the past oedipal and/or preoedipal object with whom he or she experienced conflicts. Projective identification is a primitive yet prevalent defense mechanism that consists in the tendency to project an impulse onto another person, fear of the other person under the influence of the projected impulse, the unconscious tendency to induce such an impulse in the other person, and the need to control the other person under the influence of this mechanism. If early conflicts around aggression were severe, the possibility arises of reenacting primitive, fantastically combined mother-father images that carry little resemblance to the actual characteristics of the parental objects.

Unconsciously an equilibrium is established by means of which the partners complement each other's dominant pathogenic object relation from the past, and this tends to cement the relationship in new, unpredictable ways. Descriptively, we find that couples in their intimacy interact in many small, "crazy" ways. This "private madness" (to use André Green's [1986] term) can be both frustrating and exciting because it occurs in the context of a relationship that may well have been the most exciting and satisfactory and fulfilling one that both partners could dream of. To an observer, the couple seem to enact a strange scenario, completely different from their ordinary interactions, a scenario that, however, has been enacted repeatedly in the past. For example, a dominant husband and a submissive wife become transformed, respectively, into a whining little boy and a scolding schoolmarm when he develops the flu and requires nursing; or a tactful and empathic wife with a direct and aggressive husband may become a paranoid complainer and he a reassuring, motherly caretaker when she feels slighted by a third person; or an orgy of throwing dishes may disrupt a couple's harmonious life-style from time to time. This "union in madness" ordinarily tends to be disrupted by the more normal and gratifying aspects of the couple's relationship in the sexual, emotional, intellectual, and cultural realms. In fact, a capacity for discontinuity in their relationship plays a central role in maintaining it.

Discontinuities

This capacity for discontinuity, described by Braunschweig and Fain (1971, 1975) and by André Green (1986, 1993), has its ultimate roots in the discontinuity of the relationship between mother and infant. According to Braunschweig and Fain, when a mother becomes unavailable to her baby because she has returned to her husband as a sexual partner, the infant eventually becomes aware of this fact. Ideally, a woman can alternate her two roles and move easily from being a tender, subtly erotic, affectionate mother to her infant and child to being an erotic sexual partner to her husband. And her child unconsciously identifies with her in both roles. The mother's discontinuity triggers the earliest sources of frustration and longing in the infant. Also, through identification with mother, the infant and child's capacity for discontinuity in his or her intimate relations is triggered. According to Braunschweig and Fain, the infant's autoerotism derives from repeated sequences of gratification alternating with frustration of his or her wish for fusion with mother: masturbation can represent an object relationship before it becomes a defense against that relationship.

André Green regards this discontinuity as a basic characteristic of human functioning in both normality and pathology. Discontinuity in love relations, he proposes, protects the relationship from dangerous fusion within which aggression would become paramount. The capacity for discontinuity is played out by men in their relationships with women: separating from women after sexual gratification represents an assertion of autonomy (basically, a normal narcissistic reaction to mother's withdrawal) and is typically misinterpreted in the—mostly female—cultural cliché that men have less capacity than women for establishing a dependent relationship. In women, this discontinuity is normally activated in the interaction with their infants, including the erotic dimension of that interaction. This leads to the man's frequent sense of being abandoned: once again, in the cultural cliché—this time a male one—of the incompatibility of maternal functions and heterosexual eroticism in women.

The differences between men and women in the capacity for tolerating discontinuities also show in their discontinuities regarding love relations, as Alberoni (1987) has pointed out: Women usually discontinue sexual relations with a man they no longer love and establish a radical discontinuity between an old love relationship and a new one. Men are usually able to maintain a sexual relationship with a woman even if their emotional commitment has been invested elsewhere, that is, they have a greater capacity for tolerating discontinuity between emotional and erotic investments and for a continuity of erotic investment in a woman, in reality and in fantasy, over many years, even in the absence of a real ongoing relationship with her.

Men's discontinuity between erotic and tender attitudes toward women is reflected in the "madonna-prostitute" dissociation, their most typical defense against the unconsciously never-abandoned, forbidden, and desired oedipal sexual relationship with mother. But beyond that dissociation, profound preoedipal conflicts with mother tend to reemerge in undiluted ways in men's relationships with women, interfering with their capacity to commit themselves in depth to a woman. For women, having already shifted their commitment from mother to father in early childhood, their problem is not the incapacity to commit themselves to a dependent relationship with a man. It is, rather, their incapacity to tolerate and accept their own sexual freedom in that relationship. In contrast to men's assertion of their phallic genitality from early childhood on in the context of the unconscious erotization of the mother-infant relationship, women have to rediscover their original vaginal sexuality, unconsciously inhibited in the mother-daughter relationship. One might say that men and women have to learn throughout time what the other comes prepared with in establishing a love relationship: for men, to achieve a commitment in depth, and for women, sexual freedom. Obviously, there are significant exceptions to this development, such as narcissistic pathology in women and severe types of castration anxiety of any origin in men.

Discontinuity in the love relation is also fostered by the mutual projection of dictates from the superego. Projecting onto the sexual partner the sadistic aspects of an infantile and/or oedipal superego may lead to masochistic submission and unrealistic, sadomasochistic distortions in the relationship, but also to a rebellion against the projected superego, precisely by means of the temporary separations that characterize normal discontinuities in the love relationship. A violent rejection of or attack on the guilt-inspiring object may result in temporary freedom from a projected, sadistic superego. That relief, paradoxically, may permit love to reemerge.

The central function of discontinuity explains why some couples may have a steady and durable relationship together with (in spite or because of) the aggression and violence enacted in their love life. If we categorize nonorganic psychopathology roughly into neurotic, borderline, narcissistic, and psychotic categories, partners coming from different categories of pathology may establish varying degrees of equilibrium that stabilize their relationship while permitting them to enact their world of private madness contained by protective discontinuities. For example, a neurotic man with an obsessive personality married to a borderline woman may unconsciously admire what he senses as her freedom to give vent to violent aggressive outbursts. She may be protected from the real and feared consequences of her aggressive behavior by the discontinuity achieved in the splitting processes she imposes as the most natural way of relating within the marital relationship. Her obsessive husband may be reassured by the self-containing nature of aggression that he unconsciously fears in himself. But another couple with similar pathology may destroy itself because the obsessive man cannot tolerate the woman's inconsistency, and the borderline woman cannot tolerate the persecutory nature, as she experiences it, of her obsessive husband's rational persistence and continuity.

Throughout many years of living together, a couple's intimacy may be either strengthened or destroyed by enacting certain types of unconscious scenarios that differ from the periodic enactment of ordinary, dissociated past unconscious object relations. These specific, feared, and desired unconscious scenarios are gradually built up by the cumulative effects of dissociative behaviors. The enactments may become highly destructive, sometimes simply because they trigger circular reactions that engulf the couple's love life beyond their intentions and their capability to contain them. I refer here to the enactment of oedipal scenarios representing the invasion of the couple by an excluded third party as a major disruptive force, and to various imaginary twinship relations enacted by the couple as a destructive centripetal or estranging force. Let us explore these latter relations.

Narcissistic conflicts manifest themselves not only in unconscious envy, devaluation, spoiling, and separation but also in the unconscious desire to complete oneself by means of the loved partner, who is treated as an imaginary twin. Didier Anzieu (1986), in developing Bion's (1967) work, has described the unconscious selection of the love object as a homosexual and/or heterosexual completion of the self: a homosexual completion in the sense that the heterosexual partner is treated as a mirror image of the self. Anything in the partner that does not correspond to that complementing schema is not tolerated. If the intolerance includes the other's sexuality, it may lead to severe sexual inhibition. Behind the intolerance of the other's sexuality lies the narcissistic envy of the other gender. In contrast, when the other is selected as a heterosexual twin, the unconscious fantasy of completion by being both genders in one may act as a powerful cement. Bela Grunberger (1979) first pointed to the unconscious narcissistic fantasies of being both genders in one.

It has frequently been observed that after many years of living together partners begin to resemble each other even physically; observers often marvel at how two such similar persons found each other. The narcissistic gratification in this twinship relationship, the wedding, we might say, of object love and narcissistic gratification, protects the couple against the activation of destructive aggression. Under less ideal circumstances, such twinship relations may evolve into what Anzieu (1986) has called a "skin" to the couple's relationship—a demand for complete and continuous intimacy that first seems an intimacy of love but eventually becomes an intimacy of hatred. The constantly repeated question "Do you still love me?" reflecting the need for maintaining the couple's common skin, is the counterpart of the assertion, "You always treat me like that!" signaling a shift in the quality of the relationship under the skin from love to persecution. Only the opinion of the other really counts in protecting one's safety and sanity, and that opinion may turn from a steady stream of love to an equally steady stream of hatred.

Unconsciously enacted long-range scenarios may include wish-fulfilling fantasies, unconscious guilt, the desperate search for a different ending to a feared and endlessly repeated traumatic situation, and an unwillingly, unwittingly triggered chain reaction that disrupts the internal sequence of the scenario. For example: a woman with a hysterical personality structure, an oedipal fixation to an idealized father, and profound prohibitions against sexual involvement with him is married to a man with a narcissistic personality structure and an intense unconscious resentment against women. He selected her as a desirable heterosexual twin and unconsciously expected her to be totally under his control as a support for his narcissism. Her sexual inhibition frustrates his narcissism and causes him to seek extramarital satisfaction; her disappointment in the oedipal father triggers, first, ineffectual masochistic submission to her husband and, later, a masochistic and (for the same reason) sexually gratifying love affair with a forbidden man. Her abandonment of her husband makes him aware of his dreaded dependency on her, denied by his previous treatment of her as a slave, while her now fully awakened sexual response in a threatening but unconsciously permitted relationship (because of its nonmarital nature) brings about her acceptance of her own genital sexuality. Husband and wife reencounter each other with a better understanding of their mutual needs.

It is true that both underwent psychoanalysis and, without treatment, probably would not have been able to reconstruct their relationship. He unconsciously needed to provoke her to become the rejecting mother, thus justifying retrospectively, so to speak, his devaluation of her and his search for a new idealized woman; she unconsciously needed to reconfirm the unavailability and disloyalty of father and to pay the price of a socially dangerous situation as a condition for responding sexually to a man who was not her husband.

Triangulations

Direct and reverse triangulations, which I have described in earlier work (1988), constitute the most frequent and typical unconscious scenarios, which may at worst destroy the couple or at best reinforce their intimacy and stability. I use *direct triangulation* to describe both partners' unconscious fantasy of an excluded third party, an idealized member of the subject's gender—the dreaded rival replicating the oedipal rival. Every man and every woman unconsciously or consciously fears the presence of somebody who would be more satisfactory to his or her sexual partner; this third party is the origin of emotional insecurity in sexual intimacy and of jealousy as an alarm signal protecting the couple's integrity.

Reverse triangulation defines the compensating, revengeful fantasy of involvement with a person other than one's partner, an idealized member of the other gender who stands for the desired oedipal object, thus establishing a triangular relationship in which the subject is courted by two

members of the other gender instead of having to compete with the oedipal rival of the same gender for the idealized oedipal object of the other
gender. I propose that, given these two universal fantasies, there are potentially, in fantasy, always six persons in bed together: the couple, their
respective unconscious oedipal rivals, and their respective unconscious
oedipal ideals. If this formulation brings to mind Freud's (1954) comment
to Fliess, "I am accustoming myself to the idea of regarding every sexual
act as a process in which four persons are involved" (letter 113, p. 289),
it should be noted that his comment was made in a discussion of bisexuality. My formulation arises in the context of unconscious fantasies
based on oedipal object relations and identifications.

One form that aggression related to oedipal conflicts frequently takes
(in clinical practice and in daily life) is the unconscious collusion of both
partners to find, in reality, a third person who represents a condensed ideal
of one and a rival of the other. The implication is that marital infidelity,
short-term and long-term triangular relationships, more often than not
reflects unconscious collusions between the couple, the temptation to
enact what is most dreaded and desired. Homosexual as well as heterosexual dynamics enter the picture because the unconscious rival is also a
sexually desired object in the negative oedipal conflict: the victim of infidelity often identifies unconsciously with the betraying partner in sexual
fantasies about the partner's relationship with the jealously hated rival.
When severe narcissistic pathology in one or both members of the couple
precludes the capacity for normal jealousy—a capacity that implies a certain achievement of toleration for oedipal rivalry—such triangulations
easily become enacted.

The couple that is able to maintain its sexual intimacy, to protect itself
against invasion by third parties, is not only maintaining its obvious conventional boundary but also reasserting, in its struggle against rivals, its
unconscious gratification of the fantasy of the excluded third party, an
oedipal triumph and a subtle oedipal rebellion at the same time. Fantasies
about excluded third parties are typical components of normal sexual relations. The counterpart of sexual intimacy that permits the enjoyment
of polymorphous perverse sexuality is the enjoyment of secret sexual fantasies that express, in a sublimated fashion, aggression toward the loved
object. Sexual intimacy thus presents us with one more discontinuity:
discontinuity between sexual encounters in which both partners are completely absorbed in and identified with each other and sexual encounters
in which secret fantasied scenarios are enacted, thus carrying into the
relationship the unresolved ambivalences of the oedipal situation.

The perennial questions "What do women want?" and "What do men want?" may be answered by saying that men want a woman in multiple roles—as mother, as baby girl, as twin sister, and, above all, as adult sexual woman. Women, because of their fateful shift from the primary object, want a man in fatherly roles but also in motherly roles—as father, baby boy, twin brother, and adult sexual man. And at a different level, both men and women may wish to enact a homosexual relationship or to reverse sexual roles in an ultimate search for overcoming the boundaries between the sexes that unavoidably limit narcissistic gratification in sexual intimacy: both long for complete fusion with the loved object with oedipal and preoedipal elements that can never be fulfilled.

Perversity and Boundaries

Basically, the experience of the boundaries between the genders can be overcome only when the symbolic destruction of the other as a person permits the use of his or her sexual organs as mechanical devices without emotional involvement. Sadistic murder is the extreme but logical consequence of an effort to penetrate another person to the very essence of his or her existence and to erase all sense of being excluded from that essence. Under more moderate circumstances, perversity—the recruitment of love in the service of aggression—transforms deep sexual intimacy into a mechanization of sex, which derives from the radical devaluation of the personality of the other, an observation first made by Fairbairn (1954).

Perversity in the sexual encounter may be illustrated by the developments typical of couples engaged over a period of time in group sex. After six months to a year of consistent participation in multiple polymorphous perverse activities, their capacity for sexual intimacy (and, for that matter, all intimacy) ends (Bartell 1971). Under these circumstances, the oedipal structure tends to become dismantled. This is in marked contrast to the stabilizing effects on a couple of an actual triangular love relationship. An equilibrium is reached that permits the acting out of nonintegrated aggression by splitting love from aggression in the relationship with two objects; acting out unconscious guilt over the oedipal triumph is achieved by maintaining a love relationship that is less than fully satisfactory.

In the couple's emotional relationship, a corresponding perversity may be observed in long-standing sadomasochistic relationships wherein one of the partners enacts the functions of the perfectionistic and cruel superego, thereby gratifying his or her own sadistic tendencies through self-righteous indignation, while the partner masochistically expiates his or her guilt derived from oedipal and, more frequently, preoedipal sources.

Or perhaps such a perverse equilibrium no longer involves the super-ego-sanctioned expression of aggression but is the enactment of more primitive sadomasochistic scenarios, with life-threatening types of aggression and primitive idealization of a powerful and cruel object without a moral dimension. One partner, for example, may agree to sterilization or even to actual mutilation or self-mutilation as symbolic castration. Primitive dissociative mechanisms may protect perversity within a stable equilibrium of the couple that reaches an extraordinary intimacy dominated by aggression.

Activation of dissociated primitive object relationships in the interaction of the partners can create circular reactions that acquire a fixed quality, which the ordinary discontinuity in the couple's relationship may no longer contain. For example, the rageful outbursts of one partner may evoke a response of righteous indignation and identification with primitive superego functions. This is followed by a masochistic submission of the first perpetrator to his or her partner, changing into renewed angry outbursts or an immediate reinforcement of rage as a secondary defense against unconscious guilt. These reactions may escalate until this dissociated primitive object relation becomes a recurrent feature in the life of the couple. Ethel Person (1988) has described a typical situation in which one partner has an extramarital relationship and defends himself or herself against feelings of guilt by provocative behavior toward the marital partner aimed at inducing a rejection by that partner and thus assuaging the existing guilt. This may lead to a result quite opposite to the one intended, finally destroying the couple. Generally, relentless aggression as an unconscious plea for acceptance and as the expiation of guilt triggered by that very aggression may not be contained by the partner.

Boundaries and Time

The boundaries separating the couple from its social environment protect the couple's equilibrium, for good or otherwise. Extreme social isolation of couples with perverse developments in the sexual, emotional, and/or superego areas may gradually worsen the destructive relationship because the partners lack corrective interactions with the environment and lose their normal capacity to "metabolize" aspects of the aggression generated in their social interactions. Social isolation of extremely sadomasochistic couples may pose a danger to the masochistic partner. On the positive side, the normal boundaries protect not only the couple's intimacy against triangular invasion from the surrounding social environment but also their "private madness," the necessary discontinuities in their relationship.

Certain common boundaries of couples become significant at different stages of the couple's life. First is the relationship with their children, a subject too vast and complex to explore at this point, except to stress the importance of maintaining the boundaries that separate the generations. One of the ubiquitous manifestations of unconscious guilt over the implicitly rebellious and defiant quality of any intimate relationship (representing oedipal fulfillment) is the couple's not daring to maintain firm boundaries of intimacy in relation to their children. The proverbial absence of a lock on the bedroom door may symbolize the parents' unconscious guilt over sexual intimacy and their unconscious assumption that parental functions should replace sexual ones. This regressive fantasy, projected onto the children as a fear of their reactions to being excluded from the parental bedroom, reflects the underlying fear of identifying with the parental couple in the primal scene and the unconscious collusion between the two parents in abdicating from fully identifying with their own parents.

Another boundary is with the network of couples that constitutes ordinary social life. Relationships with other couples are normally infiltrated with eroticism; among the friends and their spouses in unconscious collusion are the feared rivals and the desired and forbidden sexual objects. The teasingly exciting and forbidden boundaries among couples are the typical settings within which direct and reverse triangulations are played out.

The boundary between the couple and the group is always a combat zone. "Static warfare" is represented by the group's pressure to mold the couple into its image and is reflected in conventional morality—in ideological and theological ritualization of love, commitment, marriage, and family tradition. From this viewpoint, the couple that exists from early adolescence or even from childhood on, brought together by their relatives, sanctioned by universal benevolent perception, actually lives in a symbolic prison, although the couple may escape into a secret love relationship. The mutual temptations and seductions in the network of adult couples represent a more dynamic warfare, but also, at times, potential salvation for individuals and couples entrapped in relationships that are drowning in mutual resentment and aggression.

The group needs the couple for its own survival, for the reassurance that an oedipal triumph, breaking away from the anonymous crowd, is possible. And the group envies and resents the couple's success as contrasted with the individual's loneliness in that anonymous crowd. The couple, in turn, needs the group to discharge its aggression into the environment. Projective identification not only operates within the couple but in subtle ways includes third and fourth parties as well. Liberman (1956) has described how the patient's bitter complaints to the analyst about the marital partner may be part of a subtle acting out. The analyst becomes the repository of the aggression against the marital partner, and the patient withdraws into a "saved" relationship with the partner while abandoning the relationship with the analyst.

This is a particular example of the more general phenomenon of the "lavatory" analyst, which Herbert Rosenfeld (1964) described. A couple's intimate friends who may serve that function are often not aware that they have become the carriers of the aggression that would otherwise become intolerable for the couple.

A couple that seems to be functioning well may evoke inordinate envy within unstructured social groups, such as extended large travel groups, political parties, professional organizations, or communities of artists. The envy that is usually kept under control by the rational and mature aspects of interpersonal relationships and friendships among a network of couples becomes immediately apparent in such groups. The couple's unconscious awareness of this envy may take the form of guilt-ridden public mutual attacks to soothe those who are envious or external behavior of defiant total harmony while mutual aggression remains hidden from public view. Sometimes the partners manage to hide from others how close their relationship really is.

And a third boundary, represented by the dimension of time, is the frame for both the full development of a couple's life as such and the limited nature of that life because of death and separation. Death becomes an important consideration for couples in later years. Fear of aging and illness, fear of becoming unattractive to the partner, fear of becoming excessively dependent on the other, fear of being abandoned for somebody else, and the unconscious tendency to defy or deny the reality of time—for example, by reckless neglect of one's physical health or that of the partner—may become the field within which aggression from all sources is played out. Here, concern and mutual responsibility derived from ego and superego functions may play a major role in protecting the couple's survival, in contrast to the unconscious collusion with dangerous self-defeating patterns, as in neglecting illness or financial irresponsibility.

Men may be particularly sensitive to the aging process in women, much more so than women in their relation to men, because of an unconscious connection between idealization of the surface of mother's body as one origin of eroticism and fear of the content of mother's body as an expression of unconscious projection onto her of primitive aggressive tendencies (Meltzer and Williams 1988). This sensitivity may sexually inhibit men (and, insofar as they fear being sexually less attractive, also women) in advanced stages of their life, reactivating or reinforcing oedipal prohibitions against their sexuality. The affirmation of a couple's sexual intimacy when they are advanced in age is a last test of their sexual freedom. The common denial of sexual life in the elderly is the final edition, so to speak, of the child's efforts to deny the parents' sexuality; it is also the final edition of the parents' guilt associated with their own sexuality. Concern for the loved companion of a lifetime may become an increasingly important factor in mediating and controlling the couple's enactment of dissociated aggression.

The changes of power and authority related to changes in a couple's prestige, income, and other developments having to do with profession and work not only may affect the emotional equilibrium but, paradoxically, may often represent the unforeseen effects of unconsciously determined factors. A classic example is the nurse who puts her husband through medical school, secure in her role as a maternal provider while gratifying his dependency needs. When he later is a successful physician, he resents his dependency on mother and searches for a relationship in which he is the dominant father to a little girl-mistress. His wife struggles with her resentment over the loss of her maternal function for him and the unconscious resentment toward powerful men (penis envy) activated by his professional success.

Or a narcissistic man establishes a relationship with an adoring, inhibited, unsophisticated girl and stimulates her to study and work so that she can live up to his expectations for a narcissistic twinship, only to discover that her blossoming activates his deep envy of women and resentment of her independence. He subsequently devalues her, and their relationship is destroyed.

But time does not operate only destructively. The search for reactivation of past conflicts to heal wounds (to use Martin Bergmann's [1987] expression) may be successful in that love can be maintained in spite of the violence of mutual aggression; the survival of the couple may expose the fantastic, exaggerated nature of unconscious fears surrounding repressed or dissociated aggression. To be able to attack one's partner sadistically and yet witness the survival of his or her love; to be able to experience in oneself the transition from relentless rage and devaluation to guilt, mourning, and repair—these are invaluable experiences for the couple. When sexual intimacy and pleasure incorporate the reparative efforts linked to such awareness, guilt, and concern, then sexual excitement and emotional intimacy increase, together with the couple's commitment to joint responsibility for their lives.

Emotional growth implies an expanding identification with all the stages of life, bridging the boundaries that separate age groups. The accumulated experiences of a shared life include mourning the loss of one's parents, of one's youth, of a growing past left behind, of a future becoming remorselessly restricted. A joint life becomes the repository of love, a powerful force that provides continuity in the face of the discontinuities of daily existence.

In later life, faithfulness to the other becomes faithfulness to the internal world. The growing awareness of the limitation of all relationships through death highlights the importance of this internal world. Denial of one's personal death is limited by awareness of the necessary end, at some point, of the joint life of the couple, which initiates a mourning process that again enriches life lived together and after the death of the person one loves. The surviving member carries the responsibility for the continuation of the life lived together. The woman whose husband has died and who joins their old network of couples with a new husband activates this mourning process within the entire group.

Pathological Role Fixation

I have described perversity in love relations that destroys the sexual couple because aggressive elements predominate and control sexual excitement, because sadomasochistic patterns dominate and control the emotional relationship, and because persecutory and sadistic aspects of mutually projected superego functions also dominate and control. An additional form of perversity is the freezing of the relationship in a single pattern of an unconscious complementary object relationship from the past. Normally, enactments from the past interplay with realistic relations. An illustration of a typical flexibility in the partners' interactions would be the husband's unconscious shift from the role of the sexually dominant and excited male penetrating his wife and symbolically enacting the loving and sexually accepting father to the role of the satisfied infant who has been nourished by mother, symbolically represented by the woman who has given him the gift of her orgasm. He may then become the dependent child of a maternal woman who tucks him in, feeds him, and puts him to sleep or he may actively shift into a fatherly role toward a dependent daughter by repairing a broken lamp, which she cannot (or pretends she cannot) do.

Or the wife may shift from the role of adult sexual partner to dependent daughter of a protective mother, or to that of the motherly woman who feeds her little boy-man. Or she may become the guilty little girl who is seduced into sex by a sadistic father; or she is "raped" in her fantasy during sexual intercourse, thus confirming her lack of guilt for sexual enjoyment; or she may ashamedly exhibit herself, thus expiating her sexual pleasure while obtaining the gratification of being admired by the man who loves her.

Or a man may shift from guilt-ridden little boy being scolded by a perfectionistic mother to the envious little boy watching the mysteries of adult female concerns and interests. Or he may become resentful of a woman's dedication to her profession or to their baby because he feels like a neglected child, the counterpart to a woman's unconscious resentment of her husband's professional success because it reactivates early envy of men.

These and other role enactments may be mutually gratifying because they express both love and hatred—the integration of aggression within a loving relationship. But these unconscious collusions may break down, and aggression may be expressed by unconsciously "fixating" the self and the sexual partner in particular roles, leading to the typical scenarios that become the conscious subject matter of chronic marital conflict: the dependent, clinging, love-hungry woman and the narcissistic, indifferent, self-centered man; the dominant, powerful, and controlling woman who wants an adult man as her partner and feels frustrated by her insecure, childlike boy-man, having difficulty perceiving the self-perpetuating nature of their relationship. Or the "sex-hungry" man who cannot understand the limited sexual interest of his wife. And, of course, the guilty partner and the accusatory one in all their variations.

Rigid role fixations usually reflect enactments of underlying dissociated scenarios and an incapacity to accept or carry out the functions of discontinuity related to oedipal guilt or narcissistic fixations. One may ask whether simply a lack of harmonious correspondence of unconscious enactments may bring about clashes resulting from contradictory expectations—a man trying to be a protective father collides with a competitive mother; or both partners are frustrated because each has dependent expectations. Clinically, however, the unconsciously fine attunement in the couple's unconscious awareness of each other's disposition makes it abundantly clear to them how each will be perceived by the other. What appears to be simple misunderstanding is usually determined by unconscious needs.

The assumption that the couple's problems result from their failure to communicate touches only the surface. Sometimes communication may serve to enact barely controlled aggression, which does not mean that efforts to communicate needs and expectations are not helpful. But when deep unconscious conflicts come into play, the communicative process itself may be contaminated by them, and open communication may serve only to accentuate the conflicts.

A final word about couples vis-à-vis social and conventional values. Dicks (1967) has described the complex relationship of the couple's conscious aspirations, their cultural values, and those of the surrounding social world. I believe that there are no "objective" rules about what values should determine a couple's relationship, particularly their way of dealing with conflicts. The ideological dimension of all cultures is, I believe, implicitly directed against a couple's intimacy. It is in the very nature of conventional culture to attempt to control the basically rebellious and implicitly asocial nature of the couple as it is perceived by the conventional social environment. The couple's independence from social conventionality may therefore be crucial to its survival under conditions of conflict—and their nonconventionality may also be essential in their therapist's role with them. It is true, of course, that when extreme distortions in the enactment of dissociated object relations from the past threaten the physical or emotional integrity of one or both partners, ordinary social reality may protect the partners from a dangerous, even life-threatening deterioration. Such conditions, however, apply to only a minority of cases. There is a large majority of couples whose unconscious conflicts take on the surface mimetism of ideological battle cries of the moment, with further complications in their relationship as conventional standards become rigid slogans that reduce their flexibility to deal with their conflicts.

7.

Superego Functions

In describing the contributions of libido and aggression to the sexual and emotional relations of the couple, I referred to the crucial role played by the superego. Let us now examine the role of that agency in more detail. We have seen how the couple becomes the repository of both partners' conscious and unconscious sexual fantasies and desires and their internalized object relations. We have also seen how the couple acquires an identity of its own in addition to the identity of each of the partners. I suggest that the couple as an entity also activates both partners' conscious and unconscious superego functions, resulting in the couple's acquiring, over time, a superego system of its own in addition to its constituent ones.

The effect of this new superego system on the couple's relationship depends on the maturity of the superego of each partner. When primitive superego pathology dominates, sadistic superego precursors are enacted and have the potential for destroying the couple. A mature superego, expressed in concern for the partner—and the self—protects the couple's object relations, fosters love and commitment, but, because the superego always includes remnants of oedipal conflicts, may threaten the capacity for sexual love by inhibiting or forbidding the expressions of tender and sexual feelings for the same object. The superego may thus reinforce the capacity for lasting sexual passion, or that very agency may destroy it. Schafer (1960) clarified the benign and hostile aspects of the superego for the individual; here I am examining these functions for the couple.

Setting up the ego ideal as a substructure of the superego is a basic prerequisite for the capacity to fall in love. The idealization of the loved other reflects the projection of aspects of one's ego ideal, an ideal that represents the sublimatory realization of oedipal desires. It is a projection that coincides with attachment to this projected ideal, the sense that the loved other represents the coming alive in external reality of a desirable, profoundly longed-for ideal. In this regard, the relationship in reality with the loved other is ideally an experience of transcending one's own psychic boundaries, an ecstatic experience in dialectical contrast to the ordinary, everyday world and one that provides a new meaning to life. Romantic love thus expresses a deep emotional need, quite essential to why people form couples and not simply derived from romanticism as a cultural ideal.

As Chasseguet-Smirgel (1985) pointed out, the projection of the ego ideal onto the loved person does not reduce one's self-esteem, as Freud (1914) originally suggested, but increases it because the aspirations of the ego ideal are thereby realized. In addition, requited love increases self-esteem as part of the gratification of being in love and being loved in return. Under these conditions, self love and object love fuse—a crucial aspect of sexual passion. Unrequited love may have different outcomes—one determinant is the individual's psychic equilibrium. A mourning process might, in a person of sufficient resiliency, permit recovery without significant trauma; but if the individual is neurotically fixated to what was originally an unreachable, frustrating object, he or she will experience a loss of self-esteem. In general, the greater an individual's predisposition to oedipal defeat and preoedipal frustration (for example, the frustration of oral dependency), the greater the inferiority feelings related to unrequited love.

I am proposing that the enactment of mature superego functions in both partners is reflected in each having the capacity for a sense of responsibility for the other and for the couple, concern for their relationship, and protection of the relationship against the consequences of the unavoidable activation of aggression as a result of the equally unavoidable ambivalence in intimate relationships.

At the same time, a more subtle but extremely important superego function is activated. I refer to the healthy aspects of both partners' ego ideals, which combine to create a joint structure of values. A preconsciously adhered-to set of values is gradually mapped out, elaborated, and modified through the years, and provides a boundary function for the couple vis-à-vis the rest of the world. In short, the couple establishes its own superego. It is in the context of this joint set of values that a couple can creatively contribute to solving conflicts. An unexpected gesture of love, remorse, forgiveness, or humor may keep aggression within bounds. Tolerance for shortcomings and limitations in the other as well as in the self is silently integrated into the relationship.

The importance of this joint superego structure resides in its implicit function as a "court of appeal," a kind of last resort when one partner has inflicted a grave lesion in their jointly established value system. A transgression—actual or tempting—against this joint boundary warns the couple of an extraordinary danger to their relationship and thus constitutes an important alarm system protecting the couple from possible dissolution.

Should one or both partners have a less than mature and sturdy superego, the projection of repressed aspects of the infantile superego can make the other partner particularly susceptible to criticism from him or her. A cluster of projections from a primitive superego reinforces whatever objective criticism might be coming from the partner. A mature superego allows the criticized partner to rebel and overcome the attack and helps to maintain the couple's equilibrium.

But severe superego pathology in either of the partners can result in the employment of projective identification rather than simple projection, making rebellion against this defense more difficult. The consequence may be the destruction of the couple's equilibrium as sadistic superego introjects take over the relationship.

With normal development, the preoedipal superego precursors, characterized by primitive idealization and fantasies of being persecuted, are gradually toned down and neutralized, which in turn facilitates the internalization of the idealized and prohibitive aspects of the advanced oedipal superego. The integration of the preoedipal and oedipal levels of superego formation then facilitates the consolidation of the postoedipal superego with its characteristic abstraction, individuation, and depersonification (Jacobson 1964).

One of the complex affects that evolves as a consequence of these processes is gratitude. Gratitude is also one of the means by which love develops and perpetuates itself. The capacity for gratitude contributed to by both ego and superego is basic to reciprocity in human relations; it originates in the infant's pleasure at the reappearance in external reality of the image of the gratifying caretaker (Klein 1957). The ability to tolerate ambivalence, which indicates the shift from the rapprochement phase of separation-individuation to that of object constancy, is also marked by an increase in the capacity for gratitude. The achievement of object constancy also increases the capacity for experiencing guilt over one's aggression. Guilt, as Klein (1957) pointed out, reinforces gratitude (although guilt is not its origin).

Guilt also increases idealization. The earliest idealization is that of the mother during the symbiotic phase of development; it evolves into the idealization of the mother in the separation-individuation phase. The integration of the superego that fosters the development of the capacity for unconscious guilt stimulates the development of idealization as a reaction formation against guilt and as a direct expression of guilt. This superego-stimulated idealization acts as a powerful reinforcement to gratitude as a component of love.

The couple's capacity for idealizing each other is expressed most strongly in their capacity for experiencing gratitude for love received and the corresponding intensification of the desire to give love in return. The experience of the other's orgasm as an expression of love received as well as of the capacity to reciprocate with love contains the assurance that love and reciprocity dominate over envy and resentment.

Paradoxically, however, the capacity for gratitude resulting from idealization runs counter to certain advanced characteristics of the ego ideal in the oedipal stage of development, in which the idealized relationship with the oedipal parents derives from the renunciation of polymorphous perverse infantile eroticism and genital erotic aspects of that relationship.

As Dicks (1967) has stressed, the initial mutual idealization of the newly established couple and its conscious expectations of a sustained love relationship sooner or later conflict with the resurgence of repressed and dissociated conflictual past internalized object relations. Oedipal conflicts and the corresponding superego prohibitions will in most cases bring about a gradual breakdown of these early idealizations in the context of renewing the adolescent task of integrating eroticism and tenderness. These conflicts, frequently involving tests of the stability of the couple, may not only produce painful discoveries for both participants but may create their own healing processes as well, as the following case illustrates.

A patient had what she considered a satisfactory sexual relationship with her boyfriend before their marriage. Once they married, their sexual life deteriorated. She complained that he was not paying enough attention to her, that he seemed exclusively interested in the sexual nature of their encounter without sufficient tenderness.

She had no tolerance for the ordinary discontinuities in any long-lasting intimate relationship. She felt that she loved him and was unaware that her tendency to blame him and see herself as a helpless victim was poisoning their relationship, that her childishly clinging and guilt-raising behavior repeated aspects of her mother's relationship with her father, and her own relationship with her father during her early adolescence.

When she met a man who had been her boyfriend in early adolescence and whom she had idealized since then, she embarked on an affair with him which proved satisfying sexually. She was surprised to experience herself fully satisfied as a woman and to perceive an increase in her sense of security and self-esteem. At the same time, she found her love for her husband renewed, which made her feel both guilty about the extramarital affair and appreciative of the positive aspects of their life together. In fact, over a period of time she discovered that the emotional aspects of the relationship with her husband were much more satisfying than those with her lover, although, simultaneously, she experienced full sexual gratification with her lover, which she thought her husband would not be able to provide her. This conflict led her into psychoanalytic treatment, and to the gradual awareness of her unconscious inability to experience a fully satisfactory emotional and sexual relationship with the same man.

The chronic externalization of an infantile superego and the search for an unwaveringly loving relationship with a parental object that such a superego structure personifies may severely restrict an individual's and a couple's love life in spite of the absence of manifest conflict. Usually, however, such apparent stability and harmony are obtained at the cost of some degree of restriction of the couple's social life because potentially threatening—or confrontingly corrective—relationships have to be screened out, particularly the awareness of the possibility of more satisfactory relationships. One partner's identification with the aggressor (expressed in identification with the other's superego) may result in the couple's sadomasochistic alliance against the external world and may gratify the couple's need for a shared set of values by jointly projecting the rebellion against the infantile superego onto the environment. Couples who jointly behave as offended and humiliated victims of third parties may thus maintain a neurotic though stable relationship, which may include many healthy features of mutual concern and responsibility as well.

At the opposite extreme, shared values may provide a couple the strength and endurance to survive in a hostile environment—for example, in a totalitarian society—where culturally sanctioned dishonesty in ordinary social relationships must be tolerated and screened out by the couple's shared silent rebellion against their environment's oppressiveness and corruption. As I have already suggested, the very nature of the couple's sexual intimacy implies such a shared rebellion against conventionality and is a source of ongoing gratification in their relationship.

The struggle against infantile superego demands helps to consolidate a couple's relationship—freeing them from unthinking acceptance of conventional sexual stereotyping and ideologies, typically represented by the cultural clichés of men as sexually omnivorous and emotionally indifferent, and women as sexually passive and dependent. The couple must also become aware of the human tendency to project remnants of one's own infantile superego onto the sexual partner. A partner's implicit reassurance against such fantasied fears may have healing functions: "No, I don't think you are a timid little boy I can't take seriously sexually." "No, I will not consider you a fallen woman after having sex." "No, your aggressive behavior will not lead to eternal punishment, devaluation, resentment, or to my bearing a grudge forever." Yet another and related task is to withstand the danger that primitive superego functions in one partner will impose a symbolic reign of terror on both. Here we enter the realm of psychopathology of sadistic superego formation in one or both partners, leading to sadomasochistic relationships.

The couple has also to integrate the conscious expectations for a life lived together with the aspirations, demands, and prohibitions of the cultural surround. The conflicts produced by differences in religious, ethnic, or economic backgrounds and political and ideological views may play an important role in assuring or interfering with the couple's relationship to its social environment. A couple may choose social isolation to protect itself against potential conflicts between the current cultural environment and past internalized values. Typically, however, once children are born, the couple's isolation is threatened, and the challenge of integrating values with those of the environment may become urgent and unavoidable.

On the positive side of the projection of superego functions onto the partner is the use of the partner as a counselor and defender, a consolation after external attack, and a source of reassurance of one's worth. The way one partner idealizes the other has significance: a man who marries a woman whose admiration has bolstered his self-esteem cannot later rely on her admiration because he has devalued her. Thus the initial utilization of reassurance from the other may backfire and produce a feeling of loneliness in a person incapable of idealizing the partner.

While the frequent dissociation of tender from erotic love is the underlying dynamic of many long-term triangular relationships, so is the search for a relationship that compensates for important frustrations. Some extramarital affairs have as their major function to protect the marital relationship from an unconsciously feared aspect of that relationship, thus actually consolidating it by reducing its level of intimacy. Unconscious guilt over the gratifying and fulfilling nature of a love relationship, particularly marriage, may represent the effects of superego pathology in one or both partners.

Another superego-determined chronic triangulation may reflect the intolerance of one or both partners for the normal ambivalence of love relations, for the expression of any aggression. For example, one or both may have an idealized yet emotionally naive sense of a perfectly harmonious relationship with a partner that combines sex and tenderness and, simultaneously, another long-term relationship that combines sex and tenderness; the underlying aggression is expressed only in the unconscious enjoyment of the aggressive implications of the betrayal of both partners.

These dynamics, particularly the splitting mechanisms involved, may be a defense against sadistic superego features in the relationship of the couple that can be observed when one of the parallel relationships is dissolved. A sometimes justified but often inordinate fear that the person to whom an individual is really committed will never be able to forgive or forget the past infidelity—thus becoming a cruel, unforgiving superego—may be matched, in effect, by the loved partner's enacting such a nonforgiving, eternally resentful role. Although the narcissistic lesion of feeling abandoned and betrayed is an obviously important aspect of such unforgiving behavior, I am thinking of the corresponding projection onto the partner and/or the identification with an implacable superego on the part of the "betrayed" partner.

The capacity to forgive others is usually a sign of a mature superego, stemming from having been able to recognize aggression and ambivalence in oneself and from the related capacity to accept the ambivalence that is unavoidable in intimate relations. Authentic forgiveness is an expression of a mature sense of morality, an acceptance of the pain that comes with the loss of illusions about self and other, faith in the possibility of the recovery of trust, the possibility that love will be recreated and maintained in spite of and beyond its aggressive components. Forgiveness based on naïveté or narcissistic grandiosity, however, has much less value in reconstructing the life of a couple based on a new consolidation of their shared concern for each other and for their life together.

Fantasies about the partner's and one's own death are so common that they tell a good deal about the status of the couple. When severe illness or threat to life occurs it may be easier to tolerate the prospect of one's own death than the death of the partner: unconsciously, the essential fantasy of being preserved refers to the survival of mother. Käthe Kollwitz symbolizes death in her sculpture of a young Kollwitz falling asleep in God's arms—an expression of a basic source of anxiety and security. The ultimate loss of mother, the prototype of abandonment and loneliness, is the basic threat against which the survival of the other is a protection; this concern increases love for the other and the unconscious wish for the other's immortality.

That concern is complemented by the frightening prospect of one's own death as the final triumph of the excluded other, the danger of being replaced by the oedipal rival: "Till death do us part" is experienced as a fundamental threat, a cruel joke of destiny; symbolically, it is castration. Basic confidence in the love of the partner and in one's own love for the partner significantly reduces this fear of an excluded third party and helps one deal with anxiety regarding one's own death.

An important aspect of the enactment of superego conflicts in the couple's relationship is the development of deceptiveness. Deceptiveness may serve to protect against real or fantasied aggression from the other, or it may hide or keep under control one's aggression against the other. Deceptiveness is itself a form of aggression. It may be in reaction against feared attacks from the other, which in turn may be realistic or may reflect superego projection. A husband's statement, "I can't tell this to my wife. She would never be able to accept it," may be true and reflect her infantile superego, or may be derived from his projecting onto her his own infantile superego. Or both may be imprisoned by a joint superego structure: a couple may sometimes succumb to self-destructive collusion derived from their submission to a joint sadistic superego. Deceptiveness may also serve to protect the other from narcissistic lesion, jealousy, or disappointment. But "absolute honesty" is sometimes simply rationalized aggression. The ambivalence ordinarily under control in social interactions may go out of control in intimate ones—the inflection of the voice or a change of facial expression has the potential for escalating rapidly into serious conflict even if the original stimulus was relatively innocuous. Often a couple is not fully aware of how well each knows the other, how well each can "read" the other.

In fact, affective communication increases the danger of mutual superego projections of the uncontrolled or uncontrollable expression of the negative aspects of normal ambivalence. The very intrusion into the partner's psychic experience, fostered by both partners' heightened capacity to read each other's unexpressed feelings, accelerates the transformation of paranoid fears into defensive deceptiveness. At best, deceptiveness may be perceived by the other as a discrete degree of artificiality which increases distancing. At worst, it may be experienced as a disguised attack that triggers further paranoid reactions in the partner. Deception, though intended to protect the couple's relationship, may worsen it. Even in successful relationships, there are cycles of what might be called deceptive, paranoid (or mutually suspicious), and depressive or guilt-determined behaviors, which express as well as defend against direct affective communication. Deceptiveness can be a defense against underlying paranoid fears, and paranoid behavior may in turn be a defense against deeper depressive features. Self-blame may also be a defense against paranoid tendencies, a reaction formation against blaming the other.

Relatively Mild Superego Pathology

In milder types of superego pathology, when the relationship of the couple is maintained but the jointly established superego structure is excessively restrictive, the couple also becomes more susceptible to the restrictive demands and prohibitions of the surrounding culture, particularly in its conventional aspects. Insofar as conventionality reflects culturally shared remnants of the superego of latency, this is another way in which the failure of mature superego functions brings about a regression to restrictive infantile superego demands and prohibitions.

The following case illustrates the problem produced by a well-integrated but excessively severe and restrictive superego in both partners, jointly shared or unconsciously imposed by one of the partners on the couple's relationship.

A married couple consulted me because of growing interpersonal and sexual difficulties. She was in her early thirties and was, as described by both of them, a dedicated, efficient housewife who took loving care of their two boys, ages three and five years. He, in his late thirties, was described by both as a hardworking, responsible man who had worked his way up, in a few years, to a leading position in his business. They belonged to a Catholic, middle-class suburban community, and both were part of extended families of Latin American origin. The reason for consultation was her growing dissatisfaction with what she experienced as her husband's distancing, his emotional unavailability and neglect of her, and what he experienced as his wife's increasingly intolerant nagging and scolding, which was driving him away from home. They accepted my proposal for separate diagnostic interviews for each, interspersed with a series of joint diagnostic interviews. My objective was to assess the marital conflict and decide on possible treatment for one or both or as a couple.

The individual evaluation of the wife provided evidence for the diagnosis of a significant personality disorder with a predominance of hysterical and masochistic features, functioning on a neurotic level of personality organization. Her main difficulty appeared to be her sexual adjustment to marriage. She had a desire for sexual intimacy but a capacity for minimal sexual excitement, which would disappear moments after penetration. She loathed what she experienced as her husband's excessive sexual interest and "crudeness." She also seemed to resent his failure to replicate the warm relationship she had with her idealized, strong father. She also hated herself for beginning to sound like her submissive, nagging, guilt-provoking mother. She described the puritanical attitude about sex shared by her parents, and she manifested intense repressive defenses, such as blocking out all memories of her early childhood. She complained bitterly about the change in her husband, whose lively, outgoing, chivalrous behavior during their courtship had been replaced by sullenness and withdrawal.

The individual interviews with the husband also gave evidence of a significant personality disorder, with predominantly obsessive-compulsive features. He presented a well-integrated ego identity, a capacity for object relations in depth, and symptoms of a moderate, persistent neurotic depression. His father was a businessman whom the patient in his childhood had admired for his strength and power. But in adolescence as the patient recognized the insecurity behind his father's authoritarian behavior, his admiration changed to increasing disappointment. The patient's early childhood curiosity about the sexuality of his two older sisters had been severely reprimanded by both parents, particularly his mother, an apparently submissive wife, whose manipulative control over father was quite evident to my patient.

During his adolescence, he defiantly became involved with women of lower socioeconomic status from different cultural groups. He experienced several passionate love affairs in early adulthood. But then, to the great joy of his parents and relatives, he married a young woman from their own cultural and religious background. His wife's somewhat timid and shy demeanor, the similarity of their backgrounds, her reluctance to enter into a sexual relationship with him before their marriage, all had attracted him. Once they were married, her lack of sexual responsiveness, which he at first had dismissed as owing to inexperience, became a growing source of dissatisfaction. At the same time, he blamed himself for his inability to gratify her sexually, felt increasingly insecure in approaching her, and finally reduced his sexual advances, so that, at the time of consultation, they were having sexual intercourse only once or twice a month.

He also felt increasingly depressed, consciously guilty for not being more available to his wife and children, yet relieved when he was away from home and submerged in his work. He insisted that he loved his wife and that, if she were less critical of him and if their sexual relations were better, the other problems would disappear. The fact that they had so many interests and aspirations in common seemed important to him.

And, he underlined, he really loved the way she dealt with the children, their home, and daily life.

She in turn had stated similar convictions in her individual interviews: she loved her husband, was disappointed because of his distance and withdrawal, but hoped that the relationship could revert to how it had been earlier. The only problem was the sexual one. Sex was a duty that she was willing to fulfill, but responding to him as he wished depended, she was sure, on his adopting a gentler, more patient approach.

In the joint interviews I carried out parallel to the individual sessions over several weeks, it turned out that they indeed shared assumptions and aspirations regarding their cultural life and values and their conscious expectations of their respective roles in the marriage. Their main difficulty did seem to be in the sexual area. I wondered to what extent his depression might be secondary to his unconscious guilt over failing to live up to their joint expectations of him as a strong, successful husband; I wondered whether her sexual inhibition might reflect unconscious guilt over unresolved oedipal strivings, reinforced by her husband's incapacity to help her overcome these inhibitions.

Both, I thought, were struggling with oedipal issues in their unconsciously activated object relations. He unconsciously perceived her as a revenant of his controlling and manipulative mother, who disapproved of his sexual behavior, while he, against his will, was reenacting an identification with the failing father (the patient's perception in early adolescence). She, in unconsciously reducing him to the role of a sexually failing husband, was avoiding a sexual relationship with a strong, warm, and dominant father, which would have evoked oedipal guilt. And, against her will, she was enacting the frustrated, yet guilt-raising and controlling behaviors of her mother. Consciously, they both tried to hold onto their mutually agreed-upon ideals of the warm and giving wife and the strong and protective husband. Both of them, in unconscious collusion, were avoiding awareness of the aggressive feelings unconsciously present in their relationship.

In exploring the extent to which they would become able to acknowledge this unconscious collusion, I found that both were most reluctant to further discuss their sexual difficulty. She was strongly critical of my efforts to treat intimate aspects of sexual relations in what she called a "public and mechanical" manner, and he agreed that, given her reluctance and his having come to terms with the situation, he did not wish to "artificially inflame" their sexual conflicts. They were so skilled and mutually supportive in minimizing the importance of their sexual difficulties that I had to return to my written notes of the individual interviews to reassure myself about what they had told me regarding their sexual difficulties.

In reaffirming their consciously held image of an ideal relationship, they asserted what might be called a joint superego, placing me in the role of a tempting devil. Both expressed the wish that I provide them with recommendations and rules for how they should treat each other in order to reduce their tensions and mutual recriminations; they hoped thus to resolve their difficulties.

In the individual sessions that followed these joint interviews, a new development took place. He made it very clear that he did not believe his wife wanted to continue the diagnostic interviews and that, in fact, she felt that I was biased against her and more of a threat than a help to her marriage. At the same time, he went on, it would be acceptable to her if he continued seeing me so that I could attempt to improve his behavior toward her. He said that if I really believed that he required treatment, he would be willing to undergo treatment for himself. I asked what he would see as an objective of such treatment as contrasted with their jointly working on their marital relationship; he said that his depression, his indifference to sexual intercourse, which was so unlike his behavior before his marriage, and his helplessness in relating to her were good reasons, if there were a chance of overcoming these difficulties.

Individual meetings with her confirmed her suspicion and resentment about the joint interviews. She felt that as a man I was inclined to be on her husband's side and that I exaggerated the importance of the sexual aspects of their relationship. She said that if he needed treatment that was fine with her, but she was no longer willing to continue the joint interviews.

I finally decided to recommend individual treatment for both of them; I accepted their decision not to continue the joint interviews and, in individual interviews with her, suggested that she evaluate with another therapist, on her own, whether her acknowledged sexual difficulties might have deeper sources in herself and whether she might benefit from further treatment. With some reluctance, she entered psychoanalytic psychotherapy with a woman. However, she suspended that treatment after a few months, considering it neither helpful nor necessary.

I carried out psychoanalytic treatment with her husband during the next six years. In the course of this analysis, the nature of his conflicts with his wife, the sources of his selecting her as a partner, and the dynamics of his depression and sexual inhibition were clarified and worked through. In the early stages, he repeatedly insisted that, regardless of any other outcome, he would never want to divorce his wife: his religious conviction and his background would preclude such a step. Psychoanalytic exploration revealed how, behind this statement, he was projecting onto me his adolescent, rebellious behavior toward both parents, particularly his father's prohibitions against any relationship with women outside their cultural and religious community. I and psychoanalysis in general represented an antireligious ideology, probably the approval of free sex and immorality, and he was on guard against that.

Later on, as he became able to acknowledge this projected aspect of his personality, he came to see the dichotomized, "madonna-prostitute" morality of his adolescence and how he identified his fiancée with the idealized Catholic Latin woman who reminded him of his mother. His sexual inhibition reflected the reactivation of his profound guilt over his sexual interest in his sisters, and the perception of his wife as an ideal, disappointed, and disgusted mother. At a still later stage of his analysis, unconscious guilt over aggression related to earlier frustrations at mother, unconscious rage at feeling that she had neglected him, and guilt over a serious, life-threatening illness his mother had experienced in his early childhood, and for which he had unconsciously felt responsible, emerged as major themes. Furthermore, in connection with the inhibition of his competitive strivings in his work, unconscious guilt over his success in business emerged as a new element. He felt that a bad marriage was a fair price to pay for that success, which unconsciously represented triumph over his father.

Thus, multiple layers of conflicts related to unconscious guilt had been expressed in his depression, which gradually lifted during the first two years of treatment. At an advanced stage of his analysis, acting out oedipal rebelliousness in the form of an extramarital affair with a highly unsatisfactory woman further illuminated his profound fear of a tender and erotic relationship with the same woman. In the fifth year of his analysis, a relationship with another woman evolved. This woman was erotically responsive and culturally, intellectually, and socially gratifying. When he was in the early stages of this relationship, he told his wife about it, acting out retaliatory aggression against the frustrating mother, but also in an unconscious effort to give his wife and himself one more chance to improve their relationship. She reacted with great rage and indignation, presenting herself to her family as the innocent victim of his aggression, thus further poisoning their relationship and accelerating its demise. The patient divorced his wife and married the "other" woman, a step that also signaled the resolution of his sexual inhibition. A significant improvement in his obsessive-compulsive personality traits coincided with these changes. At the completion of his analysis his major difficulties had been resolved. A follow-up after five years confirmed the stability of this improvement and his happiness in his new marriage.

We see here several aspects of superego pathology: the mutual reinforcement of a rigid idealization of the conscious expectations of marriage and marital roles brought about by the couple's identification with the cultural values and ideology of their specific social group; their mutually projected and rigidly adhered-to ego ideal, which provided stability, but with the sacrifice of their sexual needs. The unconscious mutual projection of prohibitions against oedipal sexuality and the integration of tender and erotic feelings facilitated the unconscious activation of their corresponding oedipal relationships; their current interactions showed a growing similarity to their past relationships with oedipal figures.

On the positive side, their sense of responsibility and concern had brought them to treatment; but the underlying guilt feelings and their collusion in maintaining the idealization of the consciously adhered-to views of marriage prevented them, as a couple, from following up that concern with acceptance of the opportunity to change their present equilibrium. He proved to be the more flexible one, but the very fact of his treatment created a disequilibrium in the couple's relationship that led to its gradual destruction.

Severe Superego Pathology

Turning now from the effect on the couple's love life of the normal or mildly pathological superego to the impact of severe superego pathology, we might begin by saying that the greater the pathology, the greater the restrictions the couple places on what the partners find tolerable. Severe superego pathology is also responsible for rigid rationalizations of identification with a primitive superego on the part of either or both partners, "injustice collecting," assumed betrayal and revenge, and hostile detachment.

Further, severe psychopathology of superego functions leads to indifferently neglectful and frankly hostile behavior that expresses primitive levels of aggression, which begins to dominate and frequently destroys the couple. Paradoxically, in the early stages of the activation of such severe superego pathology, the couple's sexual life may flourish because of the denial of unconscious oedipal prohibitions or the expiation of unconscious guilt by the couple's suffering. An apparently free and enjoyable sexual interaction may obscure the deterioration of the emotional relationship.

When superego pathology is severe, both idealizing and persecutory superego precursors militate against superego integration and facilitate the inordinate reprojection of superego nuclei onto the partner, which permits one or both partners to tolerate an ongoing enactment of contradictory character patterns. One partner blames, criticizes, and derogates the other and, by means of projective identification, unconsciously induces such behaviors in the other. These projections may be reflected in a defensive emotional distancing between the partners that evolves over a period of months or years. Sometimes the couple may simply "freeze" in a distancing position that becomes reinforced over time and leads to the eventual destruction or breakdown of the love relationship.

Sometimes such distancing allows preservation of the couple's intimacy in some areas. Chronic but controlled distancing interferes with a couple's intimacy and its ordinary stabilizing discontinuities. Secondary developments may include a reactive rationalization of each partner's aggressive behavior toward the other. Mutually induced and sustained frustrations may then become the rationalization for behaviors that further increase the frustration and the distancing—for example, involvement in an extramarital affair.

The most frequent expression of superego projection, however, is one partner's experience of the other as a relentless persecutor, a moral authority who takes sadistic pleasure in making the other feel guilty and crushed; and the second partner experiences the first as unreliable, deceitful, irresponsible, and treacherous, attempting to "get away with it." These roles are often interchangeable. As a consequence of mutual projective identifications, the partners may be highly effective in reinforcing or even inducing the very characteristics they dread in the other. Persistent sadomasochistic relationships without the interventions of excluded third parties are probably the most frequent manifestations of severe superego pathology. The relationships may initially permit satisfactory sexual relations, but in the long run the sadomasochistic interactions affect the couple's sexual functioning as well.

A couple consulted me because of constant violent altercations. He presented a mixed personality disorder with obsessive, infantile, and narcissistic features; she presented a predominantly infantile personality with hysterical and paranoid features. His feelings of insecurity at work, of not being able to live up to his own expectations of being as strong as his father, were reflected in his behavior with his wife. Ordinarily attentive, somewhat submissive to her, he had to struggle with fears of approaching her sexually. Her rejection of sexuality unless he approached her in certain restricted ways she could accept had gradually reduced their sexual contacts and contributed heavily to his occasional impotence with her.

A passionate affair with a coworker had temporarily provided him a sense of sexual prowess and fulfillment, marred by intense feelings of guilt toward his wife, whom he now began to see unconsciously as his domineering, shaming, guilt-raising, sadistic mother. His mother had alternated between subservience to her husband and violent outbreaks of rage at him. My patient now started to alternate between guilt-ridden submissiveness and conciliatory moves and periodic episodes of sudden, childlike temper tantrums, when he screamed, broke dishes (as had his mother), and attempted in a fumbling and self-defeating way to emulate his father.

His wife then felt that he had mistreated and abused her, a repetition of her experience with her father. In attempting to avoid what she had experienced in her childhood as the humiliating behavior of her own, submissive mother, the wife now began to protest violently, involving as witnesses neighbors, relatives, and, above all, her own mother.

In an unconscious effort to provoke her husband to further violence, she belittled his sexual performance, and she also involved their two school-age children and other acquaintances to shame her husband. In the course of escalating violence, on one occasion he finally struck her, which promptly led her to report him to the local authorities for abusive behavior. It was at this point that marital assessment and treatment were recommended.

This account illustrates unconscious identifications, reprojection of parental images onto the marital partner, and, above all, superego introjects with "injustice collecting," "righteous indignation," strongly rationalized behavior that served to justify persecuting each other, as well as acting out of unconscious guilt because there were aspects of an adult marital relationship they both found intolerable. The wife's psychoanalytic treatment revealed the origins of her sexual inhibition in unconscious efforts to recreate a sadomasochistic relationship with an abusive father; the husband's treatment revealed, beneath a layer of ambivalence toward a teasing and rejecting mother, his unsuccessful struggle with a powerful and threatening father image.

8.

Love in the Analytic Setting

Transference Love

The analytic setting is the clinical laboratory that has permitted us to study the nature of love in its myriad forms. The transference in conjunction with the countertransference is the vehicle for our study of these forms.

The main difference between the original oedipal situation and transference love is the possibility, under optimal circumstances, of fully exploring in the transference the unconscious determinants of the oedipal situation. Working through transference love implies working through the renunciation and mourning that normally accompany the resolution of the oedipal situation. At the same time, the patient has to learn that the search for the oedipal object is going to be a permanent feature of all love relationships (Bergmann 1987). This does not mean understanding all future love relations as deriving solely from the oedipal situation; it does mean that the oedipal structure influences the framing of new experiences for both individuals and the couple.

Under optimal circumstances, the regressive experience of transference love and its working through are facilitated by the "as if" nature of transference regression—and the underlying ego strength implied in such a limited regression—and by the patient's growing capacity for gratification of oedipal longings by sublimation in an actual reciprocal love relationship. The absence of such reciprocity sharply differentiates transference love from a love relationship outside the analytic setting, just as the conscious exploration of oedipal conflicts differentiates it from the original oedipal situation. One might say that it resembles neurotic love in that transference regression fosters the development of unrequited love. But the analytic resolution of the transference in turn sharply differentiates transference love from the acting-out quality of neurotic love, when unrequited love increases the attachment rather than resolving it through mourning.

Psychoanalytic exploration of transference love provides evidence of all the components of the usual process of falling in love: the projection onto another (the analyst) of mature aspects of the ego ideal; the ambivalent relation to the oedipal object; the defenses against as well as the deployment of polymorphous perverse infantile and genital oedipal strivings. All these combine to bring about the experience of romantic love infused with sexual wishes in the transference, even if relatively briefly and transitorily. These feelings are ordinarily diluted by displacements onto the available objects in the patient's life. Indeed, there is probably no other area of psychoanalytic treatment in which the potentials for acting out and for growth experiences are so intimately condensed.

Transference love may betray its neurotic components by its intensity, rigidity, and stubborn persistence, particularly when its nature is masochistic. At the opposite extreme, the absence of evidence of transference love may reflect either strong sadomasochistic resistances against a positive oedipal relationship or a narcissistic transference within which positive oedipal developments are significantly curtailed. The nature of transference love varies with the gender of the participants, as has been widely observed (Bergmann 1971, 1980, 1982; Blum 1973; Karme 1979; Chasseguet-Smirgel 1984a; Lester 1984; Goldberger and Evans 1985; Person 1985; Silverman 1988). In brief, neurotic female patients in analysis with male analysts tend to develop typical positive oedipal transferences—witness the cases Freud (1915a) described in his classic paper on transference love. But women with narcissistic personalities in analysis with male analysts tend not to develop such transference love or to develop it only at very late stages of the treatment, usually in rather subdued form. Narcissistic resistances against dependency in the transference, part of the defense against unconscious envy of the analyst, preclude the development of transference love; the patient experiences any sexualized longings for the analyst as humiliating, as making her feel inferior.

Neurotic male patients in analysis with female analysts usually show some degree of inhibition in directly manifesting transference love, a tendency to displace it onto other objects; they instead develop intense anxieties over sexual inferiority or insufficiency as part of the reactivation of normal infantile narcissistic fantasies in regard to the oedipal mother. As Chasseguet-Smirgel (1970, 1984b) has pointed out, the little boy's unconscious fear that his small penis will not be able to satisfy his big mother is a significant dynamic here. Narcissistic male patients in analysis with

female analysts, however, often display what appears to be intense transference love but is in fact an aggressive, sexualized seductiveness reflecting transference resistance against feeling dependent on an idealized
analyst. This effort to reproduce the conventional cultural duo of the powerful, seductive male vis-à-vis the passive and idealizing female is a counterpart to the conventional cultural situation of a dependent, sexualized
relationship between the neurotic female patient and the male analyst, as
well as the reproduction, in the latter case, of the little girl's oedipal desire
for the idealized father.

Patients who have been sexually traumatized, particularly incest victims and patients with a history of sexual involvements with psychotherapists, may, owing to the trauma-induced heightened pressure for
repetition compulsion, try to seduce the analyst, their demands perhaps
dominating the transference for an extended period of time. Unconscious
identification with the aggressor plays an important role in these cases,
and careful analysis of the patient's enraged resentment of the analyst's
failure to respond to his or her sexual demands may require a great deal
of attention before the patient experiences relief and appreciation for the
maintenance of the psychoanalytic frame.

Narcissistic women with strong antisocial features may attempt to
sexually seduce the analyst in what may be erroneously understood as
oedipal transference love. But the aggression underlying their efforts to
corrupt the treatment is often quite clear in the transference. Such women
should be distinguished from masochistic women who may or may not
have a history of sexual abuse and have a predisposition to being sexually
abused and exploited. The intensity of erotized transferences in patients
with hysterical personality structure represents classic transference love:
a defensive, sexualized idealization of the analyst often hides significant
unconscious aggression derived from oedipal disappointment and unconscious oedipal guilt.

The neurotic features of transference love are evident not only in the
intensification of erotic longings in connection with unrequited love; they
are also manifest in the usual infantile narcissistic wish to be loved rather
than in the adult active love for the analyst, the wish for sexual intimacy
as a symbolic expression of symbiotic longings or preoedipal dependency,
and the general defensive accentuation of sexualized idealization as a defense against aggressive strivings from many sources. Patients with borderline personality organization may manifest particularly intense wishes
to be loved, erotic demands with strong efforts to control the therapist,
and even suicide threats as an effort to extract love by force from the
therapist.

Developments in homosexual transference love are similar in both genders, but important differences may emerge in the countertransference of the analyst. Patients with neurotic psychopathology may develop intense homosexual longings for their same-gender analyst, in which the negative oedipal complex and preoedipal, oral-dependent, and anal strivings converge; the elements of sexual wishes may be explored after the systematic analysis of resistances against the transference regression.

In narcissistic pathology, homosexual transferences usually acquire the same demanding, aggressive, and controlling characteristics as the heterosexual transferences of male narcissistic patients with female analysts and of female borderline and antisocial narcissistic patients with male analysts. As a general rule, the analyst's comfortable tolerance of the positive, sexualized transference love of the neurotic patient and maintenance of the analytic frame with the pseudo-positive transference love of narcissistic pathology are key requirements for a full analytic exploration and resolution of all these developments. The vicissitudes of the countertransference are of central importance in this process.

Countertransference

Although the countertransference as a factor in the formulation of transference interpretations has been receiving growing attention in the literature on psychoanalytic technique, far more has been written about aggressive countertransference than about erotic countertransference. The traditionally phobic attitude toward the countertransference, which has changed only in recent decades, still operates with regard to the analyst's erotic response to the erotic transference.

In general, when the patient's erotic feelings and fantasies in the transference are repressed, they usually evoke little erotic response in the countertransference. But when the patient's erotic fantasies and wishes become conscious, the analyst's countertransference response may include erotic elements that alert him or her to the possibility that the patient is consciously suppressing erotic fantasies and wishes. When the resistances against the full expression of the transference have significantly decreased and the patient experiences strong sexual wishes toward the analyst, erotic countertransference responses may become intense, fluctuating with the intensity of the erotic transference.

My emphasis here is on fluctuations of the transference: ordinarily, even intense erotic transferences wax and wane as the patient displaces transference feelings and wishes onto available opportunities for enactment, acting out, or extra-analytic gratification of sexual feelings. When the patient's erotic wishes become centered exclusively on the analyst, the resistance aspect becomes quite evident and the aggressive component of sexual demands more accentuated. This development tends to diminish the intensity of erotic countertransference feelings.

When projective identification predominates over projection—that is, when the patient attributes to the analyst sexual feelings that the patient recognizes in him or herself, rejecting these feelings as dangerous while attempting to control the analyst in order to avoid a feared sexual attack, in contrast to simple projection of unconscious impulses—erotic countertransference is usually absent. In fact, a strange discrepancy between intense projected sexual fantasies of a patient with an erotomanic transference and a countertransference response reflecting only the sense of intimidation and constraint should alert the analyst to the existence of severe narcissistic psychopathology in the patient or deep regression in the transference.

In my experience, the most intense erotic countertransference probably obtains in any of three situations: (1) in male analysts treating female patients with strong masochistic but not borderline features who develop an intense, "impossible" sexualized love for an unavailable oedipal object; (2) in analysts of both genders with strong, unresolved narcissistic characteristics; and (3) in some female analysts with strong masochistic tendencies treating highly seductive narcissistic male patients. Some female masochistic patients are able to generate marked rescue fantasies in their male analyst, "seducing" him to attempt to help them only to prove how misguided or useless that help really is. These seductions may become sexualized and may become manifest in the countertransference as rescue fantasies that have a strong erotic component. Typically, for example, the male analyst may ask himself, how is it that this extremely attractive woman patient is unable to keep any man and is always being rejected? From that question to the countertransference fantasy, "I would make a very gratifying sexual partner to this patient," is only a step.

I have found it helpful with masochistic patients having a long history of unhappy love affairs to be attentive to moments in which such rescue fantasies or erotic countertransferences develop. More often than not, such transference-countertransference seductions culminate in the patient's suddenly frustrating, disappointing, or angrily misunderstanding the analyst's comments, or shifting into inordinate demands on the analyst which instantly destroy the erotized rescue countertransference development.

I have also found it helpful for the analyst to tolerate his or her sexual fantasies about the patient, even let them develop into a narrative of an imaginary sexual relationship. Soon enough the analyst's own fantasy will cause the idea to evaporate because of his preconscious awareness of the help-rejecting, "antilibidinal," self-defeating aspects of the patient's personality; such an approach will facilitate an interpretation of the transference even before its sudden shift into negative aspects. Inconsistencies in the treatment arrangements, requests for changes in hours, allegation of the analyst's insensitivity to special circumstances, financial irresponsibility, and late payments of treatment fees are some of the obvious ways in which a patient's unconscious attempts to prevent or destroy the possibility of a steady positive relationship with the analyst are enacted; alertness to the countertransference narratives may enable the analyst to detect these tendencies before their enactment in the treatment.

Intense erotic transference manifestations must be differentiated from the patient's desire to be loved by the analyst. Beneath conscious or unconscious seductive efforts in the transference may lie the wish to become the object of the analyst's desire—to become the analyst's phallus—with fantasies of physical inferiority and of castration. I therefore like to analyze not only a patient's defenses against full expression of the erotic transference but the nature of transference fantasies themselves. Under what may look like a wish for a sexual relationship with the analyst are multiple transferences and meanings. Intense erotization, for example, frequently is a defense against aggressive transferences from many sources, an effort to escape painful conflicts around oral dependency, or the enacting of perverse transferences (the wish to seduce the analyst in order to destroy him).

The analyst who feels free to explore in his own mind his sexual feelings toward the patient will be able to assess the nature of transference developments and will thus avoid a defensive denial of his own erotic response to the patient; he must at the same time be able to explore transference love without acting out his countertransference in a seductive approach. The patient's erotic transference may be expressed in nonverbal behavior, in an erotization of his or her relationship to the analyst, to which the analyst should respond by exploring the defensive nature of nonverbalized seduction without either contributing to an erotization of the treatment situation or defensively rejecting the patient.

The analyst's unresolved narcissistic pathology is probably the major cause for countertransference acting out in the form of a contribution to the erotization of the psychoanalytic situation and even a rupture of the frame of the psychoanalytic setting. Having sexual relations with patients is, I believe, more often than not a symptom of the analyst's narcissistic character pathology and its attendant significant superego pathology.

There are, however, sometimes purely oedipal dynamics involved; it may be that the analyst's crossing of the sexual boundaries of the analytic relationship symbolically represents the crossing of the oedipal barrier, an acting out of masochistic pathology in an unconscious wish to be punished for an oedipal transgression.

The exploration of the complex and intimate aspects of the patient's erotic fantasies and desire for a sexual love relation with the analyst provides a unique opportunity for the analyst to better understand the sexual life of the other gender. Homosexual as well as heterosexual dynamics operate here, the positive as well as the negative Oedipus complex. Insofar as the analyst identifies with the emotional experiences of the other-gender patient, the concordant identification in the countertransference with the patient's erotic experiences with other heterosexual objects activates the analyst's capacity for and resistances against identification with the sexual yearnings of the other gender. The male analyst, in order to be able to establish a concordant identification in the countertransference with his female patient's interest in another man, has to be free to reach his own feminine identification. When this same female patient experiences sexual feelings toward the analyst, he may acquire a much better understanding of the sexual desire of a member of the other gender by integrating his concordant identification with his patient's sexual desire and his complementary identification as the object of her desire. This understanding on the part of the analyst includes an emotional resonance with his own bisexuality as well as the crossing of a boundary of intimacy and communication that is reached only in a sexual couple's culminating moments of intimacy.

Activation of an intense and complex countertransference that can probably be tolerated and used for work is unique to the psychoanalytic situation only because of the protection offered by the limits of the psychoanalytic relationship. An ironic confirmation of the uniqueness of this countertransference experience is that although psychoanalysts have a singular opportunity to study the psychology of the love life of the other gender, this knowledge and experience tend to evaporate when it comes to understanding their own experiences with the other gender outside the psychoanalytic situation. That is, outside the psychoanalytic situation, the analyst's love life becomes simply human.

When patient and analyst are not of the same gender, the concordant identification in the countertransference relies on the analyst's tolerance of his homosexual components, and heterosexual components prevail in complementary identification in the countertransference. This distinction becomes blurred when patients of the same gender as the analyst experience intense transference love. Homosexual transferences and the analyst's erotic response to such transferences tend to activate preoedipal as well as oedipal libidinal strivings and conflicts, particularly with patients whose homosexual conflicts and longings are expressed in the context of a neurotic personality organization. If the analyst can tolerate his own homosexual components, the countertransference exploration of his identification with the preoedipal parents should help him to analyze the negative oedipal implications of the patient's homosexual feelings. This rarely seems to become a major problem except for analysts who are struggling with a conflictual repression of their own homosexual longings or a suppressed homosexual orientation.

The transference developments in homosexual patients with narcissistic personality structure in treatment with analysts of the same gender acquire an intensely demanding, aggressive quality that reduces or eliminates strong homosexual countertransferences and their corresponding difficulties. Naturally, the lack of sexual resonance in the countertransference of a same-gender analyst with a homosexual patient who suffers from severe narcissistic pathology also requires exploration in terms of a possibly specific phobic reaction of the analyst to his or her homosexual impulses. The stronger cultural bias against male homosexuality unfortunately may represent a stronger countertransference burden for the male psychoanalyst.

From the preceding observations, it seems that the most important technical issues in the analysis of transference love are, first, the analyst's tolerance of the development of sexual feelings toward the patient, whether homosexual or heterosexual, which demands the analyst's internal freedom to utilize his or her psychological bisexuality; second, the analyst's systematic exploration of the patient's defenses against the full expression of transference love, steering a middle course between phobic reluctance to examine those defenses and the risk of being seductively invasive; third, the analyst's ability to fully analyze both the expression of the patient's transference love and the reactions to the frustration of the transference love that unavoidably will follow. Thus, in my view, the analyst's tasks include refraining from communicating his or her countertransference to the patient so as to ensure his internal freedom to fully explore his feelings and fantasies and integrating the understanding of his countertransference he has gained with the formulation of transference interpretations in terms of the patient's unconscious conflicts.

The patient's experience of the analyst's "rejection" as a confirmation of the prohibitions against oedipal longings, of narcissistic humiliation, and of the patient's sexual inferiority and castration should be explored and interpreted. When these conditions are met, periods of free and open expression of transference love, oedipal and preoedipal, may be deployed in the transference and are typically expressed in fluctuating intensities as the emotional growth in the patient's sexual life facilitates his or her efforts to obtain more gratifying relations in external reality.

The analyst has to come to terms not only with his or her own bisexual tendencies as they become activated in the erotic countertransference but also with other polymorphous perverse infantile strivings, such as the sadistic and voyeuristic implications of the interpretive explorations of the patient's sexual life. It is probably also true that, the more satisfactory the analyst's sexual life, the more he or she will be able to help the patient resolve inhibitions and limitations in this essential area of human experience. Regardless of the problematic aspects of transference love, I believe that the unique experience psychoanalytic work provides in analyzing this love while being its temporary target may contribute to the emotional and professional growth of the analyst.

A Clinical Illustration

Miss A. was a single woman in her late twenties referred to me by her internist because of chronic depression, alcohol and polysubstance abuse, and a chaotic life-style, with instability at work and in her relationships with men. I earlier referred to other aspects of her treatment (chap. 5). Miss A. impressed me as intelligent, warm, and attractive enough, but somewhat plain, neglectful of her appearance and attire. She had successfully completed studies in architecture and had been employed in several architectural firms, frequently changing her job, as I gradually found out, mostly because of unhappy love affairs with men she met at work. She had a tendency to mix work and personal relations in ways that were self-defeating.

The patient's mother died when Miss A. was six years old. Miss A.'s father, a prominent businessman, had international connections that required frequent overseas travel. During these trips, Miss A. and her two older brothers were left in the care of her father's second wife, with whom Miss A. did not get along. Miss A. described her mother in idealized but somewhat unrealistic ways. She had experienced intense mourning after her mother's death, which shifted into lasting hostility toward her stepmother, whom her father married about a year later. The relation with father, which had until then been excellent, also deteriorated. He thought her hostility to his new wife was unwarranted.

During Miss A.'s adolescence, her stepmother seemed pleased to be able to stay at home and continue her social engagements while Miss A. accompanied her father on his trips overseas. It was during her high school years that Miss A. discovered father's affairs with other women, and it became clear to her that those affairs were a major focus of his activities during his trips abroad. Miss A. became her father's confidante, and she consciously felt thrilled and happy that he trusted her. Somewhat less consciously, she felt triumph over her stepmother.

During her college years, a pattern in her behavior began to take shape which continued until she entered treatment. She would fall in love, become intensely dependent, submissive, and clinging, only invariably to be dropped. She reacted with deep depression and a tendency to resort to alcohol and minor tranquilizers to overcome the depression. She experienced a gradual deterioration of her social standing in the exclusive social group to which she belonged as she developed the reputation of being a pushover. When an unhappy love affair became complicated by an unwanted pregnancy and an induced abortion, her father became concerned, which prompted Miss A.'s internist to refer her to me.

My diagnostic impression was that of a masochistic personality, characterological depression, and symptomatic alcohol and substance abuse. Miss A. had maintained good relations with a few girlfriends over many years, was able to work effectively as long as she did not become involved in intimate relations with men at work, and impressed me as basically honest, concerned about herself, and capable of establishing object relations in depth. I recommended psychoanalysis, and the following developments took place during the third and fourth years of her treatment.

Miss A. had been involved for some time with a married man, B., who had made it very clear that he was not willing to leave his wife for her. He had offered, however, to have a child with Miss A. and to assume financial responsibility for this child. Miss A. was playing with the idea of getting pregnant as a way of cementing their relationship and hoping that this would eventually consolidate their union. To me, she repeatedly described her experiences with B. in ways that portrayed him as sadistic, deceitful, and unreliable; she complained bitterly about him. When I asked how she understood a relationship she described in such terms, she accused me of attempting to destroy what was, after all, the most meaningful relationship in her life, and of being impatient, domineering, and moralizing.

It gradually became clear that she was experiencing me as an unhelpful, critical, unsympathetic father figure, a replica of the way she experienced father's concern for her. At the same time, she was repeating her masochistic relationship pattern in the transference. What struck me as peculiar was that she described in great detail all her arguments and difficulties with her lover, but she never described the intimate aspects of their sexual relation except to say from time to time that they had a marvelous time in bed together. For some reason, I failed to explore the discrepancy between her general openness and this particular guardedness. Only slowly did I realize that I was hesitating to explore her sexual life because of my fantasy that she would immediately interpret it as seductive invasiveness. I sensed a particular countertransference reaction in myself that I did not yet fully understand.

As I explored the functions of her endless repetition of the same sadomasochistic interactions with B., I discovered that she was afraid that I would be jealous of the intensity of her relationship with him. She heard my interpretations—that she was replicating a frustrating and self-defeating relationship with me as she was experiencing it with B.—as an invitation for an erotic submission to me. I then was able to understand my previous reluctance as my intuitive awareness of her suspicions about my seductive intentions toward her. I suggested that she was afraid to share the details of her sexual life with me because she thought I wanted to exploit her sexually and seduce her into developing sexual feelings toward me.

I should add that these developments evolved in a remarkably nonerotic atmosphere; throughout this time, moments of quiet self-reflection seemed to occur in the middle of angry outbursts against her lover or at me because of my alleged intolerance for her relationship with him. She then began to explore the sexual aspects of the relationship with B. I learned that, although from the beginning she had been a willing participant in whatever sexual play or activity B. proposed and that her submissiveness provided him particular pleasure, she was not able to achieve orgasm in intercourse but experienced the same sexual inhibition with him that she had experienced with many previous lovers. It was only when one of these lovers, enraged with her, hit her that she was able to achieve full sexual excitement and orgasm.

This information clarified one aspect of her ongoing, clinging, yet provocative behavior with B.: her unconscious efforts to provoke him to hit her, so that she would be able to achieve full sexual gratification. Her abuse of alcohol and minor tranquilizers emerged as a way of presenting herself as impulsive, uncontrolled, demanding, and complaining—in contrast to her usual sweet and submissive self. Thus she both provoked men to violence—with a possibility for her sexual gratification—and made herself unattractive to them as well. Retrospectively, her alcohol abuse seemed one way to account for her eventual rejection by men. Unconscious guilt over the oedipal implications of these relationships gradually emerged as a major dynamic.

Analysis of this material accelerated the end of the relationship with B.: Miss A. became less regressively demanding and confronted B. more realistically with the inconsistencies of his behavior toward her. Faced with her alternatives regarding the future of their relationship, he decided to terminate it. In the period of mourning that followed, conscious erotic feelings toward me evolved for the first time in the transference. Miss A., who had suspected me of trying to seduce her sexually and had seen me as a replica of her hypocritical, moralistic, and promiscuous father, now perceived me as very different from her father. Her image of me became that of an idealized, loving, protective, yet also sexually responsive man, and she rather freely expressed erotic feelings about me that integrated tender and sexual fantasies and wishes. I, in turn, having regarded her as somewhat plain, now developed erotic countertransference fantasies during the sessions, together with the thought that it was really remarkable that such an attractive woman should not have been able to maintain a permanent relationship with a man.

Miss A., in the midst of apparent freedom to express her fantasies of a love relation with me—in the context of which she imagined predominantly sadomasochistic sexual interactions—also became highly sensitive to any minor frustration in the sessions. If she had to wait a few minutes, if an appointment had to be changed, if for some reason I could not accommodate a change that she requested, she felt hurt—first "depressed," and then very angry. Humiliated by my lack of response to her sexual wishes, she accused me of being cold, callous, and sadistically seductive. Images of her father's carefree relations with various women overseas, when he used her to protect himself against the suspicions of his second wife, emerged as a significant theme: I was as seductive and unreliable as her father and was betraying her in my "carefree" relations with my other patients and my female colleagues.

The intense affect of these recriminations, her accusatory, self-depreciatory, and resentful attitude, a replica of her difficulties with men and the opening of an aspect of her relationship with father that had previously been repressed, also led to a shift in my countertransference. Paradoxically, I felt freer to explore my countertransference fantasies, which ranged from sexual interactions replaying her sadomasochistic fantasies to what it would be like to live with a woman like Miss A. My fantasies about sadomasochistic sexual interactions also replicated men's aggressive behavior toward her, which she had unconsciously tended to induce in them. My fantasies culminated in the clear recognition that she would relentlessly provoke situations that frustrated her dependency needs and angry recriminations, escalating to violent interactions and public displays of depression and rage. She would present herself as my victim, which would unfailingly destroy our relationship.

As I utilized this countertransference material in my interpretation of the developments in the transference, Miss A.'s profound feelings of guilt over the sexualized aspects of the relationship with me became apparent. In contrast to earlier complaints about feeling rejected and humiliated because of my lack of a loving response to her, she now felt anxious, guilty, and upset over her wish to seduce me and evoked an idealized image of my wife (about whom she had no information or awareness). I realized in retrospect that my resistance to exploring countertransference fantasies had prevented me from following them in a direction that would have clarified the masochistic self-destructiveness of Miss A.'s erotic wishes toward me. Thinking back, I would say that my unconscious counteridentification with her seductive father interfered with my freedom to explore my erotic countertransference and thereby to perceive more clearly the masochistic pattern in the transference. I also think that my resistance against unconscious sadomasochistic impulses of my own role responsiveness to Miss A. played a part. Miss A.'s sexual fantasies about father, her past experiences of him as teasingly provocative and yet sexually rejecting, then became a dominant content in the analysis.

In the context of our exploration of the profound guilt feelings that now connected her idealized image of my wife with the idealized image of her own mother, Miss A. realized that she had defended herself against these guilt feelings by splitting the image of mother into the idealized dead one and the feared and depreciated stepmother represented by her rivals, the other women in the life of the men she could never have for herself alone. This awareness also helped to clarify her unconscious selection of "impossible" men and the unconscious prohibition against full sexual gratification under conditions other than physical or mental suffering.

Miss A. finally established a relationship with a man who in many ways was more satisfactory than her previous lovers. He was not involved with another woman at that time, and he belonged to her own social environment (from which, because of her turbulent life-style, she had felt ostracized). A lengthy period of analysis followed, in the course of which we explored the fantasies and fears in her developing relationship with C. She was able to talk in great detail about their sexual relationship, and we could examine her feelings both of guilt toward me—having abandoned me as her love object—and of triumph over me in a sexual relationship that, in her fantasy, was more satisfactory than any I might then have. In other words, a highly satisfactory love relation in external reality also served the transference function of working through a mourning process with me that repeated the mourning and a new reconciliation regarding the ambivalent relationship with her father.

9.

Masochistic Pathology

Masochism: A General Overview

In my view, masochism may be described as a broad field of phenomena, both normal and pathological, centered on motivated self-destructiveness and a conscious or unconscious pleasure in suffering. It is a field with imprecise boundaries. At one extreme, we find such severe self-destructiveness that self-elimination or elimination of self-awareness acquires a central motivational importance—Green (1983) called it the "narcissism of death"—and masochistic psychopathology merges with the psychopathology of primitive and severe aggression.

At the other extreme, a healthy capacity for self-sacrifice on behalf of family, others, or an ideal, the sublimatory functions of superego-determined willingness to suffer, does not warrant being considered pathological. Our prolonged infantile dependency and the necessary internalization of parental authority during our protracted childhood and adolescence make it almost impossible to conceive of a superego that would not include masochistic components—that is, some unconsciously motivated need for suffering and its underlying dynamics.

Between these two extremes lies a broad spectrum of masochistic psychopathology, the common elements of which center on unconscious conflicts concerning sexuality and the superego. In the realm of moral masochism, a price is paid in order to obtain pleasure: the transformation of pain into erotic pleasure, the integration of aggression within love, is played out in the relation between the self and a superego introject. Because of unconscious feelings of guilt, to suffer at the will of a punishing introject is to recover the love of the object and the union with it; in this way, aggression is absorbed into love. The same dynamic is also played out in sexual masochism as a specific perversion: the obligatory experience of pain, submission, and humiliation to obtain sexual gratification is the unconscious punishment for the forbidden oedipal implications of genital sexuality.

Masochism as part of polymorphous perverse infantile sexuality, as we have seen, constitutes a central aspect of sexual excitement, based on the potentially erotic response to the experience of discrete physical pain and the symbolic shift of this capacity (to transform pain into sexual excitement) into the capacity to absorb or integrate hatred into love (Kernberg 1991). As Braunschweig and Fain (1971, 1975) have stressed, the object of sexual desire is originally a teasing object, the sensually stimulating and frustrating mother, and erotic excitement, with its aggressive component, is a basic response to a desired, frustrating, and exciting object.

Under optimal circumstances, the painful aspects of erotic excitement are transformed into pleasure, heightening sexual excitement and the sense of closeness to the erotic object. The internalization of the erotic object, the object of desire, also includes the demands made by that object as a condition for maintaining its love. The basic unconscious fantasy might be expressed as: "You are hurting me as part of your response to my desire. I accept the pain as part of your love—it cements our closeness, I am becoming like you in enjoying the pain inflicted on me." The demands of the object also may be translated into an unconscious moral code expressed in a basic unconscious fantasy that might be verbalized as: "I submit to your punishment because, coming from you, it must be just. I deserve it to maintain your love, and in suffering I retain you and your love." The aggressive implications of pain (the aggression from or attributed to the desired object, and the rageful reaction to pain) are thus woven into or fused with love as an indispensable part of erotic excitement, as Braunschweig and Fain (1971) and Stoller (1991a) have stressed, and as part of the "moral defense" described by Fairbairn (1954).

An illustrative case is that of a woman in her early forties with a depressive-masochistic personality structure. In one session, late in her psychoanalytic treatment, during the course of which she was able to resolve an incapacity to achieve orgasm in intercourse with her husband after many years of marriage, she developed the fantasy in the transference that she would come to a session, undress totally, and I would be so impressed by her breasts and her genitals that I would become a complete slave to her desire, getting sexually excited and having intercourse with her, and she, in turn, would then be willing to become my slave, abandoning all her responsibilities and following me.

The only daughter of a prohibitive mother who was intolerant of any sexual manifestations in her daughter and of a warm yet distant father who spent time away during extended periods of her childhood, she immediately became aware of the connections between her wish for a sexual relation with me and the rebellion against mother implied in the wish to seduce father away from her; making me her slave combined the wish for my full acceptance of her genitals and her sexuality while punishing me for having preferred other women (her mother), and offering herself in turn for slavery expiated her guilt. But she also experienced the enactment of the slavery fantasy as an exciting expression of aggression without having to fear its inhibiting effects on her sexual pleasure. To the contrary, she felt that this aggression would heighten the gratification of total intimacy and fusion in the reciprocity of the slave and master relation. Following that session, she was able for the first time to ask her husband, in the middle of sexual intercourse, to pinch her nipples forcefully; he did so with intense sexual excitement, permitting her, in turn, to scratch his back so deeply that he bled, and both, for the first time, reached an intense orgasm together.

In analyzing this experience, she expressed the fantasy that her husband was like a hungry, frustrated infant biting mother's breasts, and she, as a powerful, understanding, and giving mother, could gratify his needs while tolerating his aggression. At the same time, she felt, she was a sexual woman relating to her husband-infant, who thus was not a threatening father, and also taking revenge against father who had abandoned her, as well as against her husband, who had caused her pain, by causing him in turn to bleed. And she felt that to scratch him while embracing him tightly intensified their fusion and her sense that she could participate in his orgasm while he could participate in hers. This woman, who was approaching completion of her analysis, was able to articulate important facets of normal sexual excitement and erotic desire.

Fusion with the object of desire, however, is fostered under conditions not only of intense erotic excitement and love but also of extreme pain and hatred, as proposed by Jacobson (1971). When interactions with mother are chronically aggressive or abusive, frustrating, and teasing, the intensity of the infant's physical or psychic pain cannot be absorbed into a normal erotic response or into sadistic, yet protective and reliable, superego precursors; it is instead directly transformed into aggression. Basing his proposal on observations by Stoller (1975a), Fraiberg (1982), Galenson (1983, 1988), Herzog (1983), and others, Grossman (1986, 1991) says that excessive pain is transformed into aggression and that excessive aggression distorts the development of all psychic structures and interferes with the elaboration of aggression in fantasy as opposed to its direct expression in behavior. One might also say, with André Green (1986), that excessive aggression restricts the realm of unconscious psychic experience by primordial somatization or acting out.

Under extreme circumstances, excessive aggression is reflected in primitive self-destructiveness. Severe early illness with prolonged pain, physical or sexual assault, and chronically abusive and chaotic relations with a parental object may all be reflected in severe destructiveness and self-destructiveness producing the syndrome of malignant narcissism (Kernberg 1992). This syndrome is characterized by a pathological grandiose self infiltrated with aggression, which reflects the fusion of the self with the sadistic object. The fantasy might be described as: "I am alone in my fear, rage, and pain. In becoming one with my tormentor, I can protect myself by destroying myself or my self-awareness. Now I no longer need to fear pain or death because in inflicting them upon myself or others I become superior to all others who induce or fear these calamities."

Under less extreme circumstances, the sadistic object may be internalized into an integrated yet sadistic superego and the fusion with it reflected in the morally tinged desire to destroy oneself. The delusional conviction of one's badness, in psychotic depression, the desire to destroy the fantasied bad self, and the unconscious fantasy of becoming reunited with a loved object by self-sacrifice may reflect these conditions. Under still less severe conditions, masochistic suffering may provide a sense of moral superiority; "injustice-gathering" patients typically represent the more moderate compromise formation of moral masochism.

But if aggression is absorbed into the superego in the form of internalization of a punishing yet needed object of desire, erotic masochism also may "contain" the aggression, not in the usual sadomasochistic aspects of sexual excitement, but in the condensation of sexual excitement with a total submission to the desired object and the wish to be humiliated by that object. Masochism as a restrictive, obligatory sexual practice thus transforms ordinary polymorphous perverse infantile sexuality into a "paraphilia" or perversion in a strict sense; by the same token, it may protect psychic development from the general infiltration of aggression into the superego by internalizing the sadistic object. Apparently, two kinds of mental organization are built up separately, in some patients whose physical or sexual abuse has been more limited, or when incest occurs in the context of other relatively normal object relations, or when punishment itself has been erotized in actual beating experiences and related interactions.

A sexual perversion established early might later be reinforced by defenses against castration anxiety and unconscious guilt derived from advanced oedipal conflicts, eventually "containing" these conflicts. How-

ever, the ascendance of a strict but well-integrated superego that inter-
nalizes a repressive sexual morality may contribute to the transformation
of earlier sexual masochism into moral masochism, transmuting the symbolic meanings of sexual pain, submission, and humiliation into psychic
suffering, submission to the superego, and acting out of unconscious guilt
in humiliating or self-defeating behavior.

In summary, I am describing three levels of psychic organization at
which primitive severe aggression is incorporated into the psychic apparatus: primitive self-destructiveness, erotic masochism, and moral masochism. In all types, secondary narcissistic elaborations of masochistic
trends contribute to the subject's rationalizing and secondarily defending
the characterological, behavioral manifestations of these masochistic patterns.

Optimally, primitive aggression would be integrated as the sadomasochistic element of erotic excitement or, if more severe, would be contained by a masochistic perversion, without necessarily "contaminating"
the general character structure under the effects of further pathological
superego development. But the failure of erotic masochism, even of a masochistic perversion, to carry out these containing functions would then
predispose the subject to moral masochism. Moral masochism itself, within an excessively severe but well-integrated superego structure, might
limit the self-destructive effects of masochism, might in fact contain it.
Excessive aggression, however, spilling over from primitive self-
destructiveness first into a sexual perversion and still later into sadomasochistic personality developments, may present the most severe cases of
sadomasochistic personality in which sexual perversion, severe narcissistic pathology, and sadomasochistic personality features with significant
self-destructiveness coincide.

Masochism in Men and Women

Like all sexual perversions, masochism is more frequent in men than
in women (Baumeister 1989). I am using the term *perversion* to refer to
the obligatory and exclusive organization of sexual behavior under the
dominance of a partial instinctual drive. Although the findings of empirical studies in the United States and Europe vary widely (Kinsey et al.
1953; Greene and Greene 1974; Hunt 1974; Spengler 1977; Scott 1983;
Weinberg and Kammel 1983; Baumeister 1989; Arndt 1991), it seems that
5 to 10 percent of the U.S. adult population habitually enjoy some type
of masochistic sexual activity. Cultural variations apparently exist with

regard to both the prevalence of masochism as a perversion per se and the dominant form it takes.

There are both similarities and differences in sexual masochistic fantasies and activities between men and women. Men's fantasies and sexual activities expressing the wish to be dominated, teased, excited, and forced to submit to a powerful cruel woman as a requirement for orgasm are the counterpart of women's fantasies and activities of being humiliated by exhibiting herself to others and being raped by a powerful, dangerous, unknown man. Baumeister (1989) tells us that male masochism usually involves greater pain and a stronger emphasis on humiliation, the infidelity of the sexual partner, audience participation, and transvestism. Female masochism, in contrast, involves pain more frequently but of less intensity, punishment in the context of an intimate relationship, sexual display as humiliation, and a nonparticipating audience. Male masochism usually culminates in orgasm excluding genital intercourse, whereas female masochism usually culminates in genital sex although less consistently in orgasm.

Psychoanalytic understanding helps to clarify these differences: at an oedipal level, the central dynamics of sexual masochism as well as of perversion in general involve intense castration anxiety related to intense aggressive aspects of oedipal conflicts (which may include significant preoedipal aggression as well) and defensive accentuation of pregenital sexuality as an assurance against the threat of castration. The greater intensity of castration anxiety in men is assumed to relate to their higher frequency of sexual perversions. McDougall (personal communication) has called attention to the more primitive and diffuse nature of castration anxiety in women, their unconscious fear of general bodily destruction, as a major dynamic that would explain their different defensive structures against castration anxiety.

Chasseguet-Smirgel (1984b) has described perversions, in patients with borderline pathology, as the condensation of preoedipal aggression with oedipally determined castration anxiety. Preoedipal aggression intensifies by projection the oedipally determined castration anxiety. Chasseguet-Smirgel emphasized the regression to anal sexuality as underlying the unconscious denial of the differences between generations and genders, the defensive idealization of the perversion, the devaluation of genital intercourse, and the general deterioration of object relations.

Chasseguet-Smirgel's (1970, 1984b) and Braunschweig and Fain's (1971) descriptions of the development of the oedipal situation in boys and girls provide more specific clues to the differences in the nature of fantasy in male and female masochism. For men, domination by a powerful woman replicates the little boy's fantasies of involvement with the powerful and overwhelming mother, together with the expiation of guilt for the oedipal transgression and the narcissistic fantasy that his little penis is as satisfactory to mother as father's is. Transvestite fantasies and activities integrated into male masochism, the typical "feminine masochism" of men, both symbolize and serve to deny castration anxiety. In women, the unconscious fantasy of being the preferred sexual object of the powerful, distant, and potentially threatening as well as seductive father condenses with the expiation of guilt by being forced to submit, sexually humiliated, and abandoned. In both genders, masochistic scenarios stress the teasing quality of frustrating and stimulating sexual interactions, a basic dynamic of sexual excitement traceable to the erotic quality of the mother-infant relationship (Braunschweig and Fain 1971, 1975). This teasing quality may emerge directly in male masochistic scenarios in their relations with women; women's masochistic scenarios related to father also may be condensed with a masochistic relation to mother.

If masochism as a sexual perversion is more common in men than in women, nothing indicates that moral masochism is more frequent in either gender. Psychodynamic and social factors may contribute to these findings. I believe it is reasonable to assume that a paternalistic culture reinforces characterological masochism in women and sadistic components of sexuality in men, thus reinforcing the sexualization of masochism in men while strengthening its transformation into characterological patterns in women. As feminist writers (Thompson 1942; Mitchell 1974; Benjamin 1986) have indicated about submissive relationships, it is important to differentiate objective oppression from unconscious pleasure, although one factor may complement the other. Objective oppression may deform patterns of pleasure. Cultural attitudes may, for example, reinforce sadistic patterns in women with masculine identifications: cultural stereotypes are available to be used in gender fantasies. In addition, ideology may be utilized to rationalize the unconscious origin of character structure.

The clinical characteristics of the depressive-masochistic personality (Kernberg 1992) may be found in both men and women, but they tend to crystallize around different life situations. In my experience, women's masochistic love relations are more frequent than men's, but men's masochistic submissiveness in the workplace is probably more frequent than women's. I believe that male therapists in particular may underestimate the extent to which masochistic patterns in men's submissive behaviors are played out in the workplace. Again, objective discrimination against women in the workplace must be distinguished from men's widespread, culturally adaptive submissiveness to authority and power. In addition, as one explores in depth the attitude of men toward love relations, significant unconscious masochistic elements emerge from the socially adaptive, "sadistic" surface. And exploring women's relationship to study and work reveals significant masochistic elements—for example, premature abandonment of competition and missed opportunities for advancement.

Early psychoanalytic literature, perhaps best represented by Deutsch's *Psychology of Women* (1944–45), stressed the greater predisposition of women to masochism and related it to biological factors (such as menstruation) expressed in an unconscious assumption of castration, also presumably reflected in the painful aspects of childbirth; it assumed a close relation between femininity and passivity and the underdeveloped characteristics of the female superego. These early views have since been strongly repudiated (Stoller 1968; Chasseguet-Smirgel 1970; Mitchell 1974; Schafer 1974; Blum 1976; Chodorow 1978; Person 1983). Disentangling the influence of cultural stereotypes, the adaptation to specific social and cultural challenges, ideological commitments, unconscious dynamics, and biological predispositions regarding moral masochism, remains an unfinished task.

Masochistic Love Relations

In women with depressive-masochistic personalities, masochistic love relations are often themselves the dominant psychopathology. Frequently during early or late adolescence falling in love with an idealized, unavailable, frustrating, or deeply disappointing man becomes an experience that influences the woman's future love life. Falling in love with "unavailable" men may lead either to romantic encounters in unrealistic situations that end in disappointment or to a romantic fantasy maintained over many years regarding what might have been. Falling in love with unavailable men may be considered to be a normal manifestation of the reactivation of oedipal conflicts during adolescence, but the persistence and especially the intensification of experienced love precisely after it has become clear that that love is unrequited are what characterize these particular relationships. These women do not gradually overcome the idealization of unavailable men in future relationships that become more realistically selective—as is characteristic of normal development. A fixation on the trauma carries them to endless repetitions of the same experience.

Women with masochistic psychopathology may alternate sexual fears and inhibition with impulsive sexual involvements under frustrating or even dangerous circumstances. For example, a patient had a puritanical and punitive background regarding all sexual experiences and several love relations with men in which she resisted any sexual intimacy. Her first sexual encounter was a one-night stand with a man whose aggressive, even potentially threatening qualities exerted a strong seductive influence on her.

In their sexual encounters, masochistic women with well-integrated superego functions and a neurotic personality organization may experience some degree of sexual inhibition at first, and then, sometimes as if by chance, they discover a particularly painful, humiliating, or submissive quality in their sexual interaction around which a sexual perversion crystallizes. When a patient with a depressive-masochistic personality was having intercourse with her boyfriend, as part of playful dominance of her, he twisted her arm to the point at which it became very painful; she was able to experience orgasm in intercourse for the first time. The experience initiated a pattern of masochistic sexual relations in which her arms had to be tied up in a twisted position behind her back to provide her with maximal excitement and orgasm.

Again, this development contrasts with the normal integration of sadomasochistic fantasies and experiences. Early traumatic sexual experiences may give rise to masochistic fantasies that accompany and facilitate sexual intercourse under conditions of gratifying love relations and sexual interactions. Masturbatory fantasies in particular may perpetuate what amounts to a self-limited masochistic scenario that derives from early adolescent initiation into sexual activity. The gothic romantic novel, a staple of mass culture aimed at women (and so in contrast to the standard pornographic novels for men), usually centers on the relationship of an inexperienced young woman and a famous, unavailable, often notorious and unreliable, attractive yet threatening or dangerous man. Against all odds and after numerous disappointments and failures, threatened by competition with other powerful women, the heroine is finally embraced by the great man (whose positive qualities have been reconfirmed), faints in his arms, and the story ends.

The typical male "madonna-prostitute" fantasies and experiences in early adolescence are greatly exaggerated when influenced by masochistic psychopathology. Typically, an "impossible love" involves extreme idealization of a beloved woman, available or unavailable, and an inhibition regarding her that interferes with establishing the relationship, while the man's sexual activity is limited to masturbatory fantasies about or sexual relations with depreciated women, sexual engagements that may include sadistic features but are experienced as frustrating, shameful, or degrading. The idealization is accompanied by inhibition and lack of assertiveness, an unconscious tendency to leave the field for rivals or to provoke conditions for failure.

In both men and women, unrequited love increases love instead of diminishing it, as is customary in healthy mourning. Over a period of years, one can observe in masochistic men and women a tendency to fall in love with impossible people, to submit excessively to an idealized partner, and to unconsciously undermine the relationship by this very submissiveness, while discarding the possibility of other, potentially much more gratifying relationships.

Why long strings of unhappy love affairs are more frequent in women than in men is often explained by pointing to the cultural pressures that reinforce, and even induce and facilitate, self-defeating behavior in women, to the constraints created by women's economic exploitation, to unwanted pregnancies, and to cultural reinforcement of sadistic behavior in men. Although these are indeed powerful influencing forces, equally important is women's earlier capacity than men's to develop an object relation in depth in the context of a sexual relationship, derived from the little girl's shift from mother to father at the initiation of the oedipal period in contrast to the little boy's persisting attachment and intense ambivalence toward the primary object. Women's earlier capacity for commitment to a love relation and their masochistic attachments may reinforce each other.

The sharp early differences in psychosexual development between boys and girls become attenuated in adulthood. Perhaps the greatest differences between men and women emerge in late adolescence and early adulthood, when women have to integrate their new awareness of menstruation, childbearing, and motherhood, and when men have to come to terms with their intense ambivalence to mother, the unchanged primary love object. As one examines the love relations of patients in their thirties and forties, in contrast to those in their twenties and earlier, the differences between masochistic character pathology and ordinary vicissitudes of life become sharper.

A physician enamored of his beautiful and creative artistic wife encouraged her to develop close relationships with other (male) artists while he submerged himself in his professional life to the extent that her emotional needs were more and more frustrated. When she abandoned him for one of her artist friends, he sank into a severe depression and was willing to tolerate her affairs with other men. Analytic exploration revealed that unresolved guilt over intense rivalry with the oedipal father and a related wish to submit homosexually to him caused the physician unconsciously to push his wife toward other men while identifying with her. He intensely idealized unavailable women, representing mother, who had died in his early childhood, and unconsciously recreated the fantasied relation with the lost mother.

It is important to differentiate predominantly masochistic personalities with secondary narcissistic reinforcement of masochistic patterns from narcissistic personalities whose chaotic love life may resemble masochistic patterns. Predominantly narcissistic personalities tend to idealize potential partners when they seem unavailable and then devalue them once they become available, and they have great difficulty tolerating the ordinary frustrations and ambivalences of all love relations. Masochistic personalities search for highly idealized, potentially unavailable partners but have a capacity for object relations in depth, particularly with frustrating and sadistic partners. Clinically, however, complex combinations make this prognostically important difference difficult to assess in the initial history-taking (Cooper 1988). In the course of psychoanalytic treatment, narcissistic personalities who suffered from uncontrollable sexual promiscuity may develop masochistic love relations as a consequence of the dissolution of the pathological grandiose self: the masochistic commitment may be experienced as a relief from previous isolation.

So far, I have mentioned individual masochistic patterns. The couple's unconscious collusion can transform a satisfactory relationship into a nightmare. Most frequently, the mutual projection of sadistic superego demands and prohibitions is reinforced by mutual guilt-raising behavior as the partners identify with their own sadistic superego introjects. One or both partners often show a chronic tendency to submit, out of irrational guilt, to impossible demands from the other, and then to rebel against these demands in potentially self-injurious ways.

A somewhat dependent husband was married to a woman with a severe depressive-masochistic personality and characterological depression. She easily felt slighted by him and other relatives and friends; he adjusted by attempting to engage relatives and friends to be particularly considerate toward her. While others saw him as henpecked, he blamed himself for what he considered to be his own inability to make life more tolerable for his gifted and hypersensitive wife. She, however, used his guilt-ridden behavior to strengthen her conviction that he was treating her badly, and she assumed that she had been condemned to live with an insensitive man. Projecting her unconscious guilt feelings onto him gave her temporary relief from depression. But his acceptance of her accusations reconfirmed her feelings of injury, fostering further depression. This woman was reenacting the oedipal submission to a sadistic, guilt-raising mother, unconsciously hoping to be rescued by a powerful, good father; but the husband's conciliatory behavior reinforced her submission to mother.

A man with long-standing self-defeating patterns in his work and a paranoid attitude toward authority—the source, he thought, of his short-comings, was married to a strong, protective wife who had sacrificed her career to dedicate herself to a husband whose achievements she very much admired. At home, he found a safe haven from his real and imagined slights at work, and her needs to be protective and giving were gratified. Over the years, however, she could not fail to see his contributions to his difficulties, and, afraid of her own exasperation with his behavior at work and feeling guilty for not living up to her ideal of a perfect spouse, she became even more solicitous while withdrawing socially. He, in turn, became more and more dependent on her, finding himself reinforced in his sense that the world was unfair. He began to resent his increasing dependency but had difficulty formulating this resentment even to him-self, fearing that he might lose his only support. Her guilt at being inad-equate and his fear of venting his frustrations gradually escalated; she began to abuse drugs to deal with increasing anxiety, which finally led them to treatment.

Another frequent pattern is represented by what might be called "mas-ochistic bargains": an individual or a couple unconsciously sacrifices one important area of life for success and satisfaction in all other areas. Play-ing Russian roulette with destiny, becoming involved in a potentially threatening situation that might destroy major life expectations, is an-other form of acting out deep masochistic needs.

Russian roulette can also be played by attacking the beloved person relentlessly, provoking rejection from the love object while hoping that love will still prevail. An intelligent, hardworking, creative, attractive woman was married to a man with similar characteristics. He was a strug-gling young professional with unresolved problems with authority, a ten-dency to defy what he saw as domineering father figures and to "run for cover" to powerful, protective women. He was the son of a successful, admired, but emotionally unavailable father with whom unconsciously he felt he could not compete. She, whose mother was a domineering, hypochondriacal, deeply dissatisfied woman who treated her husband as a slave and intruded into the life of all her married children, uncon-sciously replicated that behavior in her relationship with her own hus-band.

She criticized his "excessive" commitment to work and lack of atten-tion to her needs, to which he responded with an alternation between guilt-ridden behaviors and lengthy absences from their home, replicating his father's unavailability. She, unconsciously, managed to reproduce the tense, chaotic atmosphere that had characterized her parents' household, while he, feeling defeated because, unconsciously, he could not compete with his successful father, behaved in an unconsciously resigned way. Therapeutic intervention occurred just before a dangerous breakup of their relationship that, in effect, would have corresponded to the woman's masochistic submission to her own internalized mother and symbolically confirmed his oedipal failure.

Ideological rationalizations of masochistic choices have an important function in perpetuating sadomasochistic relationships. The moral confirmation or even superiority involved in maintaining a relationship with a sadistic but "inferior" partner, such as an alcoholic spouse or a member of a persecuted minority, or in rationalizing the persistence of an impossible relationship "for the sake of the children" may contribute defensive systems that need to be differentiated from objectively limiting social or economic circumstances that prevent a mistreated spouse from leaving an impossible relationship.

Using children to justify the perpetuation of a severely masochistic relationship is the counterpart of postponing pregnancy until the biological clock may objectively prevent having children, an important nucleus around which masochistic patterns may consolidate. A woman who unconsciously has managed to rationalize the postponement of marriage and of having children until she reaches her late forties, may then develop a secondary ideological system implying that the fact that she cannot have a child now justifies her unhappiness for the rest of her life.

The establishment of a joint value system that may cement a couple's union and assure their freedom from their conventional cultural environment may be infiltrated by ideological systems that rationalize masochistic developments in their relationship. Both a traditionally conventional ideology of women's tasks as restricted to "children, church, and kitchen" and an ideology of women's liberation may be co-opted to serve masochistic needs. A woman may, for example, reject the stereotyping of femininity and, with it, attention to her physical care and grooming, or she may rationalize a hostile provocativeness toward men that has an unconsciously self-defeating purpose. The reality of a past history of severe victimization, such as by physical violence or incest, may determine, on the surface, a sense of entitlement and, at a deeper level, an identification with the aggressor internalized into the superego that recreates, again and again, the situation of mistreatment and perpetuates the victimization.

Transference Developments

Among the many ways in which masochistic pathology can be displayed in psychoanalytic treatment, the following examples illustrate frequent developments in the transference. An early idealization of the analyst may coincide with the patient's focus on an external, bad, persecutory object, followed by the incapacity to leave or stand up to this bad object. Typically, a man may be involved with a woman he describes as chronically frustrating, depreciative, provocative, exhibitionistic, but is incapable of leaving her despite the apparent analysis of the unconscious roots of this disposition. In fact, the patient may end up either complaining about the analyst's incapacity to help him or accusing the analyst of attempting to destroy a potentially good relationship! Thus, the idealized analyst turns into a persecutory object.

Interpretation of this transference development may uncover the significant masochistic pathology, revealing the patient's unconscious need to transform a potentially helpful relationship into a bad one because he cannot tolerate being helped, thus expressing his unconscious guilt and the masochistic origins of the displacement of hatred from the assumed bad object to the good one. Often, at a deeper level, this transference leads to the exploration of a revengeful aggression against a needed yet frustrating past good object. The unconscious identification with the aggressor, which the patient's defense of his past object relation reveals, and the hidden gratification of his "moral superiority" as a suffering victim are other features of this transference development.

Negative therapeutic reactions from unconscious guilt are typical in the analytic treatment of patients with severe masochism. For example, a patient experienced me as critical, impatient, and overbearing precisely when she was threatened by her self-defeating patterns and I attempted to interpret her temptation to destroy her opportunities, with an obvious concern for the self-destructive processes she was generating in her life. That same patient experienced me as warm and understanding when I did not intervene interpretively under conditions when she would refer to her self-defeating behaviors. Eventually I was able to clarify and interpret her unconscious effort to create a situation in the transference in which she would tell me about terrible situations in her life, and I would warmly and emphatically listen without being able to help her, thus implicitly colluding with her self-destructiveness; or else I would attempt to help her, at which point she would experience me immediately as an attacking enemy. In the transference, she was unconsciously attempting to transform me into an envious, sadistic, maternal introject.

Some masochistic patients are able to generate powerful rescue fantasies in the analyst, "seducing" him to attempt to help them only to prove how misguided or useless that help really is. As I mentioned before (chapter 8), these attempted seductions may become sexualized and manifest themselves in the countertransference as rescue fantasies with a strong erotic component.

Masochistic patients may subtly refuse to provide full information about their own contributions to their difficulties, thus protecting their masochistic acting out. Again, the analyst is put into a position of either sympathizing with the patient or, in an attempt to assess the situation objectively, immediately encountering the angry accusation of taking the side of the patient's enemy. It is important to interpret the patient's unconsciously putting the analyst in a situation in which the analyst is condemned to frustrate the patient's needs.

Some masochistic patients may insist that they are getting worse, that the treatment is damaging them, but at the same time refuse to consider the possibility that the analyst may indeed be unable to help them and that they might be wise to ask for a consultation or consider a different therapist. Some of these patients may insist that it is "this therapist or none," or this treatment or suicide, clearly indicating their fixation to this therapeutic experience as a damaging, chronically traumatic situation, a fixation to a bad internal object projected onto the analyst. In the countertransference, the analyst may feel inclined to end the treatment of such a patient, and it is extremely important that this countertransference wish be transformed into a systematic analysis of the transference behavior geared to provoke the analyst.

In patients with an organized masochistic perversion, an early task is to analyze the defensive aspects of the idealization of their sexual masochism. Here we often find, in the unconscious meaning of the perversion and in its reflection in the transference, a pseudo-idealization of both sexual masochism and the analyst. This pseudo-idealization reflects, at an unconscious level, the replacement of the genital penis by an anal, fecal penis, a regression from an oedipal to an anal world of object relations, and a corresponding "as if" quality in the transference reflecting the denial of oedipal conflicts described by Chasseguet-Smirgel (1984b, 1991). This development requires particular attention to "as if" aspects of the associative material and the transference, a dynamic particularly prominent in men. In women, behind masochistic fantasies of being raped by sadistic men, we often find the unconscious image of an invasive, phallic mother. Not surprisingly, women with a masochistic personality structure are prone to being seduced into destructive sexual relations with unethical therapists, which makes their subsequent treatment by other therapists even more difficult. Women with narcissistic personalities may also wish to seduce the therapist as a final expression of their triumph over him.

The sense of closeness, even fusion, in the interaction with an objectively dangerous, sadistic object in the context of a sadomasochistic scenario as an essential aspect of sexual interactions usually points to severe preoedipal traumatization and fixation to an indispensable yet traumatizing object. Patients with these dynamics develop strong sadomasochistic transferences with relatively little erotization, in contrast to patients with intense erotization in the transference, whose sadomasochistic fantasies reflect the unconscious reactivation of an advanced oedipal primal scene. The fantasied identification with both parents in sexual intercourse and the masochistic expiation of guilt because of this oedipal triumph may become condensed with the narcissistic fantasy of being both sexes and therefore not needing to enter into a dreaded dependent relationship with any object—a frequent dynamic in narcissistic patients.

In earlier work (1992), I reported on my experiences in the psychoanalytic treatment of some patients with severely sadomasochistic transferences that seemed to resist all interpretive efforts over many months. The essential characteristic of these transferences was that the patients consistently directed accusations at me for my allegedly frustrating, aggressive, invasive, cold, or depreciatory behavior toward them, without any possibility of clarifying the fantastic or exaggerated nature of these claims, an expression of severe transference regression in otherwise nonborderline or psychotic patients. After painstaking investigation of each instance that, in the patients' experiences, seemed to warrant such accusations, I was unable to "clear the decks," especially since it was demonstrably impossible to refer these experiences back to their antecedents; I decided to confront the patients with my total disagreement on the matter of mistreatment. I stressed, at the same time, that my intention was not to convince them of my position but to take up the incompatibility of our experiences of reality at such points as the subject for analytic exploration. This approach permitted me gradually to map out what amounted to a veritable loss of reality testing in the transference, a "psychotic nucleus" in the transference, and to trace this incompatibility of realities to its genetic antecedents. Obviously, this approach requires careful exploration by the analyst of his or her countertransference disposition at critical points in the treatment.

10.

Narcissism

Narcissistic psychopathology in couples ranges widely. One couple makes conscious efforts to maintain an unrealistic public image of their relationship as one of total mutual gratification. Another couple unconsciously colludes in the ruthless exploitation of one partner by the other. Psychoanalytic investigation shows that the proverbial image of a narcissistic partner matched with a masochistic partner does not necessarily coincide with the character pathologies of each. More generally, a partner's unconscious identification with dissociated and projected aspects of him or herself, together with the partner's mutual induction of complementary roles by means of projective identification, may result in a role distribution that conveys an erroneous impression of each partner's psychopathology.

An inconsiderate husband's self-centered exploitation of his wife, for example, may suggest significant narcissistic psychopathology in him and victimization in his wife. An exploration of the couple's conscious and unconscious interactions, however, reveals that she is unconsciously provoking him and projecting onto him her own sadistic superego. The intactness, depth, and commitment of the husband's relationships to others reveal him to be predominantly infantile rather than narcissistic. We thus have to deal with two problems: narcissistic psychopathology in one or both partners and the "interchange" of personality aspects of both, bringing about the couple's pathological relationship that does not correspond to the individual pathology of the partners.

Characteristics of Narcissistic Love Relations

The psychoanalytic study of the love relations of the narcissistic personality might begin with a comparison between couples in which one or both partners suffer from narcissistic personality disorder and couples showing no such signs. A person with nonpathological narcissism has the capacity to fall in love and to maintain a love relationship over an extended period of time. The most severe cases of narcissistic personality do not have the capacity to fall in love, which is indeed pathognomonic of pathological narcissism. And even narcissistic personalities who are able to fall in love for brief periods of time show remarkable differences from those with the normal capacity to fall in love.

When the narcissistic personality falls in love, the idealization of the loved object may center on physical beauty as a source of admiration or on power, wealth, or fame as attributes to be admired and unconsciously incorporated as part of the self.

The oedipal resonance of all love relations causes the narcissistic person unconsciously to attempt a relationship dominated by aggression as much as or more than by love because of deep frustration and resentment from the past, a past that in fantasy will be magically overcome by sexual gratification from the new object. Oedipal rivalry, jealousy, and insecurity are compounded by preoedipal aggression displaced to the oedipal realm. Narcissistic patients evince an unconscious fear of the love object, related to projected aggression: they also show a remarkable absence of internal freedom to become interested in the personality of the other. Their sexual excitement is dominated by unconscious envy of the other gender, by deep resentment because of what has been experienced as a teasing withholding of early gratification, by greed and voracity, and by the hope of appropriating what was withheld in the past in order to eliminate longing for it.

For the narcissistic partner, life proceeds in isolation; dependency upon the other is feared insofar as it represents acknowledgment of both envy and gratitude for the dependency; dependency is replaced by self-righteous demandingness and frustration when demands are not met. Resentments build up and are difficult to undo in moments of intimacy; they are more easily resolved by splitting disparate experiences from each other, maintaining peace at the cost of fragmenting the relationship. In a worst-case scenario, a stifling sense of imprisonment and persecution by the other evolves. Unacknowledged and intolerable aspects of the self are projected onto the partner to protect an idealized self-image. Unconscious provocation of the partner to comply with the projected aspects of the self is matched by attacks on and rejection of the partner thus misperceived.

The symbolic incorporation of the admired features of the other may serve as narcissistic gratification: a narcissistic woman who has married a famous public figure may continue to bask in his public prominence. In the privacy of the home, however, she may experience unmitigated boredom, aside from unconscious conflicts around envy. The absence of joint values precludes opening an area of new interests that would provide a new view of the world or other relationships. The absence of curiosity about the other, a relationship in which immediate behaviors are to be reacted to rather than reflect concern for the other's internal reality—a central problem of the narcissistic personality related to underlying identity diffusion and lack of capacity for empathy in depth with others—close the door to understanding the other's life. Sources of gratification are lacking, and boredom, failure to contain aroused rage, chronic frustration, and a sense of being imprisoned by the relationship prevail, in addition to the unavoidable activation of unconscious conflicts from the past and the outbreak of frustration and aggression in the couple's intimate relationship. Most dramatically, in the sexual realm, unconscious envy of the other transforms the idealization of the other's body into its devaluation, fosters the transformation of sexual gratification into the sense of having successfully invaded and incorporated the other, eliminates the richness of the primitive object relations activated in normal polymorphous perverse sexuality, and descends into boredom.

The question can be raised whether narcissistic personalities can love only themselves. In my view (1984), the issue is not whether the investment is in the self or the object or the self representation as opposed to object representations. The issue is the difference between the kind of self that is invested; whether it has the capacity to integrate love and hatred under the dominance of love, or whether it is a pathological grandiose self. As Laplanche (1976) suggested in reference to Freud's (1914) essay on narcissism, both anaclitic and narcissistic love relations imply an object relationship. And as van der Waals (1965) observed, it is not that narcissists love only themselves and nobody else but that they love themselves as badly as they love others.

Let us consider the interaction of narcissistic and object-related aspects of ordinary love relations. Put another way, what in a stable love relationship is the connection between self-gratification and enjoyment of and commitment to the other? Insofar as the selected partner reflects one's own ideals, an eminently "narcissistic" quality undoubtedly permeates falling and being in love. And insofar as there is a conscious and unconscious search for complementarity—ranging from the admiration of and gratification from what the other can enjoy and tolerate in himself or herself and one cannot, to overcoming the limitations of one's own gender by establishing a "bisexual" union with a partner—even such complementarity, one might say, serves "narcissistic" purposes. At the same time, insofar as the other provides gratification of both nurturing and oedipal needs and offers gratitude for what is received, the love relationship is obviously "object-related." It has altruistic features that integrate in myriad ways self-centeredness and self-sacrifice, dedication to the other, and gratification of the self. In summary, normal narcissism and object relatedness complement each other.

For clinical purposes, what I have said implies the need to consider separately the behavior pattern at which a couple's relationship has stabilized or become frozen and the personality structure of each of the partners. The presence of a narcissistic personality disorder in one or both partners undoubtedly colors the nature of their relationship and in some cases the resolution of deep, long-term marital conflict will depend on modification of the personality structure of one or both partners. More frequently, however, the resolution of pathological interaction through psychoanalysis and psychotherapy—or separation and divorce—will reveal how much of what appeared to be narcissistic pathology in one or both partners was the result of unconscious collusion in mutual exploitiveness and aggression derived from other conflicts.

Two Clinical Illustrations

The first example is of a subtle but persisting conflict between a husband with an apparently narcissistic but in reality obsessive-compulsive personality structure and a wife with depressive-masochistic personality features. He seemed cold, distant, and inconsiderate of her needs, and she was silently suffering from his excessive expectations. He was the son of an overprotective, narcissistic mother whose concerns with order and the danger of infections and physical illness dominated his childhood. His amiable father let his wife run the household. The husband had been strongly attracted to his wife's warm and relaxed nature, and amused and relieved by her somewhat disorderly ways of dealing with things. She, the daughter of a dominating but disorderly and neglectful mother and an affectionate but frequently absent father, had been impressed by her husband's stress on order and cleanliness. But after several years of marriage, the husband's obsessive need for order and cleanliness increased in parallel with his wife's sloppiness. She harshly accused him of overloading her with tasks while neglecting his own responsibilities; he accused her of willfully trying to provoke him by her careless way of running the house.

The confrontations gradually subsided because the husband "gave up." In fact, by withdrawing and absenting himself, he unconsciously fostered his wife's disorder. He gradually separated his interests and belongings from hers, became withdrawn, and experienced her as indifferent and neglectful of him while also feeling guilty for his neglect of her. Later, in the course of his psychoanalytic treatment, it emerged that he was resenting her as if she were an indifferent mother while unconsciously identifying with his own father, who had left control of the household to mother. He thereby restricted his own authority and gratification in what in many ways might have been a very satisfactory marriage. His wife, in turn, experienced him more and more as cold, indifferent, and self-centered, and herself as the victim of a traditional patriarchal husband.

Individual psychoanalytic treatment, together with exploration of their marital conflict in a time-limited joint psychoanalytic psychotherapy by another therapist, revealed their unconscious collusion. The understanding of that collusion led to the remarkable disappearance of what had initially appeared to be severely narcissistic qualities in the husband and significant masochistic qualities in the wife.

The second case centers on developments in the psychoanalytic treatment of a man with severe narcissistic pathology who consulted me because he could not maintain a relationship with a woman that would give him emotional as well as sexual gratification. Mr. L., a successful architect in his early forties, had already been through three marriages and divorces with women whom he described, in retrospect, as dedicated to him, attractive, and intelligent. In fact, he had had gratifying sexual relationships with all three before marriage. Once married, he completely lost sexual interest in them. The marital relationships evolved into a kind of "sibling friendship" that was increasingly unsatisfactory to both partners, eventually leading to divorce. Mr. L. had not wanted children; he feared they would interfere with his life-style and freedom.

Mr. L.'s professional position and administrative skills permitted him to spend much of his time in an endless search for new experiences with women. These experiences were of two distinct types—sexual ones that were intense but of brief duration because he quickly lost interest in the woman, and platonic or largely platonic ones with women he used as confidantes or counselors or friends.

In the early part of the treatment, the most important characteristic over many months was Mr. L.'s strong defense against deepening the transference relationship, which only gradually could be understood as a defense against unconscious envy of the analyst as a married man who was able to enjoy a relationship that was both emotionally and sexually satisfying. Mr. L. spent an enormous amount of time in the sessions ridiculing friends who had been married for many years and what he considered their ludicrous attempts to convince him that theirs was a happy marital relationship. He triumphantly told me about all his sexual exploits, only to fall back into a sense of despair because of his incapacity to maintain a sexual relationship with a woman who would matter to him emotionally. At such times he felt strongly inclined to end the treatment because it was not helping him to overcome this problem. He gradually became aware that, although he hoped that I did not suffer from the same problem he did, the idea that I might have a good marital relationship filled him with a sense of inferiority and humiliation. He then began to tolerate conscious feelings of envy of me.

This gradually increasing tolerance of this envy shifted his relationship in the transference into one similar to what he had with male friends, a "men only" relationship of honesty and commitment, in contrast to the assumption that women had to be taken sexually and quickly escaped from because otherwise they would become exploitive and controlling. Homosexual fantasies in the transference now reflected his sense that only men could be trusted, and a picture of aggressive and exploitive women emerged. Still later, a renewed tendency to compare himself with me took the form of fantasies that I had children to whom I could be a giving and protective father while he was in danger of not ever having any children.

For the first time, an emotional reliving of aspects of his past emerged, with memories of the constant strife between his parents, his sense that they were always suspicious of each other, and his many futile attempts to mediate. Mr. L.'s two older sisters had long since abandoned their relationship with the parents. It was Mr. L. who continued to attend to his parents' needs, attempting to settle their disputes and getting himself embroiled in violent verbal exchanges and accusations involving all three of them.

Mr. L. conveyed the impression that neither of his parents had ever had the capacity or perhaps even the intention to be interested in him. His initial attitude of bravado and depreciation of people who were engaged in empty "psychology talk" now shifted to a growing awareness of the frustration of his needs in childhood and adolescence to be listened to and respected. It became evident that he had suspected me of wanting him to marry so that I could demonstrate my superiority as a therapist; he had never believed that the purpose of treatment was to help him find his own solutions.

Within this context, the following developments took place: Mr. L. had become increasingly interested in a young architect whose behavior was the subject of ironic comments in their professional circle, but with whom Mr. L. had established a sexual relationship he found very gratifying. He described Miss F. as aggressive, moody, arbitrary in her expectations and demands, and so openly controlling and manipulative that he could feel reassured that she was not trying to exploit him. Over the next few months, Miss F.'s behavior toward him and the past attitude of Mr. L.'s mother seemed to coincide in uncanny ways. Mr. L. insisted that he did not love Miss F. and that he quite openly told her that he felt nothing for her except enormous satisfaction with their sexual relationship. Miss F. seemed to tolerate his declarations of indifference in ways that raised the question in my mind (but not in Mr. L.'s) as to whether she was masochistic or calculating. My efforts to interpret in the transference how Mr. L. might be defending himself against similar concerns about Miss F. brought about his gradual awareness not only of how much he enjoyed the sadistic nature of his treatment of Miss F. and her tolerance of it. He also recognized that even if she was trying to manipulate him, his feeling so much in control of their relationship gave him a sense of excitement.

A new theme then emerged in the treatment: namely, Mr. L.'s fantasy that if he really wanted to marry again and have children of his own, it would be the beginning of old age and death; only a playboy existence of carefree sex and lack of responsibility guaranteed eternal youth. Now his adolescent way of presenting himself in the session (an excessively and almost inappropriately juvenile style of dress and manners) became the subject of analytic exploration; it emerged as a protective effort to avoid the sense of doom connected with the idea of adulthood. As revealed in a series of loosely connected dreams, the fantasy gradually crystallized in his mind that he would be able to have children with women who were married to somebody else, or who, after divorcing him, would permit him only casual contacts with his children.

A condensation of his fear of aggressive, frustrating, dominating, and manipulative women, on the one hand, and of doing better than his henpecked, distant, and aloof father (and a related despair over being able to compete with me as an idealized version of an unavailable father model) now pervaded the hours. In a sudden acting out, Mr. L. decided to marry Miss F. Shortly after their marriage, she became pregnant. The relationship with her continued to be tumultuous and chaotic, but now, for the first time in his life, he was totally engaged in this relationship without internal pressures for sexual affairs with other women. He was himself surprised at this development and retrospectively realized that one of his fantasies had been to engage once more in an unhappy and failing marriage that he could then place at my doorstep, confirming the failure of our analytic work—and of me as oedipal father. At the same time, however, there was also a competitive oedipal meaning to his daring to have a child, although enacted in the context of a marriage much like that of his parents.

What was most striking in the relationship with his wife was that Mr. L., who had originally treated her in rather derogatory and demeaning ways, now became strangely submissive to her, although he suspected her of wanting to divorce him in order to obtain control over part of his assets. Mr. L. himself was astonished that he, a previously independent, happy, and successful playboy, should now be so much under the control of a woman his friends perceived as both aggressive and immature. Mr. L., in short, had managed to reproduce the relationship between his father and mother and had shifted from sexual promiscuity to a sadomasochistic relationship that continued to be sexually gratifying and emotionally invested.

In his analytic sessions, Mr. L. was taken aback by this change and gradually became aware that if he really thought his wife loved him he would be willing to trust her and commit his life to her. The combination of oedipal guilt (establishing a relationship with a woman that would be more satisfactory than that of his parents) and guilt over early sadistic impulses toward a frustrating and unavailable mother now became the major subject matter of the analytic hours.

It was, in short, as if the sadistic, omnipotent control in his behavior toward women had shifted and was being enacted by his wife, and his regression to a childlike, pouting dependency had replaced his narcissistic aloofness. The domineering behavior his wife had evinced before their marriage now grossly increased, unconsciously fueled by his provocative behavior, his induction by means of projective identification of his mother in her. Working through a shift into a deeper level of transference regression, in which he perceived me as a powerful, threatening, sadistic oedipal father, eventually permitted him to overcome his masochistic submission to his wife, in the context of losing his fear over asserting himself as an adult man. Eventually, he was able to normalize their relationship, and their sadomasochistic patterns of interaction subsided: he could now combine sexual and tender feelings in a stable marital relationship.

Dynamics of Narcissistic Pathology

Most frequently, the narcissistic personality enacts his or her pathological grandiose self while projecting a devalued part of the self onto the partner, whose unending admiration confirms that grandiose self. Less often, the narcissistic personality projects the pathological grandiose self onto the partner and enacts a relationship between this grandiose self and its projected reflection. The partner in such cases is merely a vehicle for a relationship between aspects of the self. Typically, an idealized partner and an "appendix" or satellite to that ideal object constitute the couple in enactments or fantasy, or they form an unconscious "reflection" in which each partner replicates the other. They can also, in complementing each other, jointly reconstitute a fantasied and lost grandiose ideal unit.

In a review of the essential dynamics underlying these defensive maneuvers, of central importance in the unconscious conflicts is preoedipally determined envy—that is, a specific form of rage and resentment against a needed object that is experienced as frustrating and withholding. What is desired thus becomes a source of suffering as well. Developing in reaction to this suffering is a conscious or unconscious wish to destroy, to spoil, to appropriate by force what is being withheld—specifically, what is most admired and wished for. The tragedy of the narcissistic personality is that angry appropriation and greedy extraction of what is denied and envied do not lead to satisfaction because the unconscious hatred of what is needed spoils what is incorporated; the subject always ends up feeling empty and frustrated.

By the same token, given that the goodness of what the other has to offer is a source of envy, dependency upon a loved object becomes impossible and must be denied; the narcissistic personality needs to be admired rather than loved. The admiration of the other supports and reconfirms self-esteem, the self-idealization of the pathological grandiose self. The admiration of others replaces the normally protective and self-esteem-regulating functions of the weakened and distorted superego, particularly the ego ideal.

Narcissistic people need to be admired and unconsciously extract supplies of admiration from others as a revengeful defense against envy; projecting these same needs onto their partner, they fear being exploited and "robbed" of what they have. They therefore cannot tolerate their partner's dependency on them. They experience the ordinary reciprocity of human relations as exploitative and invasive. Because of conflicts around unconscious envy, they cannot experience gratitude for what they receive from the other, whose very capacity to give freely they may envy. Their lack of gratitude precludes the strengthening of the capacity for loving appreciation of love received.

In severe instances, the devaluation of others suffers a regressive "analization" (Chasseguet-Smirgel 1984b, 1989), an unconscious wish to symbolically transform all love and values into excrement, which may lead to unconscious denial of the differences between genders and generations (all differentiations are denied and devalued) in order to avoid envy of the other gender and of other generations. Unconscious envy of the oedipal couple may underlie envy of the marital partner; this need to destroy the couple derives more from primitive aggression against the oedipal couple than from oedipal guilt. That unconscious hatred and envy of the good relationship between the parental couple can be turned into destructive wishes against the individual's own functioning as part of a couple is one of the most dramatic characteristics of narcissistic pathology.

These unconscious conflicts may usually be traced back to early pathology in the mother-infant relationship. Oral aggression caused, triggered, or reinforced by cold and rejecting mothers or rejecting and overstimulating mothers, by severe and chronic early neglect, exploitation by a narcissistic mother oblivious to the emotional needs and the internal life of her infant, and secondary reinforcement by conflicts with father—or the absence of a compensating availability of father—may lead to intense envy and hatred of mother, which eventually affects the unconscious relationship to both parents and creates pathologically intense envy of the love relationship of the oedipal couple.

In men, whose early relation to mother continues to color their relations to women throughout life, pathological hatred and envy of women may become a powerful unconscious force, intensifying their oedipal conflicts. They may experience mother as sexually teasing and withholding, owing to the transformation of early oral frustrations into a kind of (projected) sexual aggression. That teasing image of mother in turn intensifies the aggressive components of sexual excitement and fosters dissociation between erotic excitement and tenderness. These men experience sexual desire for a woman as a repetition of the early teasing by mother, and thus they unconsciously hate the desired woman. The hatred may destroy the capacity for sexual excitement and result in sexual inhibition. In less severe cases, a defensive idealization of women's sexual attractiveness leads to an intensified search for sexual stimulation, excitement, and gratification, quickly followed by unconscious spoiling of the sexual experience, devaluation of the idealized woman, and boredom. Intense and defensive idealization of women and the rapid devaluation of them as sexual objects may result in sexual promiscuity.

A broad spectrum of sexual pathology derives from these dynamics. Some narcissistic men present severe sexual inhibition, a fear of being rejected and ridiculed by women, related to the projection onto women of their own unconscious hatred of them. This fear of women may also lead to intense revulsion against the female genitals—a convergence of preoedipal envy and oedipal castration. Or a radical split may occur: some women are idealized and all sexual feelings for them are denied, and other women are perceived as purely genital objects with whom sexual freedom and enjoyment are possible at the expense of tenderness or romantic idealization. This leads to a self-defeating devaluation of sexual intimacy and an endless search for new sexual partners.

Some narcissistic men may be able to maintain tender relationships with women on whom they depend as long as they unconsciously devalue them as sexual partners. It is striking that some severely inhibited narcissistic men, fearful of women, possibly experiencing impotence as a direct expression of that fear, in the course of treatment moderate their fear of women and then become sexually promiscuous. They are acting out both the search for a loving relationship and the need to split off from that search their unconscious aggression toward women. In contrast, narcissistic men who are sexually promiscuous from early adolescence frequently present a gradual deterioration of their sexual life as the defensive idealization of women in brief infatuations repeatedly breaks down. Their new sexual encounters appear more and more to be repetitions of previous ones; the erosion of defensive idealization and cumulative disappointments in the sexual experience may lead to a secondary deterioration in their sexual life and impotence, which brings them into treatment only when they reach their forties or fifties.

In both genders, narcissistic personalities frequently have the unconscious fantasy of being both genders at the same time, thus denying the need to envy the other gender (Rosenfeld 1964, 1971, 1975; Grunberger 1971). This fantasy fosters the search for sexual partners along various routes. Some male narcissistic patients search for women who unconsciously represent mirror images of themselves, "heterosexual twins," thus completing themselves unconsciously with the genitals and the corresponding psychological implications of the other gender without having to accept the reality of another, different, autonomous person. In some cases, however, unconscious envy of the genitals of the other gender is such that the devaluation of the envied sexual characteristics leads to an asexual twin relationship. This can be destructive, since it carries a severe sexual inhibition.

Sometimes the unconscious wish to acquire the characteristics of both genders leads to a relationship with a man or woman who is unconsciously devalued except for his or her sexual complementarity to the patient. Some physically attractive narcissistic patients of both genders who depend heavily on admiration from others may select an ugly partner to highlight their own attractiveness. Others select a "twin" so that the public appearance of the beautiful couple becomes a relatively reliable source of gratification of narcissistic needs. To select a woman whom other men envy may gratify both narcissistic and homosexual strivings.

The unconscious hatred of women (and fear of them owing to the projection of that hatred) is an important source of narcissistically determined homosexuality in men. The selection of another man as a homosexual twin, a defensive idealization of the penis of the other as a replica of the patient's own penis and an unconscious reassurance that he/they are no longer dependent on women's genitality, may effectively protect against envy of the other gender and even permit idealized, if desexualized, relations with women as well.

A major source of conflicts for narcissistic patients in a heterosexual or homosexual relationship, which may emerge only gradually but then dominates the interactions and eventually destroys the relationship, is the protection of the twinship fantasy. The partner has to fulfill the patient's ideal but not be better than the patient because that would trigger envy; nor can the partner be inferior to the patient because that would trigger devaluation and the destruction of the relationship. Therefore, the partner, by means of the defense mechanism of omnipotent control, is "forced" to become exactly as the patient needs him or her to be, thus restricting the freedom and autonomy of the other, in addition to implying that the patient is unable to appreciate what is unique or different about the partner. Not surprisingly, patients who restrict the freedom of their partners are most afraid of being restricted or imprisoned by the other—projective identification at work.

In the relatively milder cases of male narcissistic patients' love relations, the typical "madonna-prostitute" dichotomy from male adolescence is maintained as a lifetime pattern. Insofar as this pattern fits with the culturally tolerated and fostered double morality in patriarchal societies, male narcissistic pathology is culturally reinforced—as is female masochistic pathology in love relations.

Although sexual boredom becomes prevalent in male narcissistic personalities over the years, some continue to use sexual encounters for playing out intense ambivalence toward women, with a simultaneous search for sexual gratification, sadistic revenge, even compulsive masochistic repetition of the frustration mother caused: narcissistic and masochistic pathology converge.

The Don Juan syndrome reflects a broad spectrum of male narcissistic pathology. At one end, Don Juan might be a man who desperately needs to seduce women and is driven to a sexual relationship that results in frustrating or humiliating the woman of his momentary choice; the seduction is almost consciously, manipulatively aggressive, and abandoning her is a pleasurable relief. Or Don Juan's intense compulsive search for new adventures stems from an idealization of women and the wish to find one who will not disappoint him.

At the healthier end of this spectrum, Don Juan has a mixture of narcissistic and infantile traits, a man-child with effeminate qualities who seduces women precisely on the basis that he lacks threatening masculinity. He unconsciously denies the envy of, fear of, and rivalry with the powerful father by asserting that his "little penis" is fully satisfactory to mother (Chasseguet-Smirgel 1984b), and his sexual adventures with women gratify the fantasy that he, the little boy, is mother's favorite and all mother needs. Braunschweig and Fain (1971) have described how this Don Juan never fails to find a complementary woman whose unconscious hatred of the powerful father leads her to idealize the nonthreatening, childlike man.

The male narcissistic personality's defensive idealization of women, expressed in intense if transitory infatuations, often exerts a powerful attraction for women, particularly those who have significant masochistic potential or who are insecure about their attractiveness as women. Narcissistic women may also be attracted by men whose sense of superiority and grandiosity gratifies their own need for narcissistic completion with what we might call a heterosexual twin. The genitality without paternity offered by narcissistic men who unconsciously cannot identify with the protective, concerned, procreative aspects of a paternal identity may be reassuring to narcissistic women for whom parental functions may also represent an important unconscious threat.

Transitory idealization and rapid devaluation of men may underlie sexual promiscuity in narcissistic women. The traditional patriarchal society reinforces sexual promiscuity in men but repudiates it in women. Patriarchal mores may divert narcissistic women's hatred of men into an exploitive relationship to marriage and children. Feminism, paradoxically, may foster sexual promiscuity in women with narcissistic pathology who identify with an aggressively perceived male sexuality.

If, because of its intensity, the displacement of aggression from mother to father does not resolve the little girl's ambivalence toward mother, fear and hatred of mother may lead her to search for an idealized substitute mother, which usually means disappointment and resentment. By the same token, the search for a more gratifying relationship with men may turn into an unconscious identification with men—that is, a secondary denial of this threatening dependency—and evolve into a narcissistic woman's homosexual identification with men: she searches for a homosexual relation with women, onto whom the patient may project her own dependent needs. Sometimes narcissistically motivated homosexuality in women may gratify the unconscious fantasy of being both genders at the same time, deny dependency on the hated and envied father, and reverse the dangerous dependency on mother.

An unconscious identification with a narcissistic, cold, and rejecting mother may be expressed in a controlled exhibitionism and seductiveness toward men, an effort to dominate and exploit them, which gratifies the woman's sexual needs and protects her from envy.

Narcissistic women with some frequency accept a stable relationship with a man whom they consider "the very best," searching in an unconscious heterosexual twinship relation for a compromise solution to unconscious envy of men. This may lead to what appears to be a masochistic relationship, in the sense that these women tend to devalue a man as soon as he responds to them; they remain fixated on unavailable men whose very unavailability permits their idealization to remain unchallenged and protects them from being devalued. Some severely narcissistic women may maintain long-term self-destructive allegiances to extremely narcissistic men whose power, fame, or unusual talents give them the appearance of an ideal male figure. Other narcissistic women, socially more successful, may actually identify fully with such idealized men, unconsciously experience themselves as the true inspiration of these men, and may end up running their lives.

Some narcissistic women combine the search for an ideal man with an equally intense devaluation of their partner, which leads them to gravitate from one famous man to another; others, however, find that to be the power behind the throne gratifies narcissistic needs and compensates for the unconscious envy of men. Whereas sexual promiscuity in men is largely of a narcissistic type, sexual promiscuity in women may be of either narcissistic or masochistic origin.

Narcissistic women may express their pathology in their relationship with their children. Some show an unwillingness to have a child because they are afraid of a child's dependency which they would unconsciously experience as greedily exploitive and restrictive. Others love the children as long as they are totally dependent—that is, as long as they constitute a narcissistic extension of mother's body or personality. Or mother focuses on a child's unusual attractiveness, which brings admiration from third parties, but she shows very little interest in the child's internal life. Such a mother fosters the transmission of narcissistic pathology from one generation to another. Men may present the same reluctance to have children, an incapacity to invest in them, a deep indifference except as the child gratifies their own needs: the traditional patriarchal society, in sharply differentiating the roles of father and mother, has obscured the pathology in the relationship of narcissistic men to their children. Men leave the care of children to their wives, and their own lack of investment in their children is masked.

Another significant narcissistic symptom is the absence of the capacity for jealousy, which often indicates an inability to sufficiently commit to another, rendering infidelity irrelevant. The absence of jealousy may also suggest an unconscious fantasy of being so superior to all rivals that the partner's unfaithfulness is unthinkable.

Paradoxically, however, jealousy may emerge after the fact: a strong degree of jealousy may reflect a narcissistic lesion that a narcissistic patient experiences when a partner abandons him or her for somebody else. Narcissistic jealousy is particularly striking when the partner was previously neglected or treated with contempt. Narcissistic types of jealousy may, in triggering aggression, worsen the endangered relationship. At the same time, however, they also reflect a capacity for investment in another and for an entrance into the oedipal world. As Klein (1957) pointed out, envy is typical of preoedipal, particularly oral, aggression, but jealousy dominates oedipal aggression. Jealousy arising from a real or fantasied betrayal can trigger a wish for revenge and frequently takes the form of reverse triangulation: the unconscious or conscious wish to be the object of competition between two persons of the other gender.

In selecting a partner, narcissistic individuals are crippled by their incapacity to evaluate another person in depth. This deficit makes for a possibly dangerous combination: the partner's "ideal" qualities may become devalued because of unconscious envy while the reality of the partner's personality may be experienced as an invasion, a constraint, an imposition, which the patient interprets as exploitation and which, once again, will evoke envy. A partner who has been selected because he or she admires the qualities of the narcissistic person may be rapidly devalued as that admiration is taken for granted. In contrast, a narcissistic person's encounter with a partner who is capable of a loving relationship may evoke intense unconscious envy precisely because of this capacity—one that the narcissist knows he or she lacks.

To the degree that the narcissistic person does have some superego development and experiences guilt for not being able to reciprocate love received, he or she may have an increased sense of inferiority, which triggers secondary efforts to defend against such guilt feelings by searching for defects in the partner that would justify failure to reciprocate. Two possibilities thus exist: inadequate superego development fosters indifference, lack of concern, and callousness, which distances the couple; or the existence of some superego functioning may result in the projection of guilt feelings onto the partner, which introduces a paranoid quality into the relationship.

Sustained Relations in Narcissistic Partners

Frequently, a couple in which both partners have narcissistic personalities may find an arrangement for living together that gratifies mutual dependency needs and provides a frame for social and economic survival. The relationship may be emotionally empty, but varying degrees of mutual support, exploitiveness, and/or convenience may stabilize it. Sharing conscious expectations of their social roles, financial well-being, adaptation to the cultural environment, and interest in the children may cement the relationship. Frequently, however, unconscious object relationships from the past are activated. In a replay of the relation between a frustrating, cold, rejecting mother and a resentful, envious, revengeful child, mutual projective identification may destroy sexual life, foster the enactment of triangular relations, and threaten the relationship to the surrounding social world. Unconscious competition between the partners may destroy the relationship when one or the other meets with unusual success or failure.

As I stated earlier, intense, overriding preoedipal envy affects the entrance into the oedipal situation. The unconscious envy of mother becomes the unconscious envy of the oedipal couple. The narcissist's own marriage becomes unconsciously a replica of the oedipal couple that must be destroyed. Unconscious envy and guilt over replacing the parents in the oedipal situation converge. The "analization" of the oedipal relationship—that is, the regressive spoiling of it, and its destruction by unconsciously, symbolically, submerging it in excrement—may be expressed by a relentless effort to destroy everything that is good and valuable in the other person, in the self, and in the relationship (Chasseguet-Smirgel 1984b).

Conflict between the narcissistic forces active in destroying the relationship and the couple's desperate search for a road back to each other are usually played out in their sexual relationship. Narcissistic devaluation may have eliminated the capacity to find the partner erotically exciting. And should a sexual relationship still exist, the capacity for transitory excitement and the possibility of having sex may not protect against the couple's awareness of their distance. Indeed, repeated sexual

encounters under such circumstances may constitute a traumatic complication and result in a worsening of the relationship.

But if the idealization that is part of a normal sexual relationship is
still sufficiently available so that the mutual experience of sexual excitement and orgasm is also felt and communicated as a search for merging,
forgiveness, and dependency, an expression of gratitude and love in addition to a search for pleasure, then some hope may crystallize around such
encounters. The survival of the idealization that is part of a love relationship may take the form, first, of idealization of the other's body surface.
In fact, one of the early effects of tolerating ambivalence—the recognition
of one's own aggression in relation to the other and the beginning experience of guilt and concern over it—may be a revival of sustained appreciation of and responsiveness to the other's body.

One of the most difficult narcissistic object relations is represented by
the mutual attraction of patients with the syndrome of malignant narcissism (Kernberg 1989b), severe destructive and self-destructive strivings
and a tendency toward paranoid and/or antisocial behavior. Insofar as severe, diffuse self-directed aggression and narcissistic and primitive masochistic psychopathology may combine, there may be different degrees to
which each partner exploits or mistreats the other and neglects and mistreats him- or herself in the process.

For example, a woman with chronic suicidal tendencies and an incapacity to fall in love or experience any commitment in depth to another
person became attracted to a man whose interest in her provided a protection against her terrible sense of loneliness and whose lack of demands
and willingness to gratify hers made the relationship comfortable for her.
At the same time, however, the man grossly neglected his physical health,
although he had a potentially life-threatening illness that required constant medical care. Their self-destructive patterns of work, and their
shared indifference to the long-range consequences of inadequate job performance, further united them in what on psychoanalytic exploration
turned out to be an unconscious fascination with a heterosexual replica
of their own grandiose and self-destructive selves. Only psychoanalytic
psychotherapy for the woman eventually changed this mutually destructive alliance.

Perhaps the most dramatic illustration of the condensation of oedipal
and preoedipal conflicts in the determination of a narcissistic love relationship is the development of reverse triangulation. Typically the man
is successful in a particular social, cultural, or professional milieu, married to a woman generally recognized as exemplary and acknowledged as
such by her husband. There may be children, and both parents have a

caring, responsible attitude toward them. The man also has a mistress, usually of a different social, cultural, or professional milieu. The women know about each other and appear to suffer under this situation, and there are multiple opportunities for public embarrassment as the man's involvement with both women impinges on his business, professional, social, or political life. The man himself seems unhappy and distraught, oscillating between dedication to one woman or the other.

Friends, social acquaintances, business partners, and mental health professionals counsel treatment, and our man often enters treatment, thus demonstrating his good will and good intentions to deal with a situation that is apparently beyond his control. In the course of psychoanalytic investigation, what typically emerges is severe narcissistic psychopathology with a total split in the man's relationships with women. In the concrete interaction with one or both of them, love mostly dominates, but aggression is subtly expressed in the sadistic element of his abandoning both women, usually obscured by intensely experienced or professed guilt.

The original oedipal competition for mother between son and father here has been reversed; the man is now the object of competition between two women, the seductively childlike son. Splitting the image of mother into a maternal and desexualized wife and a sexually exciting but emotionally devalued mistress differs from more purely oedipally determined splitting. The preoedipal determinants emerge in the childlike, dependent, subtle exploitative relationship of the narcissistic man to both women, his sense of entitlement and indignation when their needs do not correspond totally with his, and the incapacity to sustain either of these relationships for an extended period of time without a compensatory relationship with other women. This same pattern may be observed in women who need to be courted simultaneously and constantly by two or more men.

Sometimes these conditions induce a genuine sense of despair and a wish to resolve the situation in the one who must hold onto two members of the other gender. More often, however, external social pressures may lead these patients to treatment; the prognosis, in my experience, depends largely on whether treatment is attempted as an unconscious alibi for perpetuating the relationships, or whether it represents an effort to escape from imprisonment. Under optimal circumstances, because of the anxiety and guilt over frustrating and implicitly attacking two women who love him, the narcissistic patient is genuinely interested in obtaining treatment.

Severe narcissistic pathology in one or both partners usually requires psychoanalytic treatment, in contrast to cases in which the couple's conflict per se exceeds or overshadows narcissistic difficulties in one or both partners. The motivation for treatment is a crucial factor because the difficult and lengthy analyses these patients require, the extent to which the couple's pathology can be fully reenacted and worked through in the transference, are, in my experience, the most important prognostic features. Many narcissistic patients need to experience the failure of repeated idealizations and love relations before becoming sufficiently concerned for themselves to be motivated for analytic treatment. Hence treatment of patients in their forties and fifties has a better prognosis than treatment of younger people. Severely narcissistic patients, however, require early treatment to prevent destruction of their work life as well as their love relations.

I have throughout contrasted the relationship of couples under the impact of narcissistic pathology in one or both partners with couples who have minimal narcissistic pathology. Highlighting the effects of narcissistic pathology introduces the risk of overemphasizing its destructive effects, just as highlighting nonpathological relations may exaggerate the ideal or idealized aspect of a love relationship. Let me complete my description by pointing to the many ways in which the pathologic and the nonpathologic intermingle. Repeated encounters with the negative consequences of narcissistic pathology can have positive effects, and interactions between partners that run counter to unconscious expectations and repetitions of past conflicts can be healing, neutralizing the effects of projective identifications and omnipotent control as well as repetitive self-defeating behaviors.

In general, acknowledging ambivalence is the most common denominator of a patient's growing awareness of his or her contributions to conflicts and frustrations. Improvement is characterized by profound mourning, during which the patient can acknowledge and work through aggression, the wish to undo its effects and to repair the damage it has done in reality or in fantasy.

Such healing processes can also occur in ordinary life outside treatment situations. A narcissistic woman with a long history of exploitive relations with powerful men and a self-centered and self-aggrandizing lifestyle was able to have a child after years of unsuccessful efforts to become pregnant. When she found out that her son had an illness that would end in his death during early childhood, rage at what she sensed as a cruel and unfair destiny shifted into a total dedication to that child. Giving his care priority over her social, professional, and personal life, she found herself at peace with herself and the world for the first time in her life. Her total dedication reflected both a narcissistic investment in him and what might be called an altruistic surrender with masochistic implications. The condensation of narcissistic and masochistic features in self-sacrifice influenced her relationships with the other important persons in her life as well and brought her to revise radically her attitude toward men. It also freed her from the need to maintain an idealized view of herself as a basis for her self-esteem. Following the death of her child, she was able to engage herself, for the first time, in a relationship with a man characterized by mutuality and commitment.

Sometimes the selection of a partner includes efforts to heal an individual's pathology. Unconsciously, a man with narcissistic self-aggrandizement, a cynical devaluation of commitments to ethical values, and the conviction that the world is hedonistic and self-centered may select a woman with a deep commitment to ethical values and a profound appreciation of such values in others. In being attracted to such a woman and tempted to trample on her values as part of a repetition compulsion of his narcissistic conflicts, he may also be enacting the unconscious hope that she will triumph morally over his cynicism. Thus, healing efforts may develop in a couple's ego-ideal systems and in unconscious past conflicts.

II.

Latency, Group Dynamics, and Conventionality

Having examined how the individual's disposition to sexual excitement and erotic desire is gradually transformed into the capacity for mature love when he or she becomes part of the sexual couple, let us now explore the relationship between the couple and its surrounding social network. My focus is particularly on the small and large groups within which couples find each other, with which they interact in complex ways, and which have an important influence on the vicissitudes of the couple's love life.

I am referring not only to actual groups but also to the fantasies that individuals and the couple develop about these groups, especially regarding the demands, threats, and gratifications to be expected when they interact as a couple with such groups. I believe that the group's and the couple's real and fantasied value judgments, moral expectations, and ideas about love relations play a significant role here. At the same time, a delicate balance is established between the couple and the surrounding group or groups, which in turn influences the psychodynamics of the couple. My understanding of these relations is based on psychoanalytic formulations regarding the psychodynamics of group processes, particularly the relationship of such group processes to individual attitudes toward sexuality and the sexual life of the couple.

The Couple and the Group

I have previously (1980b) written about psychoanalytic contributions on the relationships of individuals, couples, and groups. Freud (1921) described the regression that occurs in groups and the idealization of the leader, which has its roots in the oedipal situation. Bion (1961) proposed that the members of small groups operate according to flight-fight and

163

dependency assumptions (preoedipal in source) and a pairing assumption (oedipal in source). Rice (1965) and Turquet (1975) studied larger groups and found that loss of a sense of identity characterized the members, along with fear of aggression and of losing control.

In general, all groups that are unstructured (that is, those that are not organized around some task) foster a restrictive, regressive sense of morality. This type of morality is characteristic of social networks—the small social groups and communities within which individuals communicate with one another but are not intimate and do not necessarily have personal relations with one another. The basic shared values established under such conditions, as well as the transitional ideologies that evolve in unstructured small and large groups, are remarkably similar to the characteristics of mass psychology (individuals' reactions when they experience themselves as belonging transitorily to a large group or an impersonal mass).

I suggested in earlier work (1980b) that under such conditions, the members tend to project components of the infantile superego onto the group. They try to establish an unconsciously shared consensus on some basic values—a morality very different from the morality each member operates under as an individual. I propose that this morality, which—for reasons that will emerge throughout this chapter—I call conventional morality, is strikingly similar to the morality of children in the latency phase—following the height of the Oedipus complex, roughly from age four to six and extending to puberty and adolescence. As part of superego development, the latency period witnesses the building up of a moral system that is highly dependent on the need to adapt to the social system at school and the adult world and on the need to protect tender relationships with the parents from the sexual and aggressive conflicts of the oedipal stage. Latency-age psychology is characterized by consolidation of the positive relationships with both parents and repression of the direct expression of sexual longings toward the oedipal object and of aggressive competitiveness with the oedipal rival. Derivatives of these strivings are redirected toward the group formations that characterize the latency age, and, as part of the integration into the group, the latency child identifies him- or herself with all other group members by projection of the newly established postoedipal superego. At the same time, private longings for an exclusive love relationship derived from oedipal strivings mark the beginning of the dialectic between individual desire and conformity to an assumed group ideal.

The characteristics of latency-age group morality include both sexual knowledge and "innocence," in the sense that sexuality is something forbidden and has to do with the secret behavior of "others." There is also a derogatory devaluation of genital sexuality perceived as condensed with its anal forerunners, expressed in, for example, references to sexual organs and activities as dirty, "dirty" jokes, and the reaction of shame and disgust to sexual behavior, together with a secretly excited and wondering curiosity about sexuality. The simple morality of the latency age divides individuals and causes into good and bad, dissociates genital sexuality from tender affection and genital sex from polymorphous perverse infantile sexual components, and encourages naïveté, a motivated innocence. This latency-age morality is intolerant of ambiguity and the ambivalence that characterizes mature emotional relations; it tends to eliminate the erotic element from "legally accepted" relationships—basically, the relationship of the "official" parental couple. It is of interest that, in their private feelings and fantasies, latency-age children show a remarkable capacity for falling in love, with characteristics of romantic love that tradition has attributed only to adolescents and adults—except for the theme of having children of their own (Paulina Kernberg and Arlene Kramer Richards 1994).

Latency-age values tend to structure communication in which form predominates over content: there is a preference for the histrionic or theatrical in taking action; for sentimentality over deep feeling; and, in thinking, for the simple and trivial over the profound. The intolerance of ambivalence characteristic of latency morality is perhaps most strikingly expressed in the resolution of conflicts by separating "bad enemies" from "good friends." Latency morality in fact shows great similarity to kitsch— art forms without aesthetic merit but with great popular appeal. Kitsch is usually characterized by sentimentality, obviousness, pretentiousness, grandiosity, the easy simplification of traditionally dominant expressive styles, intellectual superficiality, and the pursuit of childlike ideals: the idealization of what is small, cozy, and amusing; images of clowns, a chimney fire against a winter landscape, the warm, protected, safe, simple, and happy environment of (fantasied) childhood.

It is this latency-age morality that lends itself to massive projection onto the group and persists throughout adolescence and even into adulthood as a common value system in unstructured groups and under conditions of group regression. Whereas the latency-age superego is easily projected by the members of unstructured groups, the later, highly individualized, and mature superego "remains in place." This mature superego will permit the integration of sexuality with tenderness, resulting in the capacity for sustained passionate love in adulthood.

The similarity of latency morality to kitsch points to the intimate connection between regressive group processes and the creations of mass culture—that is, products designed to appeal to individuals functioning under the influence of mass psychology.

Mass Psychology and Mass Culture

Serge Moscovici (1981) claimed that it was justifiable to apply Freud's theory of mass psychology (1921) to individuals sitting alone or in small groups, reading newspapers, watching TV, or listening to the radio, because knowing that what one is seeing or hearing is also being seen or heard by a vast audience causes one to feel like a part of a crowd. Mass media, in short, permit a simultaneity of communication that gives one an immediate sense of belonging to a group. Insofar as radio provides a greater simultaneity of communication than newspapers, and television intensifies the immediacy of the relation between the viewed and the viewer, radio and television are particularly conducive to converting the individual viewer to the status of a group member. Mass media communication corresponds to the characteristics of conventionality that reflect the demands of the latency superego just described.

Mass culture as transmitted by the mass media is characterized by simplicity and significantly limited intellectual demands on the consumer. The language and authority of television are addressed to an implicitly passive, equalized, "uninformed" mass. The situation-comedy story is simple and clearly understandable, the spectator's reaction predictable. The viewer is allowed a sense of amused superiority which facilitates his narcissistic gratification. Dramatic situations with clear solutions maintain the dissociation between the (bad) criminal who is punished, the sinner who repents, and the (good) triumphant defenders of what is right and pure. Sentimentality, an orientation toward childhood values, and the activation of slightly paranoid and narcissistic fantasies in thrillers and adventure stories gratify the regressive wishes of the large unstructured group.

Mass culture offers a regulated, stable, strict, and rigid conventional morality; there are final (parental) authorities that decide what is good and bad, aggression is tolerated only as justified indignation or punishment of criminals, conventional group morality is taken for granted, and sentimentality protects against an emotional depth that would be overwhelming from the perspective of childhood morality. Even when aggression appears to be the main subject, the hero's besting the aggressive monsters combines the tolerance of sadism with the triumph of the latency-age superego.

With sexual themes the same latency characteristics predominate: tender love is completely separated from any erotic element, or erotism is only slightly hinted at in connection with idealized, valued individuals. Genital sexuality is "known," but may be tolerated only when dissociated from the emotional experiences of the idealized persons. Typically, explicit sexuality is linked to devalued, depreciated, aggressive interactions or the "odd" people in the conventional drama. Direct expression of polymorphous perverse infantile sexual trends is conspicuously absent. It is characteristic of conventional films, for example, that even when there is an apparent tolerance of the depiction of sexual interaction, there is no enjoyable sex among people who are happily married, and there is a lack of erotized tenderness other than that linked to moments of "passion," usually with a clear implication of the aggressive, dangerous, or punishable quality of that particular passionate interaction.

I find that films illustrate particularly well the perennial conflict between private morality and conventionality that originates with the group processes during the latency phase. I believe that exploration of the differences among erotic, conventional, and pornographic films yields a better understanding of the unconscious motivations involved in the acceptance or intolerance of the erotic under the impact of mass culture.

The Conventional Film

The Breakfast Club (Hughes 1985) is a typical example of what I have called the conventional film. It presents adolescents' conflicts and rebellion at school—their talk about sex and sexual behavior—and conveys the impression of being very "open." However, sexually explicit scenes between adolescents take place without the participants' having any emotional relation, or such scenes clearly portray aggression. When the male protagonist, a rebel who later is the prodigal son or repenting sinner, falls in love with the female protagonist, all reference to sexual intimacy disappears.

The film *Fatal Attraction* (Lyne 1987), which was an enormous commercial success, presents exactly the same structure. The husband of a wonderful, understanding spouse has an affair with a woman who at first appears most attractive but is revealed to be severely ill—self-mutilating, demanding, and finally murderous. After threatening the life of the unfaithful but now repentant husband and terrorizing his family, she is finally killed (in self-defense) by his wife. Apart from the conventional morality of this film, it depicts the erotic relation of the lovers but avoids sexual intimacy between the husband and wife.

Another example, *Sex, Lies and Videotape* (Soderbergh 1989), shows sexual intimacy only between those who are not in love with each other; the one relationship presented as authentically loving is depicted without any such intimacy. The wife of an unfaithful lawyer (who has an affair with her negatively portrayed sister) is the pure, innocent, frustrated, disappointed, sexually inhibited heroine. After contributing to the emotional rescue of her husband's young counterculture friend (a young man whose sexual "perversion" consists of impotence and videotapes of women's sexual confessions and behavior), the lawyer's wife ends up in a love relationship with this friend, but the film reveals no sexual intimacy between them.

Erotic Art in Film

In contrast to the conventional film, *My Night at Maud's*, the classic film directed by Eric Rohmer (1969), exemplifies erotism artistically portrayed. The young obsessional hero is both timid and in love—with a girl he has seen only at a distance in church. A friend has introduced him to the intelligent, warm, independent Maud, who has just emerged from a tragic love affair and who is both amused and attracted by the rigidity and timidity of our hero. Maud, in offering him the chance to spend the night with her, makes inroads on his moral reserves; he struggles with himself and rejects her, offending her pride. When, finally, he is willing to embrace her, she rejects him, telling him that she likes men who are able to make up their mind. The subtlety of the interaction between the two characters and of their erotic relationship, and the viewer's ability to identify with both of them, are deeply moving.

Bertolucci's *Last Tango in Paris* (1974), which was also a commercial success, depicts the development of the sexual relation between the two principal characters (played by Maria Schneider and Marlon Brando). Schneider meets Brando by chance in a potentially beautiful but run-down apartment, which both are looking to rent. She is uncertain about marrying her fiancé, a young film director. Brando, whose common-law wife has just committed suicide, is in deep mourning, complicated by rage at her betrayal of him with another man. In establishing a relationship with Schneider, a much younger woman, in which he and she agree to tell each other nothing, not even their names, he attempts to deny and to overcome the recent past. A deepening sexual relation, in which love and aggression mingle, reflects his mourning, and idealization, sense of loss, and aggression emerge as part of his effort to reach out to her. Schneider, in spite of her frightened reaction to his sadism, is moved and stimulated by this strange American in Paris, and the film deals with their unsuccessful attempt to maintain and develop this relationship and its final tragic end. The combination of sexual love, interwoven object relations, and profound conflicts over values depicts the complex nature of human passion and provides an intensely erotic quality to the film.

Finally, the more recent Greenaway film *The Cook, the Thief, His Wife and Her Lover* (1990) offers a powerful description of an erotic relation as an attempt to escape from a world controlled by a sadistic tyrant. A forbidden, dangerous sexual relation slowly evolves out of an initially casual encounter. That the lovers are middle aged enhances the appeal of their trying to establish a new, meaningful life in their love.

The film integrates symbolic oral, anal, and genital meanings and a totalitarian superstructure that transforms all human relations into a world of excrement and violence. The principal action occurs in the elegant dining room of an exclusive restaurant. Here, the tyrant and his followers break all the rules of ordinary human relations. Beyond the dining room, there exists an "oral" world represented by the cook and his helpers, in which culture and civilization are preserved by the ritualized preparation of food and the background music, the angelic voice of a child helper. Outside the huge kitchen is the "anal" world, a street where we see poisonous smoke, wild dogs, and mistreated people.

The lovers, attempting to escape the watchful tyrant and meet in a hidden space in the kitchen area, are eventually forced to flee, naked, in a garbage truck full of rotten meat. They emerge from this ordeal into the refuge represented by the library of which the hero is the custodian, and the lovers' relationship is cemented, at least temporarily, by a cleansing bath that frees them from the anal world that had confined them.

The tyrant's brutal mistreatment of women, his deep hatred of knowledge and intellect, the intolerance of the couple's private and free love life are all brought together into a dramatic celebration of love. Its erotic quality moves the viewer because of its very frailty and the powerful forces against which it has to assert itself.

The Pornographic Film

In the typical pornographic film—and in typical pornographic literature—there is a clear absence of superego functions. The stories stress the easy expression of sexuality; shame is abolished. Once the rupture of conventional values and particularly of individual values is accepted, the freedom from moral judgment replicates the exciting and liberating freedom from personal responsibility Freud described as characteristic of masses.

The viewer identifies with sexual activities rather than with human relations. The lack of ambiguity, the meaninglessness of the narrative, which permits no further fantasy about the internal life of the protagonists, contribute to the mechanization of sex.

The dehumanization of the sexual relationship typically conveyed in the pornographic film activates in the spectator, particularly when he or she is viewing it in a group, polymorphous perverse infantile sexual feelings dissociated from tenderness, including the aggressive aspects of pregenital sexuality, a fetishistic degradation of the couple in sexual intimacy as a collection of exciting body parts, and an implicit aggressive destruction of the primal scene into isolated sexual components. Here, in short, a perverse decomposition of the erotic takes place, which tends to destroy the link of the erotic and the aesthetic as well as the idealization of passionate love. Insofar as the pornographic film is diametrically in defiance of conventional morality—in fact, expresses profound aggression toward conventionality as well as toward emotional intimacy—it also has shock value. But even when it is individually sought out to facilitate sexual excitement at primitive levels of emotional experience, pornography rapidly becomes boring and self-defeating. The reason is that dissociation between sexual behavior and the complexity of the couple's emotional relation robs sexuality of its preoedipal and oedipal implications; in short, it mechanizes sex.

There is a parallel between the pornographic film and the deterioration of passionate love when aggressive impulses dominate the sexual encounter, when unconscious aggression destroys the couple's object relations in depth, and the lack of an integrated superego in the partners and in the couple facilitates the dissolution of privacy and intimacy into mechanized group sex. It is no coincidence that the pornographic film, which deliberately exploits the dissociation of sex and tenderness, ends up being experienced—after the early sexually arousing impact of its defiant display of polymorphous perverse sexuality—as mechanical and boring, just as individuals engaged in group sex experience a deterioration in their capacity for sexual excitement over a period of time as a consequence of the deterioration of their object relations.

The pornographic film also has a readily available, "nonconventional" or "underground," but harmoniously responsive mass audience who tolerate and enjoy the analization of sexuality that characterizes large group processes (Kernberg 1980b). The apparent contradiction of this response and the self-defeatingly boring effects of the pornographic film is expressed in the extreme instability of its mass audience.

The characteristics of the pornographic film liberate the spectators from the shock of the invaded primal scene and from the threat of confronting an integration of tenderness and sensuality that cannot be tolerated by the latency superego. In this regard, the pornographic film is the counterpart of the conventional film and, paradoxically, in all other respects obeys the same unconscious dominance of the latency superego. In fact, apart from the depiction of sexual interaction, the pornographic film tends to be extremely conventional and often adopts a childish kind of "humor" or amusement in dealing with sexual communication; this permits the viewer to avoid any deep emotional reactions or awareness of the aggressive elements in the film's sexual content. The surprisingly consistent absence of an aesthetic frame also reflects the absence of mature superego functions, expressed in the vulgarity of the decor, the accompanying music, the gestures, and the general ambience. Typically, the aggressive, voyeuristic display of sexual behavior, the focus on the mechanical acts of penetrating and being penetrated, encompassing and encompassed genitals and related body parts, contributes to splitting the human body into isolated parts, the repetitive display of which indicates a fetishistic approach to sexual organs.

Stoller's (1991b) description of the psychology of actors, directors, and producers of pornographic films dramatically illustrates their traumatic, aggressive experiences, particularly humiliation and sexual traumatization. Stoller proposes that pornography unconsciously represents an effort, by those involved in its production, to transform such experiences by means of a dissociated expression of genital sexuality under the impact of polymorphous perverse infantile sexuality. Although the pornographic film gives the impression of being unlike the conventional film, its absolute dissociation of the sexual and sensual from the tender and idealized aspects of erotism is the same.

The Structure of the Conventional Film

The depiction of the erotic in conventional films represents the counterpart of the pornographic film. The conventional erotic film facilitates a nondemanding and immediately gratifying regression to the mass-cultural level of enjoyment, harmony with conventional morality, and the reassuring stability of a group identity based on latency-age superego values. Although such films usually include a narrative and some character development, their view of the protagonists' sexual life continues to reflect latency superego morality. Intense sexual involvements may be depicted between individuals whose relationship is largely aggressive or sensual, whereas couples who are tenderly related, particularly if they are married, are not depicted in sexual interaction: the oedipal prohibitions are in place. These films simplify emotional relations, avoid emotional depth in a way strikingly similar to pornographic films, despite the acceptable behavior and reactions of individuals, and incorporate latency ideals that provide a human if sentimental quality that is absent from pornographic films. The conventional film totally eliminates the polymorphous perverse infantile sexuality that constitutes the center of the pornographic film.

It is interesting that the conventional film allows much more frequent depiction of aggression than of erotism. While censorship (or producers' self-censorship) naturally fosters the conventional film and has very little tolerance for erotic art, the mechanisms for this selective process are probably, at least in part, unconscious, related to the intuitive identification of the censors with the latency-age psychology of the prospective audience without much analysis of the underlying principles that determine the censorship. Someone who rates commercial films explained to me that, when in doubt, raters view a film several times, and that repeated viewing of aggressive scenes has a desensitizing effect on the viewer whereas erotic scenes do not. Hence films with erotic content are given a more restrictive rating than those with aggressive content. But in all fairness to the censor, erotic art films, unlike conventional erotic films, are rarely huge commercial successes. The censors, we might say, reluctantly respect (some) erotic art; the failure of art films to achieve commercial success completes their work. The conventional intolerance of erotic art depends by far on the unfailing intuition of the producers of mass culture responding to mass psychology.

The Structure of Erotic Art in Film

In my view, erotic art has several specific dimensions: the aesthetic dimension, the presentation of the beauty of the human body as a main theme, reflects idealization of the body as central to passionate love. The artistic description of what might be called the geography of the human body, the projection of the ideals of beauty onto the body, the identification of the self with nature by means of the body, and the transcendence as well as the transitory nature of human beauty are major elements of erotic art.

Erotic art is also characterized by ambiguity. It provides multiple potential meanings in the relation of lovers and points to the reciprocity of all relationships and, implicitly, to the polymorphous quality of infantile sexuality and to the ambivalence of human relations. This ambiguity opens up the space of primitive unconscious fantasy that is activated in any erotic relationship and contributes to erotic tension.

Erotic art represents a disruption of the restrictive conventional attitude toward sexuality and reveals an erotic experience that symbolizes an implicit frame of ethical values and responsibility. The erotic in art is depicted as a serious and mature aspect of human values, a symbol of an adult ego ideal that eliminates infantile prohibitions and limitations of sexuality.

Erotic art also contains a romantic dimension, an implicit idealization of the lovers who rebel against the restrictions of conventionality and against the degradation of sexuality implied in the analization, devaluation, and dehumanization of the erotic that characterize large-group phenomena (and that are found in the psychology of pornography). The romantic aspect of the erotic also implies the simultaneous combination of an ideal fusion in love with the lovers' assertion of autonomy as a couple. The erotic relationship becomes the expression of passionate love.

Finally, erotic art stresses the individualized quality of the erotic object; it typically conveys an "unsaturated" element of secrecy, privacy, and yet a potential "shamelessness." The openness or "nakedness" of the erotic object, however, is made impenetrable by an element of distance that remains a teasingly frustrating component of successful works of such art. Erotic art is self-contained in the sense that it evokes an unfulfillable longing in the spectator; it cannot be fully assimilated and has an intangible element that interferes with the spectator's ability to totally identify with it. By the same token, the primal scene (openly depicted sexual intimacy) is subtly protected by the self-contained aspect of the work of art, so that the integration of tenderness and the erotic, of the strikingly physical and sensual with the impalpable ideal or romantic, maintains an unbridgeable gap between the work of art and the viewer.

These general characteristics of erotic art may be expressed in sculpture, painting, literature, music, dance, and theater, but perhaps in no medium so clearly as in film. That film is an obvious medium for conventional art, which reflects mass culture, may be self-evident, and this function also includes conventionality in its expression of the erotic. Given the power and immediacy of film's visual imagery, it may have a particular potential as a medium for erotism that cannot be dissociated from its ability to express simultaneously the counterpart of erotic art—namely, the split-off, conventionally taboo subject of genital and polymorphous perverse infantile pregenital sexuality in the depersonalized, analized form of pornography. It is in fact the particular power of film as a medium for the erotic that encourages us to compare conventional films, erotic art films, and pornographic films.

In its ability to isolate, aggrandize, and dissociate the representation of genitals and other body parts and their intermingling, film provides a channel for idealization as well as for fetishization of the human body. The visual and auditory properties of film allow the viewer to realize in fantasy the invasion of the oedipal couple's privacy, a sadistic and voyeuristic invasion of the primal scene, as well as its counterpart, the gratification by projection of exhibitionistic and masochistic impulses and of homosexual and heterosexual strivings linked to those impulses.

At the same time, insofar as film permits the viewer to transcend the boundaries of time and space that ordinarily control the depiction of sexual behavior and the direct observation of and participation with other couples in group sex, film permits an arbitrary acceleration, deceleration, and distortion of visual experience that resonate strongly with the nature of unconscious fantasy. The depiction of the erotic in film has the potential for breaking through the conventional barriers of shamefulness and, because it simultaneously represents all components of oedipal and preoedipal sexuality, offers a stimulus for sexual arousal.

Because film is the most effective medium for transmitting mass culture, particularly before an assembled audience, it activates in the spectators the disposition to mass psychology; the erotic element in film challenges the conventionally tolerable. Because intolerance of the erotic is characteristic of mass psychology, the erotic in film shocks the conventional audience, except for those who watch sexual films alone or have gathered to enjoy pornographic films. The erotic in film threatens the very boundaries of the conventional.

Let us explore this shock. For the audience, the observation of a couple having sexual intercourse activates ancient prohibitions against invasion of the oedipal couple and the suppressed or repressed excitement attached to it. What the audience is viewing implies defiance of both the infantile superego and the conventional superego of latency. The sexual excitement it induces, particularly in those who tolerate their capacity for sexual excitement under visual stimuli (obviously, spectators with severe sexual inhibitions will react with loathing and disgust), may be experienced as an assault on deeply held values.

The shock is exacerbated because the art film has been constructed to facilitate the viewer's identification with the protagonists (unconsciously standing for the parental couple). The initial violation of a taboo thus inspires guilt, shame, and embarrassment. Unconscious identification with the actors' exhibitionistic behavior, with the sadistic and masochistic aspects of respectively voyeuristic and exhibitionistic impulses, produces a shocking challenge to the spectator's superego.

The erotic film as a form of art demands emotional maturity, the capacity to tolerate and enjoy sexuality, to combine eroticism and tenderness, to integrate the erotic into a complex emotional relationship, to identify with others and their object relations, and to be receptive to ethical values and to aesthetics, paralleling the developments already outlined regarding the capacity for passionate love. This emotional maturity tends to be transitorily eroded under conditions of mass psychology.

In a strange way, our capacity for identifying with the couple in love in the film creates a new dimension of privacy that protects it and the spectator and is in contrast to the pornographic film's destruction of intimacy and privacy. In the art film, the voyeuristic and exhibitionistic elements of sexual arousal activated by witnessing sexual intimacy, the sadistic and masochistic elements of that invasion, are contained by identification with the characters and their values. The audience participates in the primal scene while unconsciously assuming the responsibility for maintaining the privacy of the couple. And the aggressive elements of polymorphous perverse infantile sexuality are integrated within oedipal sexuality, and aggression within erotism. This is the opposite of the deterioration of the erotic when aggression dominates, which characterizes sexuality in certain pathological conditions and in pornography.

Erotic art achieves a synthesis of sensuality, deep object relations, and mature value systems, reflected in the individuals' and the couple's capacity for passionate love and engagement.

The relationships between the conventional film, the pornographic film, and erotic art in film reflect the dynamics involving the group, conventional culture, and the couple in a passionate relationship. The couple is always, in a deep sense, asocial, secret, private, and rebellious, and a challenge to conventionally tolerated love and sexuality. While conventional morality oscillates throughout history, at least the history of Western civilization, between periods of puritanism and libertinism, the implicit opposition between couple and group, between private morality and cultural convention, remains constant. Both puritanism and libertinism reflect conventional ambivalence toward the sexual couple, and these historical swings are reflected, at this time, in the simultaneous existence of conventional mass culture and kitsch, at one extreme, and pornography, at the other. One might say that only the mature couple and erotic art are able to sustain and preserve passionate love. Conventionality and pornography are unconscious allies in their intolerance of passionate love.

The Couple and the Group

Adolescent Groups and Couples

Adolescent sexuality starts out under the impact of the reawakened sexual excitement and erotic desire evoked by the hormonal changes of puberty; the perception of bodily changes results in a heightened responsiveness to erotic stimuli. Partial regression in ego functions develops, and splitting processes are activated to deal with renewed unconscious conflicts regarding sexuality that are manifested in sharply contradictory behavior patterns, particularly the alternation between periods of guilt and suppression of sexual response (the ascetic swings characteristic of adolescents) and periods of polymorphous perverse infantile sexual strivings. The decrease in repressive ego mechanisms is related to the partial regression in and reorganization of the superego and the need to integrate the newly awakened sexual strivings with infantile superego prohibitions. Under optimal circumstances, tolerance of genital and pregenital, polymorphous perverse infantile impulses permits their integration as part of the changing experiences of the self, and the infantile prohibitions against sexual strivings toward the oedipal objects are simultaneously reconfirmed.

A major structural requirement for the development of the capacity for mature sexual love is the consolidation of an integrated ego identity in the context of the adolescent identity crisis. On the basis of my work with patients presenting borderline personality organization and patients (borderline or not) presenting narcissistic personality structure, I have concluded that ego identity is established gradually, throughout infancy and childhood, in the process of overcoming a primitive ego organization in which splitting mechanisms and related operations predominate. Ego identity depends upon and reinforces the establishment of an integrated

176

self-concept and total object relations, with repression and related defensive operations the principal mechanisms. Erikson (1956), describing the achievement of intimacy as the first stage of adulthood, stressed the dependency of this stage upon the achievement of a sense of identity in adolescence. The stages I have described in the development of the capacity for falling in love and remaining in love represent an application of this concept to normal and pathological love relationships.

Adolescence typically presents identity crises but not identity diffusion, two concepts that deserve to be clearly differentiated. An identity crisis, Erikson (1956, 1959) suggested, involves a loss of the correspondence between the internal sense of identity at a certain stage of development and the "confirmation" provided by the psychosocial environment. If the discrepancy is greater than the correspondence, the self-concept as well as external adaptation is threatened and requires the reexamination of one's sense of identity as well as one's relationship to the environment. In contrast, identity diffusion is a syndrome typical of borderline pathology (Jacobson 1964; Kernberg 1970), characterized by mutually dissociated ego states and lack of integration not only of the self but of the superego and the world of internalized object relations. A relation exists between identity crisis and ego identity: the more stable the individual's basic ego identity, the better equipped is he or she to deal with identity crises; the more severe the environmental challenges to an established ego identity, the greater the threat of breakdown for one whose identity formation is faulty.

The clinical differential diagnosis between identity crisis and identity diffusion requires careful examination of an adolescent's behavior and subjective experiences past and present. Rebellious challenging of authority may coexist with behavior radically contrary to professed rebellious convictions. Intense love relationships and loyalties may coexist with inconsiderate, neglectful, even ruthless and exploitative behavior. However, in exploring the adolescent's relation to apparently contradictory ego states and actions, we see that a basic sense of emotional continuity clearly differentiates the neurotic and normal adolescent from his or her more disorganized counterpart, who exhibits identity diffusion. The following characteristics are particularly helpful in this differentiation (Kernberg 1978): the capacity for guilt and concern and the genuine wish to repair aggressive behavior, which is recognized as such after an emotional outburst; the capacity for establishing lasting, nonexploitative relations with friends, teachers, or other grown-ups, as well as a relatively realistic assessment of such persons in depth; and a consistently expanding and deepening set of values—regardless of whether these values conform to or are in opposition to those of the prevalent culture surrounding the adolescent.

The practical value of this differential diagnosis is that a reasonable certainty about the stability of an adolescent's established ego identity provides basic reassurance that the turmoil and conflicts characteristic of falling in love and love relations in general do not reflect borderline and narcissistic personality structures. The typical clinical manifestations of sexual conflicts in adolescence—the dissociation of tenderness from sexual excitement, the dichotomy of asexual idealized objects and of sexually devaluated objects of the other gender, the coexistence of excessive guilt and impulsive expression of sexual urges—may represent conflicts from normal to severely neurotic and may constitute a diagnostic challenge. In contrast, the presence of identity diffusion indicates serious psychopathology, in which sexual conflicts constitute only the beginning of long-term interferences with a normal love life.

For the mental health professional who deals with adolescents from such deprived social groups as inner-city youths in large metropolitan areas of North America, my description of conflictual love relations based on data from middle-class American adolescents may seem inappropriate. Adolescents with a chaotic family structure, a history of chronic witnessing or being victims of violence, including sexual violence, can hardly be expected to develop the capacity for establishing an integrated world of internalized object relations, to say nothing of an integrated superego. The establishment of a love relation is seriously threatened under such conditions, and an apparent degree of full sexual "freedom" may coincide with sharp limitations in one's capacity to commit to an intimate personal relationship. It is therefore tempting to ascribe manifestations of psychopathology and an incapacity to establish love relations to upbringing and the social surround. In this context, the characteristics of normal identity formation just outlined may be helpful in differentiating adaptation to an underprivileged, perhaps antisocial, subgroup from severe psychopathology. A highly pathological social structure with disorganization of the family fosters psychopathology, but a superficial adaptation to a pathological social environment may mask the underlying strength of an adolescent's development.

The reactivation of oedipal conflicts and the struggle around repression of oedipal sexual strivings are primary unconscious motivations for the adolescent's separating from the parental objects and establishing a social life within his or her peer group. Rebellion against the previously accepted behavioral norms and values of the parental home accompanies the search for new values, ideals, and behavioral norms in admired teachers and a constantly widening world. Strict adherence to group mores in early adolescence is a sign of continuing latency-age morality, which reconfirms the dissociation between exciting yet devalued sexuality as part of those mores, on the one hand, and the capacity for tenderness and romantic love gradually evolving as a "secret" potential of the individual, on the other. The fact that early male adolescent groups consciously affirm the latency child's exciting, yet anally tinged concept of genitality dissociated from tenderness and keep to themselves the longing for tender and romantic relations with the other gender contrasts with the development in typical early adolescent female groups. The girl's ideal and romanticized acceptance of an admired male object is part of the "secret," private stirrings of genital desires.

A crucial task in later adolescence is to develop a capacity for sexual intimacy; to achieve this, the intimacy of the couple has to be established in opposition to the conventional sexual mores and values, not only of the adult social group within which the couple has evolved but of its own peer group. The relationship between these two groups now becomes important. At times of relative social stability and in relatively homogeneous social environments, the cultures of the adolescent group and the adult world may be in harmony, permitting a relatively easy transition for newly formed couples. Under these circumstances, adherence to adolescent values, the gradual liberation from such values, and adherence to adult world values without an overly rigid incorporation of conventionality are relatively simple tasks.

But when sharp discrepancies exist between the two worlds—for example, when adolescent groups are from deprived subcultures or are part of a society experiencing acute and divisive social and political conflicts— late adolescent groups may rigidly adhere to ideological positions in the surrounding adult world. Social pressures for or against "political correctness" on college campuses, for example, or attitudes toward drugs, feminism, minorities, and homosexuality may encourage regressive group processes in late adolescence and make it more difficult for a couple to establish its own space.

In addition, adolescents with severe character pathology and identity diffusion may have an especially strong need to adhere rigidly to the values of adolescent groups. It is hence useful to examine the extent to which an adolescent couple in love is able to maintain independence from surrounding group pressures. During the hippie counterculture of the 1960s, unrestricted sexual freedom was the adolescent group ideology. Many adolescents at that time masked sexual inhibition and related psychopathology with superficial "sexual liberation." Under the liberated sexual behavior of adolescent "hippies" often lay hysterical, masochistic, and narcissistic pathology. And on some college campuses in the 1990s, peer pressures may consolidate around a conventional fear of dangerous male sexuality. This may inhibit the formation of sexual couples involved in a mature love relation and facilitate regressive sadomasochistic sexual interactions. These dynamics have often been observed during the treatment of hospitalized adolescents with severe character pathology.

In such treatment, it is the social and legal responsibility of the staff to see that sexual behavior among minors is neither accepted nor tolerated, although experienced therapists generally expect adolescents to seek out sexual intimacy in defiance of the rules and regulations. The healthier the adolescents, the more they will understand, adjust to, and yet rebel—privately and discreetly—against those restrictions, in order to establish and develop a relationship as a couple. I have often found, while treating adolescents with narcissistic and borderline conditions, that they are puzzled by what they consider to be my failure to frown on sexual behavior they had expected to be forbidden. They also see me as terribly "moralistic" in areas where they had least expected it—that is, with regard to the contradictory, chaotic, split-off nature of their object relations.

Analysis of the pathological character structure of a neurotic adolescent should promote the integration of mutually dissociated or split-off ego states and the overcoming of reaction formations against instinctual urges that interfere with a full love life. However, even under optimal circumstances, when the resolution of pathological character trends has consolidated and enriched an adolescent's sense of ego identity, full ego identity can come about only with time. Certain aspects of internalized object relations can become fully integrated into a consolidated ego identity only when identification with the adult-role aspects of the parental objects takes place, a process that lasts for years. Eventually, love will have to integrate identification with the paternal and maternal functions of the oedipal objects, a process that can be "tested" only over time. Full identification with the generative roles of the parental couple consolidates with the wish to have a child with the loved other: this capacity emerges first in late adolescence and matures in adulthood. As a conscious aspiration, it is one more aspect of mature sexual love. Its inhibition in an adult couple may signal significant masochistic, and particularly narcissistic, conflicts. Obviously, such an aspiration has to be differentiated from casual, irresponsible acceptance of basically unwanted pregnancies.

In other words, adolescent love relations can become solid and deep, but for them to become stable depends upon qualities in the adolescent's personality that require time to develop; the outcome cannot be predicted.

A commitment that begins in adolescence must remain an uncertainty, an adventure. To some extent, this is also true for the mature adult couple.

For the psychotherapist who works with adolescents, it is helpful to keep in mind that there is a phase-specific, normal search for a romantic road to sexual intimacy within a full and intense relationship. If this road is not successfully traversed in adolescence, it will compromise the success of future commitments, which makes this a crucial area of human experience; therapists treating adolescents need to challenge efforts to dismiss it as unimportant.

The Adult Couple's External Challenge

Mature sexual love—the experiencing and maintaining of an exclusive love relation with another person that integrates tenderness and eroticism, that has depth and shared values—is always in open or secret opposition to the surrounding social group. It is inherently rebellious. It frees the adult couple from participation in the conventionalities of the social group, creates an experience of sexual intimacy that is eminently private and secret, and establishes a setting in which mutual ambivalences will be integrated into the love relation and both enrich and threaten it. This unconventional quality of sexual love is not to be confused with rebellious adolescent subgroups or exhibitionistic behavior reflecting various kinds of pathology. I am describing an internal attitude that cements the couple, often in very discreet ways, and that may be masked by surface adaptations to the social environment.

But the couple in a love relationship, while in opposition to the group, still needs it for survival. A truly isolated couple is endangered by a serious liberation of aggression that may destroy it or severely damage both partners. Even more often, severe psychopathology in one or both participants may bring about the activation of repressed or dissociated, conflictual, internalized object relations that are reenacted by the couple through projective experiencing of the worst of the unconscious past, rupture of the couple's union, and the return of both participants to the group in a final, desperate quest for individual freedom. In less serious circumstances, unconscious efforts by one or both partners to blend or dissolve into the group, particularly by breaching the barrier of sexual exclusiveness, may be a way of preserving the existence of the couple at the risk of invasion and deterioration of its intimacy.

Stable triangular relationships, in addition to reenacting various aspects of unresolved oedipal conflicts, represent the group's invasion of the couple. The breakdown of sexual intimacy—for example, in an "open marriage"—represents severe destruction of the couple. Group sex is an extreme form of the couple's dissolving into the group while still preserving in many ways the couple's stability. Usually group sex is just a step away from the couple's total destruction.

In sum, by rebelling against the group, the couple establishes its identity, its freedom from convention, and the beginning of its journey as a couple. Dissolution back into the group represents the final haven of freedom for the survivors of a couple that has destroyed itself.

Romantic love is the beginning of sexual love, characterized by normal idealization of the sexual partner, the experience of transcendence in the context of sexual passion, and liberation from the surrounding social group. Rebellion against the group starts in late adolescence but does not end there. The romantic relationship of the couple is a permanent characteristic. Indeed, I believe that the traditional distinction between "romantic love" and "marital affection" reflects the ongoing conflict between the couple and the group, the suspicion of the social group regarding relationships including love and sex that escape its total control. This distinction also reflects the denial of aggression in the couple's relationship, which often transforms a deep love relation into a savage one.

I see a built-in, complex, and fateful relationship between the couple and the group. Because the couple's creativity depends upon the successful establishment of its autonomy within the group setting, it cannot wholly escape from the group. Because the couple enacts and maintains the group's hope for sexual union and love, even though large group processes activate potential destructiveness, the group needs the couple. However, the couple cannot avoid experiencing hostility and envy of the group that derive from the internal sources of envy of the parents' happy and secret union and from deep unconscious guilt over forbidden oedipal strivings.

A stable couple made up of a man and a woman who dare to overcome oedipal prohibitions against uniting sex and tenderness separate themselves from the collective myths that infiltrate the sexuality of the social group within which their relationship as a couple has evolved. Group processes involving sexuality and love reach maximal intensity in adolescence, but they persist in more subtle ways in the relationships of adult couples. An ongoing excitement exists within the informal group regarding the private life of the couples of which it consists. At the same time, the members of the couple are tempted to express rage in aggressive behavior toward each other within the relative intimacy of being with close friends. Unable to contain that behavior within the privacy of its relationship, a couple may thus use the group as a channel for discharging aggression and as a theater in which to display it. That some couples who habitually fight in public have a deep and lasting private relationship should not be surprising. The danger, beautifully illustrated in Albee's (1962) play *Who's Afraid of Virginia Woolf?* is that aggression will be expressed so violently that it destroys the remnants of the couple's shared intimacy, particularly its sexual bonds, and leads to the destruction of the relationship. Friends within the immediate social group who attempt to heal the rift enjoy vicarious gratification from the couple's quarrels and reaffirm the security of their own relationship.

As to sexual excitement and eroticism involving members of a social set of couples, there is a need to search for the optimal equilibrium between the couples and the group. The informality of ordinary adult social-group formation protects couples from the large group processes that characterize a formal social or work organization. A couple that maintains its internal cohesion and at the same time exerts a powerful influence on the surrounding social group, particularly within an organizational structure, becomes a strong target for oedipal idealization, anxiety, and envy. The group's hatred of the powerful couple may protect the couple by forcing the partners to unite against the group and by masking the projection of their own, unrecognized mutual aggression. Later, though, after the couple has separated from the group, serious aggression may emerge between the partners.

As we have seen, a couple that, for realistic or neurotic reasons, isolates itself from the surrounding social group is subject to danger from the internal effects of mutual aggression. Marriage may now feel like a prison, and breaking away and joining a group may feel like an escape into freedom. The sexual promiscuity that follows many separations and divorces exemplifies such escape into the freedom and anarchy of the group. By the same token, the group may become a prison for those members who cannot or dare not enter the relationship of a stable couple.

The group's chronic invasion of a couple's relationship takes several forms, and these warrant further exploration.

Sometimes when one partner maintains a relationship with a third party, the affair is preliminary to the destruction of the couple (that is, the couple or the marriage dissolves and gives way to a new couple formation); and sometimes the marriage seems to stabilize with the presence of a third party. In the latter case, various outcomes can materialize. Frequently, when one of the partners has an affair it permits the stabilizing expression of unresolved oedipal conflicts. A woman who is frigid with her husband and sexually satisfied by her lover may experience a conscious thrill and sense of satisfaction that sustain the marriage, though unconsciously she enjoys her husband as a hated transference representative of her oedipal father. In the dual relationship, she experiences an unconscious triumph over the father who had had both her mother and her under his control, whereas now she is the one who has two men under hers. The wish for the affair may also stem from unconscious guilt over experiencing her marital relationship as an oedipal triumph while not daring to establish a total identification with the oedipal mother; thus the conflict between desire and guilt is acted out in her playing Russian roulette with the marriage.

Paradoxically, the deeper and fuller these parallel marital and extramarital relationships become, the more they tend toward self-destruction, because the splitting of the object representation attained through the triangular situation eventually tends to be lost. As illustrated by the film *The Captain's Paradise* (Kimmins, 1953), parallel relationships tend to become more and more similar with time, imposing an increasingly difficult psychological burden. Whether such relationships are maintained secretly or accepted openly of course depends upon other factors, such as the extent to which sadomasochistic conflicts play a role in the marital interaction. "Openness" about extramarital affairs more often than not is a sadomasochistic interaction and reflects the need to express aggression or defend against guilt feelings.

Sometimes a couple's actual relationship is obscured by a liaison established in response to social, political, or economic pressures. For example, a couple can have a meaningful, often secret relationship that for each partner exists parallel to a merely formal one, such as a marriage of convenience. There are other instances in which both parallel relationships in a triangular situation are basically formalistic and ritualized, as in subcultures in which having a lover is a mark of status expected of a person from a certain social stratum.

What I wish to stress is that triangular situations, especially those that include a long-term, stable extramarital relationship, may have complex, variable effects upon the relationship of the primary couple. Stable triangular relationships usually reflect various types of compromise formations involving unresolved oedipal conflicts. They may protect a couple against the direct expression of some types of aggression, but in most cases, the capacity for real depth and intimacy declines, the price exacted for this protection.

Bartell's classic study, *Group Sex* (1971), richly documents some dominant social characteristics of promiscuous sexuality in an open group situation. He examined the consciously professed ideology that group sex protects and renews the marital relationship by creating shared sexual stimuli and experiences and concluded that this is actually an illusion. Typically, the "swinging" scene is impersonal, paying attention only to the preparation and carrying out of sexual activity. While marital couples may claim that their exciting, secretive participation in the group frees them from chronic boredom, actually the social relationships, both within the swinging group and within the traditional group from which the participants derive, deteriorate even further after a relatively brief time. It seems that less than two years of participation in the swinging scene are sufficient to dissipate the illusion of new sexual excitement and stimulation. Sex becomes boring once again, even more so.

The degree to which the couple is invaded by the group or dissolved into a group situation is reflected by the extent to which their union is a purely formal one or a true emotional relationship. The more open, indiscriminate, and promiscuous the sexual behavior, the more likely it is that the psychopathology of the couple contains preoedipal features with a predominance of aggression and polymorphous perverse infantile sexual needs. There is progressive deterioration of internalized object relations and of sexual enjoyment between the members of the couple.

In evaluating a couple, I am interested in the extent to which the relationship permits a sense of internal freedom and emotional stimulation, the extent to which their sexual experiences are rich, renewing, and exciting, the extent to which they can experiment sexually without feeling imprisoned either by each other or by the social environment, and, above all, the extent to which the couple is autonomous in the sense that it can remain self-generating throughout time, regardless of changes in their children, the surrounding environment, or the social structure.

If the choice of living on the surface of one's self provides a satisfactory degree of stability and gratification, there is no reason for a therapist to challenge this on an ideological or perfectionistic basis. If the couple's presenting complaint is sexual indifference, it is helpful to remember that boredom is the most immediate manifestation of lack of contact with deeper emotional and sexual needs. But not everyone has the capacity or the willingness to open that Pandora's box.

The relationship of a couple with their children gives important information regarding the relationship of the couple to the group. The wish to have children as an expression of commitment and identification with the generative and generous role of the parental images and the wish to jointly assume responsibility for the children's development and growth express the couple's desire for definite consolidation. They indicate, as well, that the couple has achieved the mature renunciation of the constraints of adolescent groups and is willing to engage in interaction with the social and cultural environment within which its children will have to grow and achieve their own autonomy. In successfully maintaining privacy and independence as a couple while functioning as parental objects, the couple consolidates its generational boundaries as it unconsciously initiates the next generation's entrance into the world of oedipal experience. And the life cycle repeats itself as the children enter the earliest group formations during the school years and, in latency, unconsciously contribute to the creation of a group morality that will cast a shadow on the morality of later group formations, including the conventional morality that surrounds the adult couple.

From a historical perspective, one can observe repeated oscillations between "puritanical" periods during which love relations become de-eroticized and eroticism goes underground and "libertine" periods during which sexuality deteriorates into emotionally degraded group sex. In my view, such oscillations reflect the long-term equilibrium between the society's need to destroy, protect, and control the couple and the couple's aspirations to break out of the constrictions of conventional sexual morality in search of a freedom that in its extreme form becomes self-destructive. The so-called sexual revolution of the 1960s and 1970s I think reflected a mere swing of the pendulum and indicated no real change in the deeper dynamics of the relationship of the couple and the social group. Obviously a couple's adaptation to conventional morality, whether related to a lack of autonomous superego development or to the appeal of submerging itself in large group processes, is potentially present at all times, and the surface behavior of couples may vary according to pressures from its social group. However, the autonomous and mature sexual couple maintains a boundary of privacy in its capacity for secret, passionate involvement under any but the most extreme social environments.

Conventional social norms that protect public morality are crucial in protecting the sexual life of the couple. The pressures for conventional behavior, however, conflict with the individual value systems each couple has to establish for itself. The couple is also threatened by the pressures for group formation along sexual lines and for the expression in such groups of the primitive suspicion and hatred between men and women characteristic of latency and adolescence. In this connection, under the influence of mass communication and the media, it may well be that the predominant conventional ideology, particularly regarding sexuality, may shift more rapidly as new ideological currents become fashionable and die out because of the appetite for variety in mass communication. These alternating changes in conventional mores illustrate the broad spectrum of more permanent elements of the conventional attitude regarding sexuality we have been exploring.

Throughout the 1970s and 1980s, the predominant conventional ideology in the U.S. was one of relatively open discussion and expression of certain aspects of sexuality, with a simultaneous trend to engineering sexual behavior ("how to" have better sex, communication, etc.), suppression of infantile polymorphous sexual components in culturally sanctioned mass entertainment, and open tolerance of violence, including sexual violence, in the same mass media. It was as if our culture were illustrating borderline pathology with superego deterioration, regressive condensation of eroticism and aggression, and splitting of the erotic components of sexuality from the object relations matrix.

The early 1990s, however, have shown a new puritanical attitude, a focus on sexual abuse, incest, sexual harassment in the workplace, and the rise of mutual distrust between male and female groups. These trends evolved out of new findings about the importance of early physical and sexual trauma in the genesis of a broad variety of psychopathology, on the one hand, and the struggle for women's liberation from traditional, paternalistic oppression, on the other. What is interesting, however, is how rapidly these scientifically informed and politically progressive developments have evolved into the reinstatement of a conventional morality similar to that of the repressive years before the "sexual revolution" in the late 1960s and to the restrictions on sexuality that exist in Communist totalitarian societies. These restrictions in fascist and Communist countries seem more analogous to the sadistic suppression of sexuality by the primitive superego of neurosis than to borderline pathology with superego deterioration.

It is as if in recent years we have been "privileged" to observe, in simultaneous action or rapid alternation, relative extremes of sexual puritanism and sexual libertinism, with both revealing the flatness of all conventionally tolerable sexuality, in contrast to the potential richness of its private dimension in the individual couple. It is true, of course, that there is an enormous difference between a totalitarian regime's suppression of individual freedom that brutally imposes a conventional morality and a democratic society's tolerance of a significant gap between conventionality and the private freedom of individuals and couples.

To conclude, I think there is an irreducible conflict between conventional morality and the private morality that each couple has to construct as part of its total sexual life and that always implies a nonconventional degree of freedom the couple has to achieve for itself. The delicate balance of sexual freedom, emotional depth, and a value system reflecting mature superego functioning is a complex human achievement that provides the basis for a relation that is deep, passionate, conflicted, and satisfying and potentially lasting. The integration of aggression and polymorphous perverse infantile sexuality into a stable love relation is a task for the individual and the couple. It cannot be achieved by social manipulation but, fortunately, cannot be suppressed either except under the most extreme circumstances by the conventions of society.

References

Albee, E. (1962). *Who's Afraid of Virginia Woolf?* New York: Simon & Schuster Pocketbook, 1964.

Alberoni, F. (1987). *L'Erotisme.* Paris: Ramsay.

Altman, L. L. (1977). Some vicissitudes of love. *Journal of the American Psychoanalytic Association* 25: 35–52.

Anzieu, D. (1986). La scène de ménàge. In *L'Amour de la Haine, Nouvelle Revue de Psychanalyse* 33: 201–209.

Arlow, J. A. (1974). Dreams and myths. Paper presented on the occasion of the founding of the St. Louis Psychoanalytic Institute, October.

Arlow, J. A., Freud, A., Lampl-de Groot, J., & Beres, D. (1968). Panel discussion. *International Journal of Psychoanalysis* 49: 506–512.

Arndt, W. B., Jr. (1991). *Gender Disorders and the Paraphilias.* Madison, Conn.: International Universities Press.

Bak, R. C. (1973). Being in love and object loss. *International Journal of Psychoanalysis* 54: 1–8.

Balint, M. (1948). On genital love. In *Primary Love and Psychoanalytic Technique.* London: Tavistock, 1959, pp. 109–120.

Bancroft, J. (1989). *Human Sexuality and Its Problems.* New York: Churchill Livingstone.

Barnett, M. (1966). Vaginal awareness in the infancy and childhood of girls. *Journal of the American Psychoanalytic Association* 14: 129–141.

Bartell, G. D. (1971). *Group Sex.* New York: Signet Books.

Bataille, G. (1957). *L'Erotisme.* Paris: Minuit.

Baumeister, R. F. (1989). *Masochism and the Self.* Hillsdale, N.J.: Lawrence Erlbaum Associates.

Benjamin, J. (1986). The alienation of desire: Women's masochism and ideal love. In *Psychoanalysis and Women: Contemporary Reappraisals,* ed. J. L. Alpert. Hillsdale, N.J.: Lawrence Erlbaum Associates, pp. 113–138.

Bergmann, M. S. (1971). Psychoanalytic observations on the capacity to love. In *Separation-Individuation: Essays in Honor of Margaret S. Mahler,* ed. J.

McDevitt & C. Settlage. New York: International Universities Press, pp. 15–40.

———. (1980). On the intrapsychic function of falling in love. *Psychoanalytic Quarterly* 49: 56–77.

———. (1982). Platonic love, transference, and love in real life. *Journal of the American Psychoanalytic Association* 30: 87–111.

———. (1987). *The Anatomy of Loving*. New York: Columbia University Press.

Bertolucci, B. (1974). *Last Tango in Paris*.

Bion, W. R. (1961). *Experiences in Groups and Other Papers*. New York: Basic Books.

———. (1967). The imaginary turn. In *Second Thoughts: Selected Papers on Psycho-Analysis*, by W. R. Bion. Northvale, N.J.: Aronson, pp. 3–22.

Blum, H. P. (1973). The concept of erotized transference. *Journal of the American Psychoanalytic Association* 21: 61–76.

———. (1976). Masochism, the ego ideal, and the psychology of women. *Journal of the American Psychoanalytic Association* 24: 157–191.

Braunschweig, D., & Fain, M. (1971). *Eros et Anteros*. Paris: Petite Bibliothèque Payot.

———. (1975). *Le Nuit, le jour*. Paris: Presses Universitaires de France.

Chasseguet-Smirgel, J. (1970). *Female Sexuality*. Ann Arbor: University of Michigan Press.

———. (1973). *Essai sur l'idéal du moi*. Paris: Presses Universitaires de France.

———. (1974). Perversion, idealization, and sublimation. *International Journal of Psychoanalysis* 55: 349–357.

———. (1984a). The femininity of the analyst in professional practice. *International Journal of Psychoanalysis* 65: 169–178.

———. (1984b). *Creativity and Perversion*. New York: Norton.

———. (1985). *The Ego Ideal: A Psychoanalytic Essay on the Malady of the Ideal*. New York: Norton.

———. (1986). *Sexuality and Mind: The Role of the Father and the Mother in the Psyche*. New York: New York University Press.

———. (1989). The bright face of narcissism and its shadowy depths. In *The Psychiatric Clinics of North America: Narcissistic Personality Disorder*, ed. O. F. Kernberg. Philadelphia: Saunders, vol. 12, no. 3, pp. 709–722.

———. (1991). Sadomasochism in the perversions: Some thoughts on the destruction of reality. *Journal of the American Psychoanalytic Association* 39: 399–415.

Chodorow, N. (1978). *The Reproduction of Mothering*. Berkeley: University of California Press.

Cooper, A. (1988). The narcissistic-masochistic character. In *Masochism: Current Psychoanalytic Perspectives*, ed. R. B. Glick & D. J. Meyers. Hillsdale, N.J.: Analytic Press, pp. 117–138.

David, C. (1971). *L'Etat Amoureux*. Paris: Petite Bibliothèque Payot.

Deutsch, H. (1944–45). *The Psychology of Women.* 2 vols. New York: Grune & Stratton.

Dicks, H. V. (1967). *Marital Tensions.* New York: Basic Books.

Emde, R. (1987). Development terminable and interminable. Plenary presentation at the 35th International Psycho-Analytical Congress, Montreal, Canada, July 27.

Emde, R., et al. (1978). Emotional expression in infancy: 1. Initial studies of social signaling and an emergent model. In *The Development of Affect,* ed. M. Lewis & L. Rosenblum. New York: Plenum, pp. 125–148.

Endleman, R. (1989). *Love and Sex in Twelve Cultures.* New York: Psyche Press.

Erikson, E. H. (1956). The problem of ego identity. *Journal of the American Psychoanalytic Association* 4: 56–121.

––––––. (1959). Growth and crises of the healthy personality. In *Identity and the Life Cycle, Psychological Issues,* Monograph 1. New York: International Universities Press, pp. 50–100.

Fairbairn, W. R. D. (1954). *An Object-Relations Theory of the Personality.* New York: Basic Books.

Fisher, S. (1989). *Sexual Images of the Self.* Hillsdale, N.J.: Lawrence Erlbaum Associates.

Fraiberg, S. (1982). Pathological defenses in infancy. *Psychoanalytic Quarterly* 51: 612–635.

Freud, S. (1894). The neuro-psychoses of defence. In *Standard Edition,* ed. J. Strachey, 3: 43–61. London: Hogarth Press, 1962.

––––––. (1905). Three essays on the theory of sexuality. In *S.E.,* 7: 135–243. London: Hogarth Press, 1953.

––––––. (1910a). A special type of object choice made by men. In *S.E.,* 11: 163–175. London: Hogarth Press.

––––––. (1910b). On the universal tendency to debasement in the sphere of love. In *S.E.,* 11: 175–190. London: Hogarth Press.

––––––. (1910c). The taboo of virginity. In *S.E.,* 11: 190–208. London: Hogarth Press.

––––––. (1912). On the universal tendency to debasement in the sphere of love (Contributions to the psychology of love, II). In *S.E.,* 11: 178–190. London: Hogarth Press, 1957.

––––––. (1914). On narcissism. In *S. E.,* 14: 69–102. London: Hogarth Press, 1957.

––––––. (1915a). Observations on transference-love. In *S.E.,* 12: 158–171. London, Hogarth Press, 1958.

––––––. (1915b). Instincts and their vicissitudes. In *S.E.,* 14. London: Hogarth Press, 1957.

––––––. (1915c). Repression. In *S.E.,* 14: 141–158. London: Hogarth Press, 1957.

––––––. (1915d). The unconscious. In *S.E.,* 14: 159–215. London: Hogarth Press, 1957.

———. (1920). Beyond the pleasure principle. In *S.E.*, 18: 3–64. London: Hogarth Press, 1955.

———. (1921). Group psychology and the analysis of the ego. In *S.E.*, 18: 69–143.

———. (1926). Inhibitions, symptoms and anxiety. In *S.E.*, 20: 87–156. London: Hogarth Press.

———. (1930). Civilization and its discontents. In *S.E.*, 21: 59–145. London: Hogarth Press.

———. (1933). Femininity. In *S.E.*, 22: 112–125. London: Hogarth Press, 1964.

———. (1954). *The Origins of Psychoanalysis, 1887–1902*. New York: Basic Books.

Friedman, R. C., & Downey, J. (1993). Psychoanalysis, psychobiology and homosexuality. *Journal of the American Psychoanalytic Association* 41: 1159–1198.

Galenson, E. (1980). Sexual development during the second year of life. In *Sexuality: Psychiatric Clinics of North America*, ed. J. Meyer. Philadelphia: Saunders. pp. 37–44.

———. (1983). A pain-pleasure behavioral complex in mothers and infants. Unpublished.

——— (1988). The precursors of masochism. In *Fantasy, Myth and Reality: Essays in Honor of Jacob Arlow*, ed. H. P. Blum et al. Madison, Conn.: International Universities Press, pp. 371–379.

Galenson, E., & Roiphe, H. (1974). The emergence of genital awareness during the second year of life. In *Sex Differences in Behavior*, ed. R. Friedman, R. Richardt, & R. Van de Wiele. New York: Wiley, pp. 233–258.

———. (1977). Some suggested revisions concerning early female development. *Journal of the American Psychoanalytic Association* 24: 29–57.

Goldberger, M., & Evans, D. (1985). On transference manifestations in male patients with female analysts. *International Journal of Psychoanalysis* 66: 295–309.

Green, A. (1983). *Narcissisme de vie, narcissisme de mort*. Paris: Minuit.

———. (1986). *On Private Madness*. London: Hogarth Press.

———. (1993). *Le Travail du négatif*. Paris: Minuit.

Green, R. (1976). One hundred ten feminine and masculine boys: Behavioral contrasts and demographic similarities. *Archives of Sexual Behavior* 5: 425–446.

———. (1987). *The "Sissy Boy Syndrome."* New Haven: Yale University Press.

Greenaway, P. (1990). *The Cook, the Thief, His Wife and Her Lover*.

Greene, G., & Greene, C. (1974). *S-M: The Last Taboo*. New York: Grove Press.

Grossman, W. I. (1986). Notes on masochism: A discussion of the history and development of a psychoanalytic concept. *Psychoanalytic Quarterly* 55: 379–413.

———. (1991). Pain, aggression, fantasy, and the concept of sadomasochism. *Psychoanalytic Quarterly* 60: 22–52.

Grunberger, B. (1979). *Narcissism: Psychoanalytic Essays.* New York: International Universities Press.

Harlow, H. F. and Harlow, M. D. (1965). *The Affectional Systems in Behavior of Non-Human Primates.* Vol. 2, ed. A. M. Schrier, H. F. Harlow, & F. Stollnitz. New York: Academic Press.

Herzog, J. M. (1983). A neonatal intensive care syndrome: A pain complex involving neuroplasticity and psychic trauma. In *Frontiers in Infant Psychiatry,* ed. J. D. Call et al. New York: Basic Books, pp. 291–300.

Holder, A. (1970). Instinct and drive. In *Basic Psychoanalytic Concepts of the Theory of Instincts,* vol. 3, ed. H. Nagera. New York: Basic Books, pp. 19–22.

Horney, K. (1967). *Feminine Psychology.* London: Routledge & Kegan Paul.

Hughes, J. (1985). *The Breakfast Club.*

Hunt, M. (1974). *Sexual Behavior in the 1970s.* New York: Dell.

Izard, C. (1978). On the ontogenesis of emotions and emotion-cognition relationships in infancy. In *The Development of Affect,* ed. M. Lewis & L. Rosenblum. New York: Plenum, pp. 389–413.

Jacobson, E. (1964). *The Self and the Object World.* New York: International Universities Press.

———. (1971). *Depression.* New York: International Universities Press.

Jones, E. (1935). Early female sexuality. *International Journal of Psychoanalysis* 16: 263–273.

Josselyn, I. M. (1971). The capacity to love: A possible reformulation. *Journal of the American Academy of Child Psychiatry* 10: 6–22.

Karme, L. (1979). The analysis of a male patient by a female analyst: The problem of the negative oedipal transference. *International Journal of Psychoanalysis* 60: 253–261.

Kernberg, O. F. (1970). A psychoanalytic classification of character pathology. *Journal of the American Psychoanalytic Association* 18: 800–822.

———. (1974). Mature love: Prerequisites and characteristics. *Journal of the American Psychoanalytic Association* 22: 743–768.

———. (1976). *Object Relations Theory and Clinical Psychoanalysis.* New York: Jason Aronson.

———. (1978). The diagnosis of borderline conditions in adolescence. In *Adolescent Psychiatry,* vol. 6: *Developmental and Clinical Studies,* ed. S. Feinstein & P. L. Giovacchini. Chicago: University of Chicago Press, pp. 298–319.

———. (1980a). *Internal World and External Reality.* New York: Jason Aronson.

———. (1980b). Love, the couple and the group: A psychoanalytic frame. *Psychoanalytic Quarterly* 49: 78–108.

———. (1984). Contemporary psychoanalytic approaches to narcissism. In *Severe Personality Disorders.* New Haven: Yale University Press, pp. 179–196.

———. (1987). Las tentaciónes del convencionalismo. *Revista de Psicoanálisis* (Buenos Aires) 44: 963–988.

———. (1988). Between conventionality and aggression: The boundaries of passion. In *Passionate Attachments: Thinking About Love,* ed. W. Gaylin & E. Person. New York: Free Press, pp. 63–83.

———. (1989a). A theoretical frame for the study of sexual perversions. In *The Psychoanalytic Core: Festschrift in honor of Dr. Leo Rangell,* ed. H. P. Blum, E. M. Weinshel, & F. R. Rodman. New York: International Universities Press, pp. 243–263.

———. (1989b). An ego psychology–object relations theory of the structure and treatment of pathologic narcissism. In *The Psychiatric Clinics of North America: Narcissistic Personality Disorder,* ed. O. F. Kernberg. Philadelphia: Saunders, vol. 12, no. 3, pp. 723–730.

———. (1991). Sadomasochism, sexual excitement, and perversion. *Journal of the American Psychoanalytic Association* 39: 333–362.

———. (1992). *Aggression in Personality Disorders and Perversion.* New Haven: Yale University Press.

Kernberg, P. (1971). The course of the analysis of a narcissistic personality with hysterical and compulsive features. *Journal of the American Psychoanalytic Association* 19: 451–471.

Kernberg, P., & Richards, A. K. (1994). An application of psychoanalysis: The psychology of love as seen through children's letters. In *The Spectrum of Psychoanalysis,* ed. A. K. Richards & A. D. Richards. Madison, Conn.: International Universities Press, pp. 199–218.

Kimmins, A. (1953). *Captain's Paradise.*

Kinsey, A. C., Pomeroy, W. B., Martin, C. E., & Gebhard, P. H. (1953). *Sexual Behavior in the Human Female.* Philadelphia: Saunders.

Klein, M. (1945). The Oedipus complex in the light of early anxieties. In *Contributions to Psychoanalysis, 1921–1945.* London: Hogarth Press, 1948, pp. 377–390.

———. (1957). *Envy and Gratitude.* New York: Basic Books.

Kolodny, R., Masters, W., & Johnson, V. (1979). *Textbook of Sexual Medicine.* Boston: Little, Brown.

Krause, R. (1990). Psychodynamik der Emotionsstorungen. In *Enzyklopädie der Psychologie der Emotion,* ed. K. R. Scherer. Göttingen: Verlag für Psychologie–Dr. C. Hogrefe, pp. 630–705.

Laplanche, J. (1976). *Life and Death in Psychoanalysis.* Baltimore: Johns Hopkins University Press.

Laplanche, J. & Pontalis, J. B. (1973). *The Language of Psycho-Analysis.* New York: Norton.

Lester, E. (1984). The female analyst and the erotized transference. *International Journal of Psychoanalysis* 66: 283–293.

Liberman, D. (1956). Identificación proyectiva y conflicto matrimonial. *Revista de Psicoanálisis* (Buenos Aires) 13: 1–20.

Lichtenstein, H. (1961). Identity and sexuality: A study of their interrelationship in man. *Journal of the American Psychoanalytic Association* 9: 179–260.

———. (1970). Changing implications of the concept of psychosexual development: An inquiry concerning the validity of classical psychoanalytic assumptions concerning sexuality. *Journal of the American Psychoanalytic Association* 18: 300–318.

Lorenz, K. (1963). *On Aggression*. New York: Bantam Books.

Lussier, A. (1982). *Les Déviations du désir: Etude sur le fétichisme*. Paris: Presses Universitaires de France.

Lyne, A. (1987). *Fatal Attraction*.

Maccoby, E., & Jacklin, C. (1974). *The Psychology of Sex Differences*. Stanford: Stanford University Press.

Maclean, P. D. (1976). Brain mechanisms of elemental sexual functions. In *The Sexual Experience*, ed. B. Sadock, H. Kaplan, & A. Freeman. Baltimore: Williams & Wilkins, pp. 119–127.

Mahler, M. S. (1968). *On Human Symbiosis and the Vicissitudes of Individuation*. Vol. 1, *Infantile Psychosis*. New York: International Universities Press.

Mahler, M., Pine, F., & Bergman, A. (1975). *The Psychological Birth of the Human Infant*. New York: Basic Books.

Mann, T. (1924). *Der Zauberberg*. Vol. 1. Frankfurt. Fischer Bücherei, 1967, pp. 361–362.

May, R. (1969). *Love and Will*. New York: Norton.

McConaghy, N. (1993). *Sexual Behavior: Problems and Management*. New York: Plenum.

Mellen, J. (1973). *Women and Their Sexuality in the New Film*. New York: Dell.

Meltzer, D. (1973). *Sexual States of Mind*. Perthshire: Clunie.

Meltzer, D., & Williams, M. H. (1988). *The Apprehension of Beauty*. Old Ballechin, Strath Toy: Clunie.

Meyer, J. (1980). Body ego, selfness, and gender sense: The development of gender identity. *Sexuality: Psychiatric Clinics of North America*, ed. J. Meyer. Philadelphia: Saunders. pp. 21–36.

Mitchell, J. (1974). *Psychoanalysis and Feminism*. New York: Vintage Books.

Money, J. (1980). *Love and Love Sickness: The Science of Sex, Gender Difference, and Pair-Bonding*. Baltimore: Johns Hopkins University Press.

———. (1986). *Lovemaps*. Buffalo, N.Y.: Prometheus Press.

———. (1988). *Gay, Straight, and In-Between*. New York: Oxford University Press.

Money, J., & Ehrhardt, A. (1972). *Man & Woman: Boy & Girl*. Baltimore: Johns Hopkins University Press.

Montherlant, H. de (1936). *Les Jeunes Filles*. In *Romans et oeuvres de fiction non théatrales de Montherlant*. Paris: Gallimard, 1959, pp. 1010–1012.

Moscovici, S. (1981). *L'Age des foules*. Paris: Fayard.

Oshima N. (1976). *In the Realm of the Senses.*

Ovesey, L., & Person, E. (1973). Gender identity and sexual psychopathology in men: A psychodynamic analysis of homosexuality, transsexualism and transvestism. *Journal of the American Academy of Psychoanalysis* 1: 54–72.

——. (1976). Transvestism: A disorder of the sense of self. *International Journal of Psychoanalytic Therapy* 5: 219–236.

Paz, O. (1974). *Teatro de Signos/Transparencias,* ed. Julian Rios. Madrid: Espiral/Fundamentos.

Perper, T. (1985). *Sex Signals: The Biology of Love.* Philadelphia: ISI Press.

Person, E. (1974). Some new observations on the origins of femininity. In *Women and Analysis,* ed. J. Strouse. New York: Viking, pp. 250–261.

——. (1983). The influence of values in psychoanalysis: The case of female psychology. *Psychiatry Update* 2: 36–50.

——. (1985). The erotic transference in women and in men: Differences and consequences. *Journal of the American Academy of Psychoanalysis* 13: 159–180.

——. (1988). *Dreams of Love and Fateful Encounters.* New York: Norton.

Person, E., & Ovesey, L. (1983). Psychoanalytic theories of gender identity. *Journal of the American Academy of Psychoanalysis* 11: 203–226.

——. (1984). Homosexual cross-dressers. *Journal of the American Academy of Psychoanalysis* 12: 167–186.

Rapaport, D. (1953). On the psychoanalytic theory of affects. In *The Collected Papers of David Rapaport,* ed. M. M. Gill. New York: Basic Books, 1967, pp. 476–512.

Rice, A. K. (1965). *Learning for Leadership.* London: Tavistock.

Riviere, J. (1937). Hate, greed, and aggression. In *Love, Hate and Reparation,* ed. M. Klein & J. Riviere. London: Hogarth Press, pp. 3–53.

Rohmer, E. (1969). Ma Nuit chez Maud. *L'Avant-Scène* 98: 10–40.

——. (1969). *My Night at Maud's.*

Rosenfeld, H. (1964). On the psychopathology of narcissism: A clinical approach. *International Journal of Psychoanalysis* 45: 332–337.

——. (1971). A clinical approach to the psychoanalytic theory of the life and death instincts: An investigation into the aggressive aspects of narcissism. *International Journal of Psychoanalysis* 52: 169–179.

——. (1975). Negative therapeutic reaction. In *Tactics and Techniques in Psychoanalytic Therapy,* vol. 2, *Countertransference,* ed. P. L. Giovacchini. New York: Jason Aronson, pp. 217–228.

Ross, J. M. (1990). The eye of the beholder: On the developmental dialogue of fathers and daughters. In *New Dimensions in Adult Development,* ed. R. Nemiroff and C. Colarusso, pp. 47–70.

Schafer, R. (1960). The loving and beloved superego in Freud's structural theory. *Psychoanalytic Study of the Child* 15: 163–188.

——. (1974). Problems in Freud's psychology of women. *Journal of the American Psychoanalytic Association* 22: 459–489.

Scott, G. G. (1983). *Erotic power: An exploration of dominance and submission.* Secaucus, N.J.: Citadel Press.

Silverman, H. W. (1988). Aspects of erotic transference. In *Love: Psychoanalytic Perspectives,* ed. J. F. Lasky & H. W. Silverman. New York: New York University Press, pp. 173–191.

Soderbergh, S. (1989). *Sex, Lies and Videotape.*

Spengler, A. (1977). Manifest sadomasochism of males: Results of an empirical study. *Archives of Sexual Behavior* 6: 441–456.

Stendhal, M. (1822). *Love.* Harmondsworth, Middlesex: Penguin Books, 1975.

Stern, D. N. (1985). *The Interpersonal World of the Infant.* New York: Basic Books.

Stoller, R. J. (1968). *Sex and Gender.* New York: Aronson.

———. (1973). Overview: The impact of new advances in sex research on psychoanalytic theory. *American Journal of Psychiatry* 130: 30.

———. (1974). Facts and fancies: An examination of Freud's concept of bisexuality. In: *Women and Analysis,* ed. J. Strouse. New York: Viking, pp. 343–364.

———. (1975a). *Perversion: The Erotic Form of Hatred.* Washington, D.C.: American Psychiatric Press.

———. (1975b). *Sex and Gender.* Vol. 2, *The Transsexual Experiment.* London: Hogarth Press.

———. (1979). *Sexual Excitement.* New York: Pantheon.

———. (1985). *Presentations of Gender.* New Haven: Yale University Press.

———. (1991a). *Pain and Passion.* New York: Plenum.

———. (1991b). *Porn.* New Haven: Yale University Press.

Thompson, C. (1942). Cultural pressures in the psychology of women. *Psychiatry* 5: 331–339.

Tinbergen, N. (1951). An attempt at synthesis. In *The Study of Instinct.* New York: Oxford University Press, pp. 101–127.

Turquet, P. (1975). Threats to identity in the large group. In *The Large Group: Dynamics and Therapy,* ed. L. Kreeger. London: Constable, pp. 87–144.

van der Waals, H. G. (1965). Problems of narcissism. *Bulletin of the Menninger Clinic* 29: 293–311.

Weinberg, T., & Kammel, W. L. (1983). *S and M: Studies in Sadomasochism.* Buffalo, N.Y.: Prometheus Press.

Wilson, E. O. (1975). *Sociobiology: The New Synthesis.* Cambridge: Harvard University Press.

Winnicott, D. W. (1955). The depressive position in normal emotional development. *British Journal of Medical Psychology* 28: 89–100.

———. (1963). The development of the capacity for concern. *Bulletin of the Menninger Clinic* 27: 167–176.

Wisdom, J. O. (1970). Freud and Melanie Klein: Psychology, ontology, and *Weltanschauung.* In *Psychoanalysis and Philosophy,* ed. C. Hanly & M. Lazerowitz. New York: International Universities Press, pp. 327–362.

Index